Bad Chaucer

Bad Chaucer

THE GREAT POET'S GREATEST MISTAKES IN THE *CANTERBURY TALES*

Tison Pugh

University of Michigan Press
Ann Arbor

Copyright © 2024 by Tison Pugh
All rights reserved

For questions or permissions, please contact um.press.perms@umich.edu

Published in the United States of America by the
University of Michigan Press
Manufactured in the United States of America
Printed on acid-free paper
First published January 2024

A CIP catalog record for this book is available from the British Library.

Library of Congress Cataloging-in-Publication data has been applied for.

ISBN 978-0-472-13344-4 (hardcover : alk. paper)
ISBN 978-0-472-22125-7 (e-book)

This book will be made open access within three years of publication thanks to
Path to Open, a program developed in partnership between JSTOR, the American
Council of Learned Societies (ACLS), University of Michigan Press, and The Uni-
versity of North Carolina Press to bring about equitable access and impact for the
entire scholarly community, including authors, researchers, libraries, and univer-
sity presses around the world. Learn more at https://about.jstor.org/path-to-open/

To Angela Jane Weisl,
Because she understands
the Goodness
of Badness

Contents

Thematic Table of Contents

A Note on Texts

Quotations of *The Canterbury Tales* and Chaucer's other works are taken from Geoffrey Chaucer, *The Riverside Chaucer*, ed. Larry D. Benson, 3rd ed. (Boston: Houghton Mifflin, 1987). Quotations of the Christian Bible are taken from *Holy Bible: Douay Rheims Version* (Charlotte, NC: St. Benedict Press, 2009). The *Middle English Dictionary* (*MED*) is cited from quod.lib.umich.edu/m/middle-english-dictionary, and the *Oxford English Dictionary* (*OED*) is cited from www.oed.com.

Introduction

On Chaucer's Badness

Of human work none but what is bad can be perfect, in its
   own bad way.
   —JOHN RUSKIN[1]

A bad book is as much of a labour to write as a good one; it
   comes as sincerely from the author's soul.
   —ALDOUS HUXLEY[2]

Even bad books are books and therefore sacred.
   —GÜNTER GRASS[3]

Bad Chaucer, taking an errant cue from Shakespeare's Mark Antony,
comes neither to praise the author and his literature nor to bury them.
Chaucer has been exalted, voluminously and passionately, over the more
than six hundred years since his death, and rightfully so, for his writings
have enchanted and entranced audiences with their comic brio, endur-
ing themes, and heartfelt emotion. And, of course, a single book—or even
many, many books—could never metaphorically bury Chaucer, even if that
were its aim. The musings of a twenty-first-century literary critic would
be unlikely to stanch the scholarly tide of centuries, and it would be mas-
ochistically counterproductive to attempt to bury a man who has provided
so many readers, including this author, with so much pleasure.

   At the same time, after one reads and rereads Chaucer's *Canterbury
Tales* over the years, it becomes apparent that his writing features rough
passages of poetry, moments of inscrutable narrative development, and
deus ex machina conclusions, among other such infelicities. In these
instances, Chaucer's poetry descends from the sublime to the, in a word,
bad, and it is Chaucer's very badness that serves as the subject of this book.
Following the order of the Canterbury pilgrimage from the *Knight's Tale* to

the *Parson's Tale* (and with the conclusion addressing the Retraction), each of the following chapters examines an individual tale and investigates the ways in which Chaucer goes most awry in his otherwise engrossing narratives. Literary scholars rarely focus on the apparently simple issue of an author's or a text's lapses and blunders, and so this approach may appear counterintuitive to contemporary critical traditions that plumb a text's ideological, historical, and cultural resonances. But we need a sense of badness to guide our appreciation of literature for, as Quentin Bell proposes, "Our perception of the goodness of good art is determined by some opposite quality with which we compare it. . . . [I]t is always useful to take an object and look at it from a new point of view, to consider it, so to speak, backside on or upside down."[4] Bad art has long encouraged a unique subculture of aficionados in those who delight in the off-kilter, the odd, and the inelegant.[5] More so, book and movie reviewers in the popular press regularly tackle such questions, weighing a cultural artifact's strengths and weaknesses and generally offering an endorsement or a condemnation. *Bad Chaucer*, in many ways, marries these traditions by scouring the *Canterbury Tales* for its blunders, muddles, and shortcomings. Readers benefit from a kaleidoscopic and complementary range of views on authors and their texts, of which their accompanying gaffes should serve a key role.

Although it is beyond the scope of this brief introduction to offer a detailed overview of the critical tradition, it is worth noting that many famous voices over the years have decried—even lambasted—Chaucer's artistry. In the centuries following the initial circulation of the *Canterbury Tales*, several readers denounced it as spiritually corruptive. Edmund Becke, in a 1549 essay, contrasts the moral value of reading either the Bible or the *Canterbury Tales* and advocates the former over the latter: "If all magistrates & the nobilitie . . . wolde . . . willingly vouchsafe to suffurate & spare an houre or [two] in a day, from theyr worldly busines, emploing it about the reading of this boke [the Bible], as they have bene used to do in Cronicles & Canterbury tales, then . . . what a florishing commune wealth should your grace injoy."[6] In *The Defense of Poesie* (1582), Sir Philip Sidney praises Chaucer while admitting and overlooking his faults: "Yet had hee great wants, fit to be forgiven in so reverent an Antiquitie."[7] As Chaucer's Middle English rendered his poetry less accessible to later readers, several noted critics relegated him to the ashbin of literary history. Joseph Addison, in "An Account of the Greatest English Poets" (1694), first praises Chaucer but then dismisses him as irrelevant:

Long had our dull forefathers slept supine
Nor felt the raptures of the tunefull Nine [Muses]
Till Chaucer first, the merry Bard, arose;
And many a story told in rhyme and prose.
But age has rusted what the poet writ,
Worn out his language and obscured his wit;
In vain he jests in his unpolished strain,
And tries to make his readers laugh in vain.[8]

Similarly attacking Chaucer simply owing to the age in which he lived, Daniel Defoe, in a 1718 letter published in *Mist's Weekly Journal*, condemns him in excoriating terms: "Jeffrey Chaucer is forgotten upon the same Account; and tho' that Author is excused, by the unpoliteness of the Age he lived in, yet his Works are diligently buried, by most Readers, on that very Principle, that they are not fit for modest Persons to read."[9] Defoe's hypocrisy is somewhat dazzling, as many of his contemporaries would soon label his *Moll Flanders* (1722) as similarly unfit for the consumption of modest readers owing to his heroine's scandalous adventures.

As the centuries passed, later critics echoed these voices. Like Sidney and Addison, Samuel Johnson, in the prefatory essay of his *A Dictionary of the English Language* (1755), initially praises Chaucer as "the illustrious *Geoffry Chaucer*, who may, perhaps, with great justice, be stiled the first of our versifiers who wrote poetically." He then declares in mixed terms: "He does not, however, appear to have deserved all the praise which he has received, or all the censure that he has suffered."[10] Following Defoe's example, in 1807 the notorious George Gordon, Lord Byron, blasted Chaucer's poetry—"Chaucer. notwithstanding the praises bestowed on him, I think obscene and contemptible:—he owes his celebrity merely to his antiquity"—while also censuring all poets contemporary to himself ("English living poets I have avoided mentioning:—we have none will survive their productions. Taste is over with us").[11] Matthew Arnold, while asserting that with Chaucer "is born our real poetry," also criticizes him sharply in an echo of Becke: "To our praise, therefore, of Chaucer as a poet there must be this limitation; he lacks the high seriousness of the great classics, and therewith an important part of their virtue."[12] With the rise of Chaucerian scholarship as a subfield of the modern university in the late 1800s and early 1900s, Thomas Lounsbury summarizes such varying viewpoints in his *Studies in Chaucer: His Life and Writings*: "[Chaucer's] earlier works exhibited decided deficiencies when contrasted with the best of his later ones. They frequently contain as fine passages. It is in their completed effect that they fail."[13] Since his death in 1400, Chaucer has received countless more accolades than insults, yet these sharp criticisms reveal as well the fact that, despite his revered status today, his place in the literary canon was by no means assured. And as most teachers of medieval English literature know to expect, some students will offer their own scathing assessments of Chaucer and his accomplishments, such as in the vividly voiced opinion recorded on a colleague's course evaluation: "Chaucer has NO RESPECT," with the concluding words underscored several times.

In reviewing this brief survey of condemnations of Chaucer's literature, several themes recur: disapproval of the moral timbre of his fictions; distaste for his bawdy and irreverent humor; and the conviction that his archaic Middle English renders his literature inaccessible. Questions of literary goodness and badness are inherently subjective, however, and the subsequent chapters of *Bad Chaucer* do not amplify any of these points documented in the literary record for the simple fact that they do not align with my perceptions of Chaucer's missteps. Those who believe narratives should preach virtue mistake moralism for literary merit; those who find bawdy humor distasteful fall to the tautological logic that such subject matter necessitates its condemnation; and those who find Middle English an insurmountable barrier to enjoying Chaucer's tales deprive themselves of the metrical eloquence of his words. Literary analysis, while often assuming an air of moderation and impartiality, almost inevitably reveals the particular idiosyncrasies of a given reader. These conditions are not to be lamented or overlooked as much as they are to be recognized and, indeed, appreciated. The subjective opinions of Becke, Sidney, Addison, Defoe, Johnson, Byron, and Arnold focused on the purported badness of Chaucer's literature as reflective of their beliefs about what constitutes good literature, and likewise this volume's assessment of Chaucer's badness can only be ascribed to the particularities and idiosyncrasies of my readings of the *Canterbury Tales*. It is, of course, my aim to convince readers of the justness of these opinions while also recognizing—indeed, celebrating—the impossibility of universal accord.

Further along these lines, *Bad Chaucer* does not attempt to rebut arguments about the aesthetic pleasure to be found in Chaucer's literature or to engage in a debate grounded on aesthetic philosophies. A simplistic binary of the aesthetic as the good and the unaesthetic as the bad pervades much criticism, yet the two are forever mingled in the vast majority of literary and other artworks. As Pierre Bourdieu argues, aesthetic judgments arise from a cultural ethics of distinction that are presented as if collectively acclaimed: "The pure aesthetic is rooted in an ethic, or rather, an ethos of elective distance from the necessities of the natural and social world, which may take the form of moral agnosticism . . . or of an aestheticism which presents the aesthetic disposition as a universally valid principle."[14] In seeking to define beauty, taste, and truth, aesthetics balances between general theories and specific artifacts, attempting to identify comprehensive principles that are then upheld or flouted by a given artwork. As an interpretive gateway, aesthetics has inspired astute explorations of Chaucer's literature, including such works as Robert M. Jordan's *Chaucer and the Shape of Creation: The Aesthetic Possibilities of Inorganic Structure*, Peggy A. Knapp's *Chaucerian Aesthetics*, and the special issue of *Chaucer Review* titled *Chaucer and Aesthetics*.[15] Appraising the critical landscape, Knapp eloquently defends aesthetically based criticism and argues against any "antiaesthetic" ethos, which is often employed to expose "the naiveté of aesthetic analysis with its admission of pleasure" and which has redirected critical attention to "unmasking the ways in which literary art reinforces aspects of hegemony by offering the bribe of beautiful form."[16] Succinctly phrased, aesthetics ceded supremacy to ideology for many critics, who turned their attention to the ways in which literature and other artworks reflect the political, historical, and social conventions in which they were inextricably enmeshed. A return to aesthetical inquiries, as Knapp passionately demonstrates, need not turn aside from ideological inquiries but instead seeks to understand the creation of beauty in its cultural moment.

Although *Bad Chaucer* does not aim to refute aesthetically based readings of the *Canterbury Tales*, it is not the purpose of this volume to establish a theory of antiaesthetics, one that would define not only for Chaucer but for a range of authors and other creators (playwrights, directors, artists, video-game designers) a set of protocols to assist in evaluating the badness of their works. Like many (if not most) theories of aesthetics, any such attempt would inevitably devolve into a morass of internal contradictions, historicist contextualizations, notable exceptions, and inherently fallible evaluations. As Robert Graves ponders in his classic essay, "What Is Bad Poetry?," this eponymous query "is so often put and so variously answered that I am inclined to break away altogether from the traditional view that the question can be answered in terms of any particular literary formula."[17] Indeed, imagining this critical discussion as a conversation, Graves posits that the answer to the question of what constitutes bad poetry might be, "Yours, when I do not understand you and when your work has no help to offer me."[18] *Bad Chaucer* eschews aesthetically (and antiaesthetically) based analysis and, taking inspiration from Graves, rejects the necessity of proposing a literary formula that would forever define literary badness; instead, this volume tackles the issue of Chaucer's badness from an alternate perspective and explores the benefits (and sometimes pleasures) of attuning oneself to an author's missteps and locating each on an individual basis. Rather than searching for universal principles, this motley collection of readings examines a vibrant vortex of anomalies that undermine, but never collapse, the integrity of Chaucer's *Canterbury Tales*—the moments when, at their simplest, readers might expect Chaucer to have done better.

For the purposes of this book, then, a simple yet compelling definition of literary badness blossoms forth from the conjoint recognition that reading offers one of life's greatest pleasures but that badness momentarily blots these pleasures. And so what is bad? Badness is when readers pause in their reading because a character really wouldn't do that, or because the sense of a story becomes mired in senselessness, or because the tedium of clichés counterbalance works of otherwise daring originality, or because suspensions of disbelief becomes unsuspended. When readers' pleasures are curtailed, badness might just be the culprit. Discerning badness is a highly idiosyncratic venture, one that perhaps tells more about the reader than the text but that is simultaneously enlightening about both. In today's media landscape, badness often propels fan-fiction authors to rewrite a story that they otherwise enjoy, to erase its annoyances and to fill its omissions with their preferred story lines (and it is worthwhile to consider Chaucer as a proto-fanfic author of Ovid, Dante, Jean de Meun, and the many other writers whose work he adapted to his own ends). Badness is what sticks in your craw when authors should have thought through the implications of their words a bit more thoroughly, should have paid more attention to complexities they overlooked. Cataloging badness is the literary equivalent of backseat driving, or Monday morning quarterbacking, or any other such endeavor that might be dismissed as annoying to our friends in real life but matters deeply to our sense of value. (Indeed, backseat driving might annoy the driver, but it has doubtless saved innumerable lives—although I make no such promises of the salutary effects of *Bad Chaucer*.)

In tracking my sense of Chaucer's badness, several patterns recur over the course of the following chapters: genre troubles; themeless themes; mischaracterized characters; pleasureful, purposeful, and purposeless badness; and outmoded perspectives. (As mentioned previously, this book proceeds in order of the *Canterbury Tales* from the Knight's to the Parson's, but it also includes a thematic table of contents so that readers can better see these overlapping specimens of Chaucer's badness in conversation with one another.) At times Chaucer's polyphony of genres become a cacophony, such as when epic and romance collide in the *Knight's Tale*, resulting in a narratively exasperating catalog of trees, and when the *Friar's Tale* fails to uphold the generic expectations of the exemplum, resulting in a moral lesson curiously unmoored from the narrative supposedly illustrating it. The riotous humor of the *Summoner's Tale* clashes awkwardly with the anti-carnivalesque humor arising from images of dead children, and certainly, if Chaucer's Knight can be trusted, the compendium of tragedies proffered in the *Monk's Tale* do not create a pleasureful literary experience. One would hardly think Chaucer needed to be warned to avoid textbook rhetorics in his otherwise engaging tales, but the *Canon's Yeoman's Tale* indicates that this lesson remained unlearned. Genres guide authors in writing and readers in interpreting texts, but they bear as well the potential to enforce rigid narrative conventions unnecessary for a tale to succeed on its own merits. In poker, players must "know when to hold 'em, known when to fold 'em," and with genres, authors must intuit when to adhere to their expected protocols, when to jettison them, and how to balance their conflicting impulses.

In other instances, Chaucer's tales do not cohere with their purported themes, as evident in the conflicted portrayal of poverty in the *Man of Law's Tale* and in the confused (and confusing) treatment of the theodicy theme—the question of why a benevolent God allows evil in the world— that undercuts any thematic consistency to the *Clerk's Tale*. The *Physician's Tale* offers a bewildering mishmash of messages in its story line and conclusion, thereby failing to illustrate any lesson to be learned from the distressing execution of the virtuous Virginia, and the *Tale of Melibee* allegorizes a man's battle with and ultimate forgiveness of characters representing the flesh, the devil, and the world, but why would a text ostensibly espousing a Christian lesson of forgiveness and redemption advocate reconciliation with evil? The *Manciple's Tale* tells the story of Apollo expelling his crow from his home for disclosing his wife's adultery but leaves curiously unanswered whether this pet would perceive its punishment as such, thus undermining any theme the narrative ostensibly promotes. A cohesive theme stands as one of the hallmarks of great literature, but Chaucer's conflicted and chaotic themes frequently subvert any organic unity between his narratives and their messages.

On several occasions Chaucer's characters fail to adhere to a tale's conventions or to act in a manner congruent with their motivations, which goads readers to contemplate the inconsistences of their actions. Such in the case with the unexpected sympathy some readers might feel for John in the *Miller's Tale*, a character repeatedly mischaracterized by the tale's narrator, or with the inscrutable and self-contradictory narrator of the *Merchant's Tale*, who seems shocked by the scandalous content of the tale he chose to tell. Dorigen in the *Franklin's Tale* is rendered a strangely impenetrable character owing to the contradictions implicit in amatory discourses of the Middle Ages, and in the *Pardoner's Tale* Chaucer includes a mysterious old man who creates an unnecessary crux in an otherwise engaging story. The *Second Nun's Tale* surprisingly unites themes of erotic abstinence with subtexts of flaming desire, but Chaucer assigns this tale to the Second Nun, a character virtually invisible on the Canterbury pilgrimage, and he consequently misses the opportunity to develop connections between his frame narrative, this stunningly sensual saint's life, and the blank figure who links them. As a final example of Chaucer's mischaracterized characters, readers have long debated whether the Parson reveals himself to be a heretic in his *Parson's Tale*—but surely such a key aspect of this character should be clearly communicated to readers. With these and other such mischaracterized characters, Chaucer depicts not merely unexpected but wholly unwarranted actions in his tales, thus handicapping the coherency of their narrative action.

Complicating these matters of badness further, Chaucer wrote some tales to create purposeful and pleasureful badness—notably the *Squire's Tale* and the *Tale of Sir Thopas*—which necessitates that readers consider his view of the unexpected delights arising from bad literature. In these and other such instances, many readers of the *Canterbury Tales* are momentarily jolted from the necessary suspension of disbelief to enjoy Chaucer's fictions and instead must ponder the awkward juxtaposition of the clunky with the sublime. These tales also spark the realization that some types of badness create their own unique sense of readerly pleasure, in the unexpected moments when readers realize that something is just so terribly bad that it transforms into a shimmering specimen of great literature— one of those rare works that, through an unfathomable alchemy of text and interpretation, becomes so bad that it is good. Puns are often derided as the lowest form of humor, and their repetition in the *Shipman's Tale* shows Chaucer's propensity to emphasize an otherwise appealing joke into tediousness, and the *Cook's Tale*, a sui generis example of Chaucer's badness, has stumped readers for centuries, as we cannot agree on such a basic issue as whether the tale is completed or was left abandoned at its rather scrawny length of fifty-eight lines.

The passing of over six hundred years has seismically shifted the social landscape from Chaucer's penning of his tales to their current reception, and his outmoded perspectives—the ostensibly comic rape of the *Reeve's Tale*, the undermining of women's agency in the *Wife of Bath's Tale*, the antisemitism of the *Prioress's Tale*, and the gendered jokes of the *Nun's Priest's Tale*—undermine the pleasure many readers otherwise discover in his literature, while also highlighting the fact that these troubling topics were troubling in Chaucer's age as well. As Sarah Baechle and Carissa M. Harris observe in their examination of the ethical challenges of teaching Chaucer in the twenty-first century, scholars are increasingly "breaking new ground in interrogating Chaucer's formative role in enduring discourses of misogyny, racism, rape culture, and antisemitism," while also recognizing that many Chaucerians "are still reluctant to acknowledge the magnitude of [his] role" in the perpetuation of lasting bigotries.[19] The critical tides are shifting to address these issues more candidly, evident in the recent work of such scholars as Nahir I. Otaño Gracia, who demonstrates the ways in which the *Canterbury Tales* "argues for the inevitability of an English, imperial, Christian Europe,"[20] and Cord J. Whitaker, who unpacks the ways in which metaphors of blackness and whiteness operate in Chaucer's fictions, notably in the *Miller's Tale*, exposing the presence of racialized discourse in a text ostensibly unconcerned with such matters.[21] When readers scrutinize his outmoded perspectives, Chaucer's defenders are quick to cry "Anachronism!"—thus to insulate their beloved author from criticisms deemed inappropriate owing to the simple fact that most people, to some degree or another, cannot help but to reflect the culture in which they lived.

True as this may be, Chaucer's defenders at times virtually deify him as a beacon of benevolent genius during historically tumultuous times, and so examining his outmoded perspectives can give readers a clearer picture of the man, his culture, and their mutual, and at times overlapping, limitations. Some of Chaucer's hagiographers fret that his outmoded perspectives will result in his immolation by the frenzied furies of political correctness, evident in A. S. G. Edwards's concern that Chaucer will be "canceled" owing to the efforts of some readers "to suppress literary history by the invention of grounds for seeing it as offensive."[22] Such an outcome seems unlikely given Chaucer's foundational role in English literature and the many pleasures of his fiction, but any attempt to grapple with the meaning and relevance of his outmoded perspectives is not necessarily helped by those devotees who insist upon the reality of Chaucer's fictional persona while knowing extremely little of his historical personality. Not to put too fine a point of it, but many horrific human beings—do I need to give examples?—have camouflaged their atrocities under winsome personas, until the truth of their personality finally emerges. Some Chaucerians simply echo Chaucer's presentation of himself as a genial, kind-hearted humanist satirizing the foibles of his contemporary society, and thus reiterate the author's vision of himself as he encouraged his contemporaries to see him through his fictions. For example, many Chaucerians insist Chaucer could not have been a misogynist because of the *Wife of Bath's Prologue* but then ignore that Chaucer apologizes for his misogynistic fictions in the *Legend of Good Women*, or they insist that Chaucer could not have been antisemitic because the antisemitism expressed in the *Prioress's Tale* is intended to satirize the Prioress, while overlooking the fact that the Parson also expresses antisemitic perspectives. The author's viewpoints cannot be disentangled from his fictions, but his outmoded perspectives can be plumbed for a deeper understanding of his literature, his historical milieu, and how we respond to them in the present. In sum, the objective of analyzing Chaucer's outmoded perspectives is not to "cancel" him, not to label him as a "bad" person, but to reckon with the ways in which these troubling aspects of his literature influence contemporary reader's engagement with his works without simply dismissing their concerns. To cry "Anachronism" is to refuse to engage with matters of pressing importance.

In a closing caveat, it should be noted that many of the readings of badness in the *Canterbury Tales* that this volume offers can be cast aside with the fallback excuse of Chaucer's deification squad: that the infelicities of his tales reflect intentional choices for his characters, and thus that any literary lapses reflect upon them rather than him. That is to say, should Chaucer or his Knight be held responsible for the generic missteps of the *Knight's Tale*, or is the author or his Miller responsible for the unwarranted sympathies generated in the *Miller's Tale*? H. Marshall Leicester Jr. explains of Chaucer's narrative technique and the metaconstruction of himself as author and character, that "by dividing speakers into parts and denying them the full import of their speaking," the *Canterbury Tales* "puts us in the difficult position of trying to decide which parts of a single narrative are to be assigned to the pilgrim teller and which to the 'author'; in these circumstances it is not surprising that different critics make the cut in different places."[23] Such lines of inquiry can build perceptive readings of the *Canterbury Tales*, notably in such monographs as R. M. Lumiansky's *Of Sondry Folk: The Dramatic Principle of the "Canterbury Tales,"* David Lawton's *Chaucer's Narrators*, C. David Benson's *Chaucer's Drama of Style: Poetic Variety and Contrast in the "Canterbury Tales,"* and John Ganim's *Chaucerian Theatricality*. On a foundational level, however, such questions remain unanswerable, for in the vast majority of cases, readers cannot determine definitively whether a particular solecism in Chaucer's tales exposes his unintentional missteps or the intentional missteps assigned to one of his characters. Blaming the characters absolves Chaucer of any culpability, and extended to its logical endpoint, this viewpoint shields Chaucer from virtually any infelicity, any literary infraction, whatsoever.

Ironically, this defense of Chaucer brings with it a paradoxical, if often unspoken, assessment of the *Canterbury Tales*, as Helen Cooper asserts: "Assigning the weakness of a tale to the weakness of the teller is a widespread, and comfortable, critical practice, but raises the awkward question of how many bad tales the complete work can hold."[24] If readers can suspend their disbelief sufficiently to accept the inherent implausibility of the *Canterbury Tales*—that a group of pilgrims would tell tales in rhymed, metrical verse; that they could hear one another on horseback and on foot while traveling over fifty miles; that a cross section of English society would be so well versed in various literary genres, in cross-cultural sources and analogues, and in classical and contemporary authors—then they can suspend their disbelief sufficiently to excuse Chaucer of his tales' faults. *Bad Chaucer* cannot definitively resolve such interpretive cruxes, just as there can never emerge a singular, definitive reading of the *Canterbury Tales* as a whole. Yet in turning our attention to these lapses for extended examination, readers are better able to see these stunning works in their full complexity, blemishes and all, and to ponder for themselves which belong to the author, which to his creations, and which affect their enjoyment, whether positively or negatively, of the tale in their hands.

And certainly, if one listens to Chaucer himself, one should expect rough patches in his otherwise peerless works. In his complementary roles as author, narrator, and character of his fictions, Chaucer frequently declares that he offers his best efforts, which simultaneously implies his realization of his inability to fully recognize his vision—even when he makes such points ironically. At the close of the *Book of the Duchess*, he states, "I wol, be processe of tyme, / Fonde to put this sweven [dream] in ryme / As I kan best" (1331-33). Similarly, in the comic conclusion of his *Tale of Sir Thopas*, he proclaims that "it is the beste rym I kan" (7.928). In his Retraction, he apologizes to his readers for the faults of his fictions: "And if ther be any thyng that displese hem [them], I preye hem also that they arrette [attribute] it to the defaute of myn unkonnynge and nat to my wyl, that wolde ful fayn [gladly] have seyd bettre if I hadde had konnynge" (10.1082). Perceptive readers know better than to take these caveats at face value: the modesty trope of the *Book of the Duchess* bespeaks Chaucer's humility; the virtuoso humor of the *Tale of Sir Thopas* depends on his telling such a bad tale; and the Retraction echoes a number of medieval apologies of questionable sincerity for one's writings, including those of Andreas Capellanus in *De amore* and Giovanni Boccaccio in *Il decameron*. One should not naively believe Chaucer when he acknowledges his badness, for in many of these instances he employs the possibility of literary badness to apologize and thus to excuse himself from censure. To these voices *Bad Chaucer* adds a necessary assessment of what Chaucer really did get wrong.

CHAPTER 1

The Catalog of Trees and Epic Digressions of the *Knight's Tale*

Is the Knight a bit of a literary windbag, breathlessly blowing stylistic tropes into his tale and then negating them in the next—and sometimes the same—sentence? In so many of his *Canterbury Tales*, Chaucer vibrantly threads together a tapestry of disparate genres, including epic, romance, fabliau, hagiography, exemplum, legend, sermon, and fable, among others. And while it is certainly true that these interweavings of genre illuminate and enliven the Canterbury pilgrimage, it is also true that Chaucer's many genres occasionally clash with, rather than complement, one another, resulting in the unraveling of a tale's organic unity. Such a disjuncture arises in the *Knight's Tale*, a narrative that stands on the border between romance and epic, as the Knight repeatedly falters in his attempts to conjoin them into a harmonious whole. At its best, the *Knight's Tale* stirs the emotions with its tragic account of the cousins Palamon and Arcite fighting for the affections of the beautiful Emelye, their shared beloved; in its weaker moments, the tale digresses into aspects of the epic tradition that highlight the mismatch between the Knight's stirring subject matter and his long-winded and apologetic narration. As Winthrop Wetherbee observes, "Every medieval poet who engaged the classical tradition must . . . come to terms with the conflicting tendencies of the literary modes he seeks to align,"[1] and it is precisely this failure to unite the "conflicting tendencies" of epic and romance that exposes the *Knight's Tale*'s greatest flaws, as strikingly evident in the Knight's tedious digression cataloging species of trees.

In brief, epics are lengthy works written in an elevated diction that recall the heroic achievements of their protagonists, who are men of historical, national, or legendary importance, as recounted in such classic works as Homer's *Iliad*, Virgil's *Aeneid*, *Beowulf*, and John Milton's *Paradise Lost*.[2] In contrast, romance traffics in adventure, chivalry, aristocratic manners, and courtly love, as Derek Pearsall outlines of its chief tropes: "The hero . . . chooses to go out from a secure bastion of wealth and privilege . . . to seek adventures in which the values of chivalry and service to ladies . . . will be submitted to test and proved."[3] On first consideration, these genres correspond in key ways, particularly in their attention to heroic protagonists bravely confronting untold dangers, yet they have long been viewed as contrasting forms, if not outright antitheses, as tacitly signaled in the title of W. P. Ker's foundational study, *Epic and Romance*. Ker acknowledges the difficulty of differentiating between these terms but nonetheless postulates: "Whatever Epic may mean, it implies some weight and solidity; Romance means nothing, if it does not convey some notion of mystery and fantasy."[4] Alexandra Cook similarly distinguishes between epic and romance, discerning "the public, external forces of epic history" in contrast to the "general figuring of romantic love as private, internal, and ahistorical."[5] Although the marriage of epic and romance has long been viewed askance, there is no inherent reason to discount the aesthetic benefits of their literary union, and other readers have demonstrated the potential synthesis of these forms. Colin Burrow, in his monograph *Epic Romance: Homer to Milton*, proposes that the merger of these genres "present[s] a structure of emotion . . . concerned with the nature of sympathy and its relation to complex social rituals."[6] The protagonists of the *Knight's Tale* are inspired by the classical and epic traditions yet adhere to the tropes and practices of medieval courtship, which indicates Chaucer's attention to synthesizing Greek and Roman legends with contemporary ideals concerning courtly love. In a strange twist of narrative desire, the Knight repeatedly digresses into distracting epic elements although his story's deeper interests lie in romance, with this conflict frequently impeding the flow of his narrative.

Certainly, either an epic or a romance would provide an appropriate subject for this aristocratic figure's tale. Chaucer the pilgrim introduces the Knight as one of the three model pilgrims of the *General Prologue* (along with the Parson and the Plowman), and Harry Bailly recognizes him as the journey's assumed leader by referring to him as "my mayster and my lord" (1.837).[7] He is a "worthy man" who "loved chivalrie, / Trouthe and honour, fredom and curteisie" (1.43, 1.45-46), as well as a valiant warrior: "Ful worthy was he in his lordes werre [war]" (1.47). Robert Haller proposes that "the Knight is the only pilgrim qualified by birth and character to speak authoritatively of the qualities of *gentilesse*," and also notes that "the classical epic, and it alone, is sufficient . . . to define those characteristics of men which deserve to be called noble."[8] The epic aspects of the

Knight's Tale celebrate the virtues of a noble and martial, if quasi-histori-cal, elite, whereas its romance aspects celebrate the chivalric values of the contemporary aristocracy. The *General Prologue* praises the Knight with terms suggestive of both genres, foreshadowing their alliances in his tale.

Despite embodying the values of epic and romance, the Knight under-mines their union through his dilatory and hesitant narration, often prov-ing himself an ineloquent storyteller who cannot identify an appropriate tone, pacing, or timbre. The Knight begins with an epigraph taken from Statius's *Thebaid*—"*Iamque domos patrias, Scithice post aspera gentis / Pre-lia, laurigero, &c*" (And now [Theseus, drawing nigh his] native land in lau-relled car after fierce battling with the Scithian folk, etc.). These lines are taken from the twelfth book of Statius's Latin epic, but the bulk of the first part of the *Knight's Tale* depicts events portrayed in Boccaccio's *Il Tese-ida*, as Theseus heeds the weeping women's plea to defeat the tyrannous Creon, who refuses to return, bury, or burn the bodies of their deceased husbands. From the tale's epigraph, audiences would likely expect an epic rather than a romance, but the opening lines of the *Knight's Tale* lack a key feature of epic: the Knight does not begin with an invocation of the Muse, in contrast to Chaucer's *Troilus and Criseyde*, which indicates its debts to the epic tradition by invoking Muses in the initial stanzas of four of its five books (respectively to Thesiphone, Clio, Venus, and the Furies). Epic is both signified and overlooked in the opening lines of the *Knight's Tale*, in a telling sign of forthcoming disjunctures.

Having introduced Theseus, Hippolyta, and Emelye as they journey to Athens following the Amazons' defeat, the Knight divulges his desire to tell more of his tale's epic backstory:

> And certes, if it nere to long to heere,
> I wolde have toold yow fully the manere
> How wonnen was the regne of Femenye
> By Theseus and by his chivalrye;
> And of the grete bataille for the nones [on that occasion]
> Bitwixen Atthenes and Amazones. (1.875-80)

These lines highlight the interpretive clash inherent in the Knight's med-ley of epic and romance, as he stresses that Theseus defeated the Ama-zons not merely through martial prowess but "by his chivalrye," yet it is difficult to imagine the Amazons regarding their conquest in battle as the actions of a chivalrous man. Were the Knight to regress in his narration and recall events prior to its beginning, he would adhere to one of the dominant tropes of the epic tradition: that the narrative should begin *in medias res* and then recount key events prior to its present moment. Here the Knight's digression privileges an epic tale rather than the hybrid one at hand—a martial tale of Theseus's military defeat of the Amazons rather than the romantic story of Palamon and Arcite battling for Emelye's hand.

In many ways, the structural problems inherent in uniting epic and romance align with their respective protagonists. Epics foreground the heroic achievements of men such as Odysseus, Aeneas, and Beowulf, whose heteroerotic relationships, if any, are relegated to the backstory (e.g., Odysseus seeks to reunite with Penelope after a twenty-year separation, Aeneas jilts Dido to continue his fated journey to Rome, Beowulf dies with neither a wife nor heir to perpetuate his reign). In contrast, romances highlight both the heroic and the amatory pursuits of their knightly protagonists, and so they must pay attention to their antagonists and to their female beloveds. As John Finlayson summarizes, "Epic character is expressed in action; romance character . . . is totally dependent on stereotyped actions whose purpose is to present an abstracted ideal."[9] Concerning the *Knight's Tale*, Theseus stands as the primary figure of the tale's epic elements, whereas Palamon, Arcite, and Emelye are the lead characters of its romance story line, and so the intersection of epic and romance produces an unsettling conflict of genre. With Theseus aligned with epic and Palamon and Arcite aligned with romance, the tale lacks a strong focalizing character. Further to this point, Theseus, as much as he directs the unfolding action of the *Knight's Tale*, serves more as an intercessionary figure than as its hero. Regardless of whether epic unsettles romance or romance unsettles epic in the tale's opening lines about Theseus's defeat of the Amazons, the Knight must begin his story anew— "And ther I lefte, I wol ayeyn bigynne" (1.892)—an inept beginning for an otherwise engaging tale.

Despite this misstep, the Knight soon achieves a powerful synthesis of epic and romance. Cappaneus's wife begs Theseus to halt Creon's desecration of soldiers' bodies; a rousing battle scene then introduces Palamon and Arcite, who are imprisoned following their capture. Smoothly segueing from epic battle to romantic conflict, both men fall passionately in love upon espying beautiful Emelye, with their declarations of love and their sophistic argumentation testifying to the depths of their emotions and their stratagems for outmaneuvering their amatory foe. Palamon cries out, "But I was hurt right now thurghout myn ye [eye] / Into myn herte, that wol my bane be" (1.1096-97), and Arcite similarly speaks of the painful pleasures of love: "The fresshe beautee sleeth me sodeynly" (1.1118). The outline of the romance plot is now apparent: both Palamon and Arcite cannot win Emelye's affections, and so the remainder of the tale will elucidate the events leading one man to triumph over the other.

As the Knight stumbles in beginning his tale owing to his urge to narrate additional backstory from Boccaccio's *Il Teseida*, thus to build an *in medias res* scaffolding for it, additional digressions, such as the introduction of Theseus's friend Perotheus, fail either to advance its plot or to enhance its literary qualities. For the purposes of his tale, the Knight should either employ this legend to fulfill the *in medias res* expectation of epic or discard it as irrelevant to the trajectory of his romance. Instead, the Knight eagerly digresses into the depth of Theseus and Perotheus's friendship but then veers sharply away from this material: "So wel they lovede, as olde bookes sayn, / That whan that oon was deed, soothly to telle, / His felawe wente and soughte hym doun in helle— / But of that storie list me nat to write" (1.1198-201). Boccaccio's *Il Teseida* includes an account of Theseus and Perotheus's friendship, yet the Knight's allusions to other story lines do not provide the *in medias res* framework he apparently desires and thus devolve into frustrating and irrelevant digressions.[10] Chaucer masterfully encodes several digressions into his tales, such as the Ovidian passage in the *Wife of Bath's Tale* (3.952-82), but these digressions thematically bolster the stories at hand. In this instance, it is virtually impossible to imagine the garrulous Wife of Bath telling a story without metaphorically "wandrynge by the weye" (1.467). In other words, all digressions digress, but some do so with a purpose. The Knight's departures from his subject matter highlight his inefficacy as a storyteller and destabilize the image that Chaucer otherwise projects for him as the pilgrimage's esteemed leader.

In accord with his dilatory epic imagination, the Knight inserts certain tropes of the genre despite realizing that his audience will find them wearisome. As is well known, epics typically include catalogs as a mnemonic device, as evident in the *Iliad*'s and the *Aeneid*'s catalogs of ships (respectively located in book 2, lines 494-759 and book 10, lines 163-214). The Knight, with his catalog of the trees needed for Arcite's pyre, respects this tradition while acknowledging its likely tediousness:

But how the fyr was maked upon highte,
Ne eek the names that the trees highte,

As ook, firre, birch, aspe, alder, holm, popler,
Wylugh [willow], elm, plane, assh, box, chasteyn [chestnut], lynde,
    laurer,
Mapul, thorn, bech, hasel, ew [yew], whippeltree [dogwood]—
How they weren feld shal nat be toold for me. (1.2919-24)

The Knight's narration falters here, as he first promises to skip this epic
catalog of trees, then records twenty-one separate species, and lastly reit-
erates that he will not address what he has already addressed. And while
any catalog of trees might strike some readers as inherently humdrum,
Edmund Spenser includes one effectively in the opening stanzas of *The
Faerie Queene* to establish his setting: "A Gentle Knight was pricking on
the plaine," he begins, as he then details the journey of this knight and his
"louely lady" through a landscape where "they prayse the trees so straight
and hy."[11] As with most literary matters, the aesthetic utility of a partic-
ular device depends on its context and its execution, and in the case of
these epic catalogs of trees, Spenser succeeds with an amusing nod to the
epic tradition to establish his lighthearted scene, whereas the Knight slav-
ishly adheres to it without accomplishing any effect other than apparently
checking an item off a stylistic checklist.

The catalog of trees signals an increasingly unsteady stream of narra-
tion, as the Knight stammers about what he will not address in his tale.
In the following forty-two lines, fifteen begin with the phrase "Ne how,"
as the Knight repeatedly tells his audiences of the many plot points that
they will not learn from him—of the gods running up and down (1.2925),
of the animals' fearful flight from the forest (1.2929-30), of Emelye's
swoon (1.2943), among other such points that are thus told through their
negation. These anaphoras—repeated phrasings used to emphasize a key
point—become grating, and more so, they introduce the rhetorical figure
of *occupatio*, in which a speaker broaches a subject by refusing to address
it further. As the Knight informs his audience that he will not divulge so
many aspects of his narrative, his words paradoxically reiterate an absence
that can never be filled. Like Gertrude Stein's famous snub of Oakland,
California—"There is no there there"[12]—the Knight's use of anaphoras
and the *occupatio* figure achieve little of literary or narrative consequence,
no rhetorical effect other than nothingness.

Likewise, in another misstep attributable to the epic tradition, the
"moral" of the *Knight's Tale* offers precious little insight into the events
befalling Palamon, Arcite, and Emelye, thus again pointing to the disjunc-

tion between epic and romance. The Knight grants Theseus the authority to guide his immediate audience, and thus to guide as well the Canterbury pilgrims and Chaucer's readers, to a deeper understanding of the meaning of Palamon's amatory triumph and Arcite's unexpected death. His words fall short: "Thanne is it wysdom, as it thynketh me, / To maken vertu of necessitee" (1.3041-42). Theseus's words are inspired by the epic tradition, which, as Northrop Frye writes, "demonstrat[es] that the fall of an enemy, no less than of a friend or a leader, is tragic and not comic." Elaborating on this point, Frye explains that "an objective and disinterested element enters into the poet's vision of human life" and that such a perspective "acquires . . . an authority based . . . on the vision of nature as an impersonal order."[13] As much as Theseus's stoic moral with its call to make virtue out of necessity reflects the ethos of many epics, it cannot appropriately segue into the tale's concluding celebration of romance. Theseus, as the chief representative of the narrative's epic ethos, highlights the Knight's inability to infuse his romance with deeper meaning.

The Knight turns again to romance and imbues his denouement with the grace and harmony typical of this genre, accentuating the "blisse and melodye" of Palamon and Emelye's marriage (1.3097). The romance ending is problematic for many readers, for as feminist critics have rightly noted, Emelye's desires remain overlooked throughout the *Knight's Tale*. She would prefer to remain a virgin rather than to marry either Palamon or Arcite, as the narrator affirms: "She woot namoore of al this hoote fare, / By God, than woot a cokkow or an hare!" (1.1809-10). Despite her prayer to Diana to remain a virgin, Saturn overlooks her wishes and instead grants the apparently contradictory wishes of Palamon and Arcite. While it is important to acknowledge these criticisms concerning the tale's treatment of Emelye, its romance conclusion is nonetheless structurally and thematically earned in light of the genre's protocols during the Middle Ages. By the end of his tale, the Knight accentuates its romance aspects, detailing the happy nuptials of Palamon and Emelye and assuring his audience that the couple are "lyvynge in blisse, in richesse, and in heele" (1.3102). Romance triumphs as epic falters, with the Knight recuperating his story from the intrusions of epic but revealing his weakness as a narrator throughout its telling. Yet in an unexpected irony, Theseus's epic adjuration to make virtue out of necessity applies well to Emelye when she is compelled to marry Palamon, which thus undercuts the marital bliss that the romance ending is intended to evoke.

Although epic tropes and digressions derail key aspects of the *Knight's*

Tale, it would be remiss not to mention that other elements of this tradition contribute powerfully to its visceral impact. The Knight vividly narrates accounts of combat with striking details, such as when Palamon and Arcite battle so fiercely that "Up to the ancle foghte they in hir blood" (1.1660). Most of the tale's third section, in which Palamon, Arcite, and Emelye pray respectively to Venus, Mars, and Diana, is indebted to the epic tradition, particularly in Saturn's intervention that will, seemingly inexplicably, allow both Venus and Mars to grant Palamon's and Arcite's wishes. Epics contain epic similes, long passages that intensify the poet's themes through an extended comparison, and the Knight employs this trope effectively in a passage that begins, "Right as the hunters in the regne of Trace" (1.1638), in which he likens Palamon and Arcite to wild animals: "Thou myghtest wene [think] that this Palamon / In his fightyng were a wood leon [crazed lion], / And as a crueel tigre was Arcite; / As wilde bores gonne they to smyte" (1.1655-58). The two are soon compared to boars again: "[They] foughten breme [fiercely] as it were bores two" (1.1699). The tournament scene strikingly combines epic and romance, uniting the hard-fought battles expected of epic with the chivalric contests expected of romance, in which "every wight that lovede chivalrye" (1.2106) joins the fray. In contrast to the somewhat stylized tournaments of many romances, the battles of the *Knight's Tale* come alive through their evocation of epic struggles between equally valiant competitors.

As a final note, and as noted in the introduction, one could posit Chaucer's satiric aim in this disjuncture between genres and the tale's narrating voice: some readers discern a pointed social commentary through the tale's metanarrative characterization of a knight who cannot satisfy the rhetorical demands of epic. But if Chaucer aimed to satirize the military culture of the aristocracy in the *Knight's Tale*, his aim at the Knight is unsteady, teetering between the character's image as an ideal representative of the warrior class and as a tale-teller tongue-tied by the desire to integrate so many epic elements into his hybrid account of Palamon and Arcite's battle for love. In contrast, Chaucer succeeds in mocking the storytelling abilities of a youthful member of the aristocracy in the notoriously, but purposefully, wretched romance of the *Squire's Tale*. In the *General Prologue*, Chaucer portrays the Knight as a battle-hardened warrior, one who has traveled vast distances to fight on his lord's behalf, whereas his son—"a lovyere and a lusty bacheler" (1.80)—represents an effete devolution of the masculine ideal embodied by his father. In sum, the father is epic, the son is romance, and the contrast between them would be heightened if the

Knight's Tale did not falter in its endorsement of epic themes. Despite the many virtues of the *Knight's Tale*, Chaucer's digressive difficulties in uniting epic and romance result in the tale's frustrating passages, memorable for their bathos amid the otherwise rarefied setting of classical courtly lovers predestined for death and marriage amid an epic world where one must be very, very careful for what one wishes.

CHAPTER 2

The Broken Arm and Sympathetic Cuckold of the *Miller's Tale*

With its riotous climax triggered by an explosive fart, Chaucer's *Miller's Tale* revels in the outrageous humor occasioned by the fabliau, with this tale famously allowing the Miller to narratively avenge himself on the Knight. "I kan a noble tale for the nones [for this occasion] / With which I wol now quite the Knyghtes tale" (1.3126-27), the Miller avows, with his ribald narrative demolishing the pretensions of courtly love so gallantly celebrated in the Knight's epic romance. Derek Brewer defines the fabliau as a "versified short story designed to make you laugh, and its subject matter is most often indecent, concerned either with sexual or excretory functions. The plot is usually in the form of a practical joke carried out for love or revenge,"[1] and Chaucer's genius arises in the Miller's deployment of this genre to wage narrative war with the Knight. Few would deny the masterful thematic and structural subversions of the *Miller's Tale*: the Knight employs the narrative structure of an erotic triangle, as Palamon and Arcite vie for Emelye's affections; the Miller accelerates this formula as Nicholas and Absolon compete for Alison's sexual favors, despite her marriage to John. Exploiting the inherent similarities between romance and fabliau in their attention to erotic pursuits, Chaucer's bawdy Miller mercilessly ridicules the artifice of the former genre and its knightly devotee. Only the most grimly dour and thematically myopic of readers would not respect the *Miller's Tale* as a masterwork both outrageously funny and intellectually impressive.

As much as the *Miller's Tale* succeeds on so many levels, a vexing fault line arises in its treatment of the character John—the *senex amans*, or loving old man—of the comic tradition. Along with the *senex amans*, a variety of stock characters populate fabliaux, including scheming suitors, dimwitted husbands, lascivious priests, and lusty wives, with cleverness often the defining feature of a given tale's protagonist—a role, in this instance, filled by "hende [courteous] Nicholas" (1.3199). Stock characters serve many useful functions for authors by cuing readers to a narrative's likely trajectory, thereby accelerating its pacing. Chaucer's introduction of a *senex amans* and his young wife outlines the likely plot for readers sufficiently versed in this literary tradition to infer that John will find himself cuckolded by the tale's completion. Stock characters simultaneously pose challenges for writers, for if they rely too heavily on yesteryear's clichés, they are unlikely to do more than to rehash a hackneyed plot. Authors must simultaneously be cautious not to innovate too far afield from a successful formula, lest they unmoor stock characters from their recognizable narrative positions. John of the *Miller's Tale* illustrates this paradox, in that he adheres to the parameters of the *senex amans* tradition while Chaucer, by individualizing him, liberates him in key ways from the prevailing expectations of this role. Like a standard *senex amans*, he is obsessed with fears of his wife's adultery, but he is also a gentle-hearted man sincerely concerned for her safety and consistently sympathetic to the needs of others. John's unexpected duality leaves the rambunctious conclusion of the *Miller's Tale* wavering between his narrative fate as comically warranted (owing to readerly expectations for a *senex amans*'s typical comeuppance) and morally unwarranted (owing to his unexpected divergence from standard protocols of characterization). Fabliaux do not typically elicit sympathy for their duped and cuckolded husbands, yet the *Miller's Tale* undermines its humor by depicting John as the only kindhearted character, whose virtue cannot redeem him from the machinations of others.

Over the course of the *Miller's Tale*, readers witness a stark disjunction between descriptions of John and his actions, with the two rarely aligning. Notably, the narrator, despite any premise of impartial omniscience, misrepresents John's motivations in the tale's opening passages. First, he establishes the age difference between John and Alison, stressing that she is merely eighteen years old (1.3221-23), and he then emphasizes that John is foredoomed to an ignoble end owing to his status as a *senex amans*: "But sith that he was fallen in the snare, / He moste endure, as oother folk, his care" (1.3231-32). Although the facts of this description cannot be denied—John is indeed significantly older than his teenage wife Alison—the narrator repeatedly records John's jealousy: "Jalous he was, and heeld hire narwe in cage, / For she was wylde and yong, and he was old / And demed hymself been lik a cokewold" (1.3224-26). John, however, never demonstrates jealousy, possessiveness, or an overweening fear of cuckoldry, and so the reader is encouraged to view him through an interpretive lens unaligned with his actions. The narrator repeats this mischaracterization when detailing Nicholas's stratagems for fornicating with Alison: "That Nicholas shal shapen hym a wyle / This sely jalous housbonde to bigyle" (1.3403-4). In his role as one of the Canterbury pilgrims, Chaucer frequently plays the role of an untrustworthy narrator who blithely accepts his fellow pilgrims' self-descriptions that the portraits themselves contradict. In describing John, the narrator of the *Miller's Tale* is similarly untrustworthy, for he introduces characters by affirming their adherence to the codes of fabliau, regardless of whether they truly fit these interpretive paradigms.

The introduction of a sympathetic *senex amans* appears—but cannot be conclusively determined—to be Chaucer's innovation to the sources of his tale. No direct origin for Chaucer's *Miller's Tale* has been discovered, and most scholars agree that it was likely a lost French fabliau. Its closest extant analogues include the Dutch tale *Heile of Beersele*, the French fabliau *Le chevalier a la corbeille* (The Knight of the Basket), and Boccaccio's *Decameron* (day 3, tale 4), each of which features characters who more fully inhabit their positions as stock figures and thus do not complicate their humor through sympathy. *Heile of Beersele* details the sexual hijinks of its eponymous character, a prostitute, and her three suitors.[2] These men's positions align with John's, Nicholas's, and Absolon's, but the male characters of *Heile of Beersele* are only distinguishable by their professions, not by their personalities, and none evince any motivation beyond lust. *Le chevalier a la corbeille* depicts a love triangle between a knight, a lady, and the lady's husband, who employs an old woman to safeguard his wife's virtue. Like John, this crone figure finds herself unexpectedly punished when, trapped in an unexpectedly descending basket, the knight's men then "See who it is [and] . . . begin / To devil her out of her skin" (lines 222-23).[3] Unlike John, however, this woman serves merely as a plot device, an obstacle that the knight must overcome if he is to enjoy the rewards of his cleverness by outwitting the lady's husband and his ally. Boccaccio's *Decameron* includes the loosely similar tale of Friar Puccio, who is deceived by his wife Monna Isabetta and her lover Dom Felice. Friar Puccio, like John, fulfills the role of a *senex amans*: young Monna Isabetta is sexually dissatisfied "because of her husband's godliness and possibly on account of his age."[4] In each of these tales the characters remain firmly in their roles as stock characters, and thus the humor of these narratives, while simpler than Chaucer's, does not suffer from the sort of conflicts engendered by his sympathetic *senex amans*.

With falsehoods similar to the narrator's, Alison alleges that John will react wrathfully, even violently, if he learns of her adultery, warning Nicholas of her fears: "Myn housbonde is so ful of jalousie / That but ye wayte wel and been privee [secretive], / I woot [know] right wel I nam but deed" (1.3294-96). According to both the narrator and Alison, John's marital possessiveness stands as his defining trait—not merely jealous but murderously so—and such a stock character would serve as an appropriate target of narrative vengeance in a fabliau. Indeed, in the *Merchant's Tale*, Chaucer depicts January's jealousy over May in similar terms, with the key difference between these tales in that the actions of this *senex amans* match his descriptions: "That he nas jalous everemoore in oon; / Which jalousye it was so outrageous / . . . / He nolde suffre hire for to ryde or go, / But if that he had hond on hire alway" (4.2086-87, 2090-91). January suspiciously monitors May's every move, and so the tale's sense of comic justice prevails when she proves herself sexually uncontrollable; in contrast, John is repeatedly envisioned as jealously attempting to control Alison, yet his actions belie this characterization. For the *Miller's Tale*, the introduction of a sympathetic *senex amans* results in a disharmony between the fabliau's humorous pursuit of comic justice and John's undeserved fate.

The clearest evidence that the narrator and Alison mischaracterize John as jealous occurs when Absolon hopes to seduce Alison despite his (John's) presence. Hoping to serenade his beloved, Absolon stands outside the couple's home and calls: "Now, deere lady, if thy wille be, / I praye yow that ye wole rewe [take pity] on me" (1.3361-62). John awakens to his rival's amatory plea, but his response evinces surprise and annoyance, perhaps even exasperation, rather than jealousy, rage, or anger. "What! Alison! Herestow nat Absolon, / That chaunteth thus under oure boures wal?" (1.3366-67), he queries, to which Alison nonchalantly replies, "Yis, God woot, John, I heere it every deel" (1.3369). The lines following this encounter catalog the extent of Absolon's efforts to woo Alison by singing to her, sending her cakes, and offering her money. These seductive efforts are recounted only cursorily, yet it strains credibility, even in this most exaggerated of tales, to assume that John could remain ignorant of his rival's repeated and blatant attempts to seduce his wife. When Absolon again seeks to woo Alison toward the tale's conclusion, he asks a "cloisterer" (1.3661) of John's whereabouts; the monk replies, "I trowe that he be went / For tymber, ther oure abbot hath hym sent; / For he is wont for tymber for to go / And dwellen at the grange a day or two" (1.3665-68). It again strains credibility to imagine a murderously jealous husband leaving his wife unattended during his frequent overnight journeys, which further discredits these aspersions against John's character; indeed, John's frequent travels grant Nicholas and Alison the necessary freedom to plan their liaison. Moreover, these circumstances ironically highlight the farcical nature of Chaucer's plot, in that it appears John's many trips would provide sufficient opportunities for sex without such fantastical plotting, although the narrator adds that Nicholas, while not apparently a very romantic figure, hopes to deceive John so that Alison "sholde slepen in his arm al nyght" (1.3406). The monk further informs Absolon that he can only conjecture because he does not know John's location: "Or elles he is at his hous, certeyn. / Where that he be, I kan nat soothly seyn" (1.3669-70). Absolon then proceeds with his plan to seduce Alison without knowing—or apparently caring— whether John, the purportedly murderously jealous *senex amans*, remains with her at home.

Rather than jealousy, John's primary characteristics appear to be his devoted affection for Alison, his sincere concern for Nicholas, and his utter ambivalence toward Absolon. When Nicholas initiates his convoluted scheme to sleep with Alison, which necessitates that he convince John of an imminent cataclysm requiring the three of them to sleep separately in tubs tied to the ceiling, he hides himself in his room for a weekend, and John grows increasingly worried. "I am adrad, by Seint Thomas, / It stondeth nat aright with Nicholas" (1.3425-26), he frets, and soon repeats his apprehension: "Me reweth soore of hende Nicholas. / He shal be rated of [reprimanded for] his studiyng, / If that I may, by Jhesus, hevene kyng!" (1.3462-64). When Nicholas warns him of this impending flood, John agonizes over the vision of his wife in jeopardy: "Allas, my wyf! / And shal she drenche [drown]? Allas, myn Alisoun!" he cries, as the narrator then adds, "For sorwe of this he fil almoost adoun" (1.3522-24). Later, while preparing for the promised flood, John is visibly distraught: "He wepeth, weyleth, maketh sory cheere; / He siketh [sighs] with ful many a sory swogh [groan]" (1.3618-19). Such an outburst of emotion evinces John's sympathy for others, which in turn creates sympathy for John among readers, although critics disagree over the extent to which this sympathy should influence an interpretation of the tale.

From these passages it is apparent that the narrator and Alison inaccurately yet repeatedly describe John as jealous, yet he exhibits another flaw common to the dupes of fabliau, in that he appears to be a man of rather limited intelligence. The narrator declares that John "knew nat Catoun, for his wit was rude" (1.3227), and John says approvingly of himself, "Ye, blessed

be alwey a lewed man / That noght but oonly his bileve kan!" (1.3455-56).
Lewed here means uneducated, ignorant, and unlettered, which comple-
ments his frequent description as *sely*.[5] As Jennifer Bryan observes, the
word *sely* was "undergoing significant semantic shift and consequently
able to slide all the way from *blessed, happy, pious*, or *innocent* at the one
pole, to *feeble, pitiable,* or *silly* at the other."[6] Additional meanings attested
to in the *Middle English Dictionary* include guileless, foolish, and gullible.[7]
In a masterful pairing of dialogue, John states, "Men sholde nat knowe
of Goddes pryvetee" (1.3454), and Nicholas states that he will not share
such information: "Axe nat why, for though thou aske me, / I wol nat tellen
Goddes pryvetee" (1.3557-58). John rejects the possibility of questioning
Nicholas about the source of his supposed vision, thereby foreclosing any
possibility that he could avert the trickster's plans. Although asserting his
knowledge of Christian teachings, John instead proves himself ignorant of
widely known narratives, particularly the account of Noah's flood. In pre-
dicting a new deluge of biblical proportions, Nicholas alludes to the flood
story in Genesis, and John affirms that he knows this passage (1.3534-
37). Notably, Nicholas's subsequent references to Noah's wife place this
biblical story in the context of medieval drama, in which she is cast in
the comic role of a shrewish woman.[8] Whether from church readings or
from dramatic performances, John should remember that God promised
not to flood humanity again ("I will establish my covenant with you, and
all flesh shall be no more destroyed with the waters of a flood"; Genesis
9.11). Nicholas also tells John that, if he heeds his advice, "thanne shul
we be lordes al oure lyf / Of al the world, as Noe and his wyf" (1.3581-82),
with John apparently not contemplating the disjunction between a vision
of Noah and his wife as a couple and the triad of Nicholas, Alison, and him-
self. Ignorance, not jealousy, is John's defining flaw, and as Dawn Simmons
Walts argues, "The carpenter's familiarity with the original tale coupled
with his lack of learning . . . provides Nicholas the opportunity to invent
his own version."[9] Nicholas, Alison, and the narrator all create fictions
that cloud readers' perceptions of John and John's perception of the world
around him: both he and we are challenged to see clearly through these
swirling duplicities.

The comic climax of the *Miller's Tale* unfolds in rapid succession. Ali-
son tricks Absolon into kissing her posteriors; Nicholas farts in Absolon's
face; and Absolon strikes Nicholas in his buttocks with a hot iron. The
antics continue as Nicholas calls out for water, John hears his cry, believes
the flood has come, cuts the cord that holds his tub to the ceiling, and

falls to the floor. The audience of the *Miller's Tale* surely laughs at the comic fates of these three men, yet it is noteworthy that the townspeople depicted in the tale laugh solely at John:

> The folk gan laughen at his fantasye;
> Into the roof they kiken [stare] and they cape [gape],
> And turned al his harm unto a jape.
> For what so that this carpenter answerde,
> It was for noght; no man his reson herde.
> With othes [oaths] grete he was so sworn adoun
> That he was holde wood [deemed insane] in al the toun;
> For every clerk anonright heeld with oother.
> They seyde, "The man is wood, my leeve brother";
> And every wight gan laughen at this stryf. (1.3840-49)

The shift in focalization—from the pains inflicted on Nicholas, Absolon, and John to John alone—distends the fabliau's humor, as the audience is encouraged to laugh specifically at one man for his shortcomings, despite the fact that the primary shortcoming for which he should receive his comeuppance—his jealousy—is nowhere evident in the tale. The townspeople apparently never learn of Nicholas, Alison, and Absolon's collective antics preceding John's downfall, which limits their comprehension of the full range of comic repercussions for the various characters, with the exception of Alison, who emerges from the tale unscathed. The unexpected irony of the tale, then, is that readers are encouraged to direct their comic derision at the tale's most generous character, which calls into question the timbre of its humor. Derek Pearsall, for instance, argues that the fabliau's unabashed humor quickly restores John to his position as the butt of the tale's joke: "There is enough here to give us a twinge of sympathy, but no more. Chaucer . . . allows the delightful apprehension of a momentary intrusion of feeling, and then resumes his splendid fooling."[10] On the other hand, by infusing his fabliau with emotions deeper than those typically expressed by the genre's stock characters, Chaucer recalibrates the emotional responses warranted by the form. In this tale in which Nicholas and Absolon single-mindedly pursue their adulterous desires, and in which Alison, after her initial demurral, readily enjoys Nicholas's attentions with little regard for betraying her spouse, John is the only character who expresses a selfless concern for the well-being of others. His sympathy functions both textually (in his actions toward

CHAPTER 3

The Stoic Dawn Song and Comic Rapes of the *Reeve's Tale*

Few genres are as funny as the fabliau, few crimes are as vicious as rape, and hence the inherent instability of the *Reeve's Tale*. It is a narrative joke that hinges on sexual violence, and it cloaks the violation at its heart by reframing fabliau-rape as parodic romance. Key to this transition is Malyne's love song at dawn, a poetic form referred to as an aubade, which shifts the tale's story line from Aleyn and John's farcical revenge against the miller Symkyn to Malyne's pining desire for Aleyn. Gale Sigal defines the aubade as "a lament for the brevity of human love and a celebration of its irrepressibility," noting as well that it paradoxically "prolongs a love affair while its subject is the love's dissolution."[1] Malyne's aubade allows readers deeper insights into her view of the night's chaotic events, elevating her from the stock figures of most fabliaux into a character of surprising depth, but it is precisely this complexity that obscures interpretive clarity of a tale teetering on the unsteady border between comic shenanigans and erotic abuse. As a key example of Chaucer's outmoded perspectives, the *Reeve's Tale* is founded on the inherently unsteady humor of sexual violence against women, which undercuts the comedy to which it aspires. Between the shifting comic valences of the fourteenth century and today, what are the literary and ethical repercussions of viewing this fabliau's humor as undercut, if not wholly undone, by its dismissive treatment of rape?

As the Miller crudely expressed his antagonism to the Knight in his prologue and tale, so too does Oswald the Reeve express his contempt for the Miller, and it soon becomes apparent that this rivalry will be waged through narrative treatments of sexual violence. A carpenter by trade, the Reeve is angered by the Miller's depiction of the cuckolded carpenter John in the *Miller's Tale* (cf. 1.614, 1.3861) and vows to avenge himself on his fellow pilgrim: "I shal hym quite [pay him back] anoon," he declares, and then adds, "Right in his cherles termes wol I speke" (1.3916-17). The phrase "cherles terms" recalls Chaucer's description of the *Miller's Tale* as a "cherles tale" (1.3169) and idiomatically denotes the genre of fabliau. Stock characters typically progress through stock story lines, and the opening passages of Chaucer's *Reeve's Tale* adhere to this formula. The narrator introduces the jealous miller Symkyn and his wife, which alerts perceptive readers to the comic reversals forthcoming. Unlike John in the *Miller's Tale*, who is repeatedly described as jealous but never evinces any jealousy, Symkyn's violently obsessive concern for his wife's fidelity is symbolized by the many knives and swords he carries (1.3929-33). Because the Reeve mentions Symkyn's intense jealousy over his wife, such that the local men know they will face his violent wrath should they attempt to "rage or ones pleye" with her (1.3958), readers versed in comic traditions should expect this jealous miller to be cuckolded, with violent repercussions ensuing.

Throughout the *Reeve's Tale*, Symkyn's wife and daughter Malyne are viewed more through a lens of erotic and financial instrumentality than of desire, which aligns them with many other female characters of fabliau who are marginalized as vessels through whom men seek aggrandizement over one another via sexual conquest. In other words, romance—both the genre and the concept—remains absent from their lives. For instance, Symkyn's jealousy is intimately connected to his ambition for upward social mobility—no matter the inherent ridiculousness of a social-climbing miller in the Middle Ages—and he views his wife and daughter as tools for achieving financial gain. He married his wife to enhance his social status, with the narrator reporting that he "wolde no wyf, as he sayde, / But she were wel ynorissed [raised] and a mayde [virgin], / To saven his estaat of yomanrye" (1.3947-49). Notably, Symkyn insisted on his wife's virginity prior to their marriage, with this line ironically foreshadowing Malyne's loss of hers. Symkyn similarly views his daughter as a means to stronger financial alliances. Like her father and mother before her, she is initially described as a stock character of the fabliau tradition: "This wenche thikke and wel ygrowen was, / With kamus [pug] nose and eyen greye as glas, / With buttokes brode and brestes rounde and hye. / But right fair was hire heer; I wol nat lye" (1.3973-76). This portrait focuses exclusively on Malyne's physical characteristics: her size, her facial features, her physique. Readers perceive no sense of this young woman's amatory desires, even as they learn of her grandfather's ambition to profit by marrying her to a wealthy family: "His purpos was for to bistowe hire hye / Into som worthy blood of auncetrye" (1.3981-82). These lines prepare readers to view Malyne as familial chattel in financial, although perhaps under the veneer of amatory, negotiations. In the introduction of the tale, she is presented as a plot device rather than as a fully individualized character, which serves as an effective strategy in maintaining the farcical humor of fabliaux.

As the plot progresses, readers learn that Symkyn regularly steals grain from Aleyn and John's college; the clerks devise a plan to end his ill-gotten gains, but Symkyn outwits them and steals the grain yet again. Because night has fallen, Aleyn and John must stay the night at Symkyn's house, and Aleyn decides to avenge himself for this loss, explaining to John the quasi-legal grounds of his actions: "For, John, ther is a lawe that says thus: / That gif a man in a point be agreved, / That in another he sal be releved" (1.4180-82). He further declares, "And syn I sal have neen amendement / Agayn my los, I will have esement" (1.4185-86). The resolution that will allow Aleyn to be "releved" and to find "esement" is Malyne, whom he determines to "seduce" in a manner congruent with fabliau plotlines:

> And up he rist, and by the wenche he crepte.
> This wenche lay uprighte and faste slepte,
> Til he so ny was, er she myghte espie,
> That it had been to late for to crie,
> And shortly for to seyn, they were aton.
> Now pley, Aleyn, for I wol speke of John. (1.4193-98)

Many readers interpret this scene not as a lighthearted romp in the sack but as a rape. Indeed, the telltale words "to late for to crie" expose Aleyn's attack as a rape, for it tacitly posits that Malyne would cry out if she were allowed sufficient opportunity to do so, even as the narration sanitizes Alyen's actions. In contrast, in the corresponding scene of the *Miller's Tale*, Nicholas "seduces" Alison with similarly aggressive acts, yet the encounter cannot be construed as rape because Alison grants her consent. Even though he "caughte hire by the queynte [vagina]" (1.3276) and "heeld hire harde by the haunchebones" (1.3279), Alison responds sharply to these unsolicited advances and warns him, "Why, lat be! . . . Lat be, Nicholas, / Or I wol crie 'out, harrow' and 'allas'!" (1.3285-86). Nicholas begs her mercy, and the narrator reports that "she hir love hym graunted atte laste" (1.3290). In this short passage, Nicholas acts in a sexually invasive manner, but Alison rebuts his advances until she determines on her own volition to accept him as her lover. At their most fundamental difference, Alison speaks during this key exchange of the *Miller's Tale*, whereas Malyne remains silent in the corresponding scene of the *Reeve's Tale*. In another relevant scene featured in the *Man of Law's Tale*, a narrative with debts to romance and hagiography, Chaucer depicts Constance resisting rape. When her attacker "seyde he sholde / Hir lemman [lover] be, wher-so she wolde or nolde" (2.916-17), she resists, "struglyng wel and myghtily" until the "theef fil over bord" and drowns (2.921-22). Notable, too, in the *Reeve's Tale* is the narrator's closing adjuration for Aleyn to "pley," as this voice attempts to imbue the scene with the frivolity of ribald comedy rather than the darkness of sexual violence.

Despite the fabliau humor of this passage—or at least, its ostensible humor—many modern readers cannot overlook the ways in which it elides the rape at its heart. In broad terms, the *Reeve's Tale* constructs its ideal reader as one who enjoys its masculinist humor, and such expectations of masculine narrative pleasure often accompany depictions of rape. As Pamela Barnett explains, "Male writers have altered the import of rape in their texts by rhetorically eliding women's protest and resistance, by replacing women's voices with the words of male discourses on female sexuality, and by deflecting the violence of the act itself—letting it hide under a rubric of playfulness, seduction, or the euphemization 'ravishment.'"[2] With a male author (Chaucer) depicting in his frame narrative a male character (the Reeve), who tells a ribald tale from the perspective of his swindled male protagonist (Aleyn), who seeks reparations for the injustice committed against him by the ostentatiously unappealing antagonist (Symkyn), the *Reeve's Tale* is suffused with a masculinist bias that leaves women characters bereft of speech until nearly its end. Noting this plenitude of male voices speaking over the tale's mostly silent women, Carissa M. Harris views the *Reeve's Tale* as celebrating a particularly vicious form of medieval masculinity that is "centered on men teaching their peers to perpetuate rape culture."[3]

At the same time that it would be ethically inappropriate to elide the rape depicted in the *Reeve's Tale*, this act of sexual violence should be contextualized within its historical period and its literary genre. As Holly Crocker explains of the legal requirements for adjudicating rape in medieval England, "The tale deploys legal standards for determining the crime of rape.... Between Aleyn's stealth and Malyne's affection, neither the girl nor Symkyn has a legal claim to rape."[4] Within the world of fabliau, a common character pairing involves a randy young man and a young woman initially hesitant to have sex with him who then accedes to his wishes—and, it is implied, to her own desires now unleashed. As with his sources, including

Le meunier et les .II. clers, Een bispel van .ij. clerken, and Boccaccio's *Decam-eron* (day 9, tale 6), Chaucer's *Reeve's Tale* tells the story of two young men who are cheated by their host, who then avenge themselves by fornicating with his daughter and wife, with a plot point involving the deceptive relocation of a cradle. In *Le meunier et les .II. clers*, the first student deceives the Malyne character with a golden ring, promising that "however much she's been a run-around, / however impure and unvirginal she is, / she will be by morning, if she has it on her finger" (214-16). In *Een bispel van .ij. clerken*, the first clerk approaches the daughter "timidly . . . feeling cold with fear" (66-67) and offers her a "ring of red gold . . . worth almost ten pounds" (84-86).[5] Boccaccio's *Decameron* most closely matches Chaucer's *Reeve's Tale* on the crucial point of Aleyn's stealthy approach of Malyne: "Pinuccio waited until he was sure that everyone was asleep, then quietly left his bed, stole across to the bed in which his lady-love was sleeping, and lay down beside her. Although she was somewhat alarmed, the girl received him joyously in her arms, and they then proceeded to take their fill of that sweet pleasure for which they yearned above all else."[6] Boccaccio's tale grants a modicum of agency to this character: first surprise and alarm but then ready acquiescence.

While not a direct source for the *Reeve's Tale*, the French fabliau *Auberée* similarly showcases a coercive sex act that borders on rape and thus further illuminates Chaucer's handling of Aleyn and Malyne's sexual encounter. In this tale a young man enlists Auberée's assistance so that he can sleep with a young woman; Auberée tricks the young woman into staying at her house and invites the young man to indulge his desires. He worries that she will view the experience as rape, asking Auberée, "What tactics, lady, should I use / if she turns proud and starts in screeching?" (356-57). Like Alison in the *Miller's Tale* the young woman threatens him with exposure: "I'll scream with might and main. / Before your eyes to me will flock / every last person on the block" (384-86). The young woman fears the damage to her reputation should this incident be divulged, and the narrator explains the coercive force of her fears: "What can she do but acquiesce? / She has to quietly submit" (402-3). Given these circumstances, "She accepts him as a lover" (411); the tale then emphasizes her enjoyment of their tryst: "The two of them all through the night / remained awake, taking delight / in close embrace and in unbounded / plea-sure" (429-32).[7] Given the comic framework of fabliaux, the narration of these stories typically presents such encounters as unexpected but then welcome seductions, necessitating readers to heed Chaucer's admonition that one should "nat maken ernest of game" (1.3186) even when it becomes rather challenging to follow.

On the whole, the sexual encounter between Aleyn and Malyne, as well as those in Chaucer's sources and analogues, asks readers to envision the paradox of rape without violation, and therefore to concentrate on erotic humor over sexual horror. Still, even when viewing Aleyn's "seduction" of Malyne within its contemporary historical and generic parameters, the *Reeve's Tale* is notably darker and more violent than the *Miller's Tale*. Nicole Nolan Sidhu persuasively observes, "Although the tale's milieu and characters suggest comical fabliau trickery, it depicts extremes of brutality, desperation, and social anxiety that are unusual in the genre."[8] Furthermore, many readers are increasingly uncomfortable excusing male characters of sexual violence, particularly when the textual evidence against them is incontrovertible. Given these conflicting interpretive impulses, and rather than simply labeling Aleyn's "seduction" of Malyne a rape, it would provide appropriate context in many discussions of medieval literature to prefix this term with the genre in which the act appears, thus to distinguish between the reactions Chaucer intended to solicit with the fabliau-genre rape of the *Reeve's Tale* and, for example, the romance-genre rape of the *Wife of Bath's Tale*.

Following Aleyn's fabliau-rape of Malyne, the tale turns to John's machinations to sleep with Symkyn's wife, as he moves her son's cradle from the foot of her bed to the foot of his. This far-fetched plan soon proves successful, for after she "wente . . . out to pisse" (1.4215), she gropes for the cradle, finds it, and unwittingly joins John in bed. Again, the tale encourages readers to privilege fabliau humor over sexual violation, recording the pleasure that Symkyn's wife unexpectedly experiences: "Withinne a while this John the clerk up leep, / And on this goode wyf he leith on soore. / So myrie a fit ne hadde she nat ful yoore [for a long time]; / He priketh harde and depe as he were mad" (1.4228-31). In several ways this passage would appear more violent than the one recounting Malyne's rape, as John leaps upon Symkyn's wife and "pricks" her with the single-minded frenzy of a madman. Yet Chaucer dilutes the violation depicted in this passage by characterizing it as a "myrie . . . fit," as well as by contrasting Symkyn's wife's energetic evening with John to her apparently unsatisfying sex life with Symkyn. (Along with the statement that "So myrie a fit ne hadde she nat ful yore," the separation of almost twenty years in age between her infant son and Malyne would suggest that Symkyn's wife does not enjoy a particularly affectionate marriage.) Critical discussions of the *Reeve's Tale* often focus more on the violation of Malyne than of Symkyn's wife, and the distinction between the two characters—the former as transcending her role as a stock figure, the latter remaining firmly within it—explains the diverging ways in which readers respond to their narrative fates.

The narrator returns to Aleyn and Malyne as the morning approaches, as the two exchange parting words of affection and regret in a passage inspired by the aubade tradition. Their names link them as lovers, as they are anagrams of each other aside from the added *m* of Malyne. While many aubades delicately elide the fact that the couple recently copulated, the *Reeve's Tale*, true to its fabliau debts, reminds readers that "Aleyn wax wery in the dawenynge, / For he had swonken [worked] al the longe nyght" (1.4234-35). Given the vulgarity typical of fabliau and the sexual violence lightly hidden under a frame of comic seduction, his words are surprisingly tender—"Fare weel, Malyne, sweete wight!" (1.4236)—as they also frame him as her devoted lover: "I is thyn awen [own] clerk, swa have I seel [as I may prosper]!" (1.4239). Although voicing the words of a courtly lover, Aleyn cannot overwrite his identity as a student, which thus undercuts the emotions purportedly on display. Malyne, voiceless when Aleyn violated her, now speaks in an extended passage of affection and instruction. "Now, deere lemman," (1.4240), she begins, as she then discloses to him the location of the cake made of their stolen meal. She bids Aleyn farewell—"And, goode lemman, God thee save and kepe!"—as the narrator records her emotional state: "And with that word almoost she gan to wepe" (1.4247-48). In a fabliau populated with unseemly and unsympathetic characters concerned more about financial gain and revenge than human emotion, Malyne evinces a depth of feeling and affection elsewhere absent in the tale. As John Plummer muses, Malyne performs "the only act in the tale that is even marginally charitable," postulating further that "as embarrassing as it might feel to do so, one ought to admit here a sense of pathos."[9] Malyne's aubade reconfigures the fabliau-rape of the previous evening into a romance-genre rape, thus destabilizing efforts to view Aleyn's encounter with her through the comic lens of fabliau.

Malyne's dawn song, however, is notable in how little it focuses either on love or on Aleyn. Other than twice referring to him as her "lemman," she speaks more about the location of the stolen grain than about the beauty or pleasure of their love. It is a strangely stoic and utilitarian aubade, one designed more to avenge herself on her father than to celebrate love's transcendence. Indeed, Chaucer's qualification that Malyne "almoost" weeps suggests an unexpected resilience that undermines the emotionality of her words, pointing to a parody of the aubade tradition more than simply its unexpected deployment in a fabliau. One suspects that Malyne recognizes her father's utilitarian view of her unbroken hymen as little more than a "proof of purchase" for whichever spouse he might eventually select for her, and that she therefore recalibrates these crude terms of exchange to posit one in which romance, no matter how far-fetched, can be envisioned as part of the unexpected encounter she experienced, whether energetically enjoyed or stoically endured, the previous evening. In complementary contrast to her daughter, Symkyn's wife also speaks near the tale's conclusion, yet her words affirm her allegiance to her husband and thus do not shift between the interpretive planes of fabliau and romance. Awoken by the brawl occasioned by Aleyn's accidental confession to Symkyn, she calls for her husband's aid: "Awak, Symond! The feend is on me falle. / Myn herte is broken; help! I nam but deed!" (1.4288-89). By adding her voice to the melee, Symkyn's wife participates in the fabliau humor that Malyne eludes through her odd, affecting, yet emotionless aubade.

Thus, the interpretive crux posed by the *Reeve's Tale* asks readers to balance the farcical humor of fabliau, the misplaced emotionalism of Malyne's morning dawn song, and the sexual violence that the narrative camouflages but cannot fully disavow in the tension between fabliau-rape and romance-genre rape. In his foundational essay identifying Malyne's speech as an aubade, R. E. Kaske noted this interpretive difficulty, proposing that the tale appears to "generat[e] a sporadic and unsatisfied sympathy for Malyne" but ultimately concluding that "Malyne remains the undifferentiated 'daughter of the house' who is *swyved* for the story's sake; and the fabliau remains consistently a fabliau."[10] Speaking sharply against such readings, Tamarah Kohanski sees Aleyn's rape of Malyne as the pivotal moment of the tale: "Because Chaucer has 'humanized' Malyne, refusing to define her explicitly as a type, we are empowered to see and understand the terrible effects of her dehumanization at the hands of men."[11] One could posit an interpretation somewhere between these two poles—that it is a darker fabliau than the *Miller's Tale* but humorous nonetheless, that readings of its sexual violence, while enlightening, must concurrently acknowledge that fabliau narrators often construct their women characters as willing participants in sexual acts coded as shenanigans rather than as violations—but the challenge of the *Reeve's Tale* stands in the unbreakable yoke between its attempted humor and its depicted violence.

As a final twist to this interpretive dilemma spanning the sensibilities of the fourteenth century to the present day, the thorny issue of whether Chaucer was himself a rapist has long complicated readers' enjoyment of his rape jokes in the *Reeve's Tale.* According to contemporary court records Cecily Chaumpaigne in 1380 "released Geoffrey Chaucer from *omnimodas acciones tam de raptu meo tam* [*sic*] *de aliqua alia re vel causa*—'actions of whatever kind either concerning my rape or any other matter.'"[12] Little context is given for this statement, and the Latin word *raptus* could refer to a rape but also to a seizure or kidnapping, although Christopher Cannon, in his detailed research on this issue, concludes that *"raptus* in fourteenth-century English law meant forced coitus."[13] Notwithstanding any historical haziness of this event, Rachel E. Moss persuasively argues, "It is absolutely critical to address the issue of Chaucer being a man who raped a woman, because it forces us to think of how Chaucer may not just have been a passive recipient of the values embedded into rape culture, but also an active promoter of those values."[14]

More recently discovered evidence would apparently exculpate Chaucer from rape charges, as Euan Roger and Sebastian Sobecki's archival research led them to the following conclusions: "a) Chaucer and Chaumpaigne were not rival parties in a legal dispute, but instead codefendants against a third party, Thomas Staundon; b) the accusations brought against Chaucer and Chaumpaigne were not charges of rape, nor were they likely charges of abduction, but instead a labor dispute under the Statute of Laborers; and c) the quitclaims of Easter 1380 represented a legal strategy by Chaucer and Chaumpaigne, in which the language of the releases was framed and formulated within existing legal frameworks."[15] Long accused of rape, now apparently cleared of the charges, Chaucer, the author, nonetheless repeatedly returned to this topic. The archaic humor of Chaucer's rape joke does not transcend its medieval temporality for many readers, which leaves the bitter aftertaste of comedy dependent on violence against women. Moreover, as Samantha Katz Seal poignantly observes in her rich reading of Chaucer's many (primarily male) defenders over the nineteenth and twentieth centuries, "Chaucer may have been freed of the suspicion of rape. But Chaucer studies will never be free of Cecily Chaumpaigne and the threat she represented to a hegemonic order founded upon race and class and gender."[16] In other words, the gendered dynamics of this critical imbroglio continue to matter, for they reveal telling cultural assumptions about authorship and identity that some readers would prefer to overlook altogether—despite the necessity of examining them critically to better understand the unsteady correlation between great artworks and the only too human individuals who created them.

From a strictly literary perspective, the chief failure of the *Reeve's Tale*, then, emerges in Chaucer's inability to maintain the comic ethos of the fabliau with the sympathies generated by an aubade of the romance tradition. In effect, Malyne's fabliau dawn song is a destabilizing oxymoron that forestalls either comedy or romance from guiding the tale to a steady conclusion. Malyne eludes the stereotypes of the wanton women of fabliau, proving herself a character of surprising depth in a tale populated primarily by types. In her unique figuration, she is subjected to sexual acts that are challenging to dismiss as a joke, and in her reformulation of the aubade, she voices her desire in terms less passionate than prosaic. While literary scholars typically appreciate narrative complexity, it is this very complexity of Malyne's aubade that undermines many readers' efforts to enjoy her fabliau, to position themselves such that they can laugh at the tale's humor without confronting the brutal force of rape. As she unsteadily moves from a fabliau-rape to a romance aubade, Chaucer's Malyne speaks of women's amatory desires in a tale that constructs them in the service of men's economic desires, with her enigmatic words frustrating attempts to view her simply as a stock character unharmed by the violence that befalls her. And for today's readers who realize, like Lindy West, that "comedy doesn't just reflect the world, it shapes it,"[17] Chaucer's rape jokes, both in their past and their present, continue to serve as a reminder of the masculinist bias behind much humor and the ways in which men's laughter at times springs forth from women's suffering.

CHAPTER 4

The Fornicating Wife and Incomplete Completion of the *Cook's Tale*

All stories must end. If for some peculiar reason one does not end, it should at least register as incomplete or otherwise unfinished so that readers can brace themselves for its disconcerting lack of closure. Several noted novels remain perpetually unfinished due to their author's death—for example, Charles Dickens's *The Mystery of Edwin Drood*, Edith Wharton's *The Buccaneers*, and Ralph Ellison's *Juneteenth*—yet through some strange alchemy of chance, mischance, and happenstance, Chaucer's *Cook's Tale* eludes categorization as either complete or incomplete, as either achieving or failing to achieve closure. Given these puzzling circumstances, readers remain dangling in an interpretive limbo, unsure whether Perkyn Revelour's revels come to a timely end or an untimely yet eternal interruption. In accomplishing—or more likely, stumbling upon—this paradoxical balance of incomplete completion, Chaucer frustrates countless readers with his *Cook's Tale*, as they are confronted with the irresolvable conundrum of a tale without an ending or of an ending without much of a tale.

Endings are of critical importance to narratives and their meaning, for authors, whether successfully or unsuccessfully, determinately or indeterminately, decide on an appropriate scene for the final encounter of their chief characters, which grants them the opportunity to weave together, organically and meaningfully, their plotlines and themes. Various narratologists have affirmed that closure is of critical importance to virtually every work of textual art. As Barbara Herrnstein Smith states of closure in poetry:

> Closure occurs when the concluding portion of a poem creates in the reader a sense of appropriate cessation. It announces and justifies the absence of further development; it reinforces the feeling of finality, completion, and composure which we value in all works of art; and it gives ultimate unity and coherence to the reader's experience of the poem.[1]

In a similar vein, Rachel Blau Duplessis discusses the importance of closure for narrative forms: "One of the greatest moments of ideological negotiation in any work occurs in the choice of resolution. . . . Any artistic resolution (especially of a linear form that must unroll in time) can, with greater or lesser success, attempt an ideological solution to the fundamental contradictions that animate the work."[2] To imagine virtually any poem without its final stanzas, any novel without its last chapter, any symphony without its final bars, any film without its final ten minutes, or any video game without its final boss fight, is to contemplate the unsteady feeling of an abrupt yet permanent interruption rather than an earned and appreciated conclusion.

From his tale's prologue, it appears that the Cook will follow the examples of the Miller and the Reeve and tell a tale about hospitality and its discontents. Such a theme is thematically captured in the word *herbergage*, which the *Middle English Dictionary* defines as "lodgings in general, capacity for entertaining strangers" and "the action of providing quarters for people."[3] The *Miller's Tale* takes *herbergage* as a key theme in Nicholas's position as a lodger in John and Alison's home, as does the *Reeve's Tale* when Aleyn and John stay the night at Symkyn's home: "But for the love of God they hym bisoght [asked him] / Of herberwe and of ese, as for hir peny" (1.4118-19). These preceding tales, with their fabliau plots of adultery and sexual deception, highlight the comic potential of themes of *herbergage*. The Cook states approvingly of the *Reeve's Tale*, "For Cristes passion, / This millere hadde a sharp conclusion / Upon his argument of herbergage" (1.4327-29), and then cites Solomon's admonition, "Ne bring nat every man into thyn hous" (1.4331), to conclude that "herberwynge by nyghte is perilous" (1.4332).[4] By establishing this theme of *herbergage*, Chaucer appears to lay the framework for the Cook's ensuing tale, one that will similarly address the humorous possibilities of hospitality's dangers.

Moreover, because Harry Bailly insults the Cook in the *Cook's Prologue*, accusing him of selling stale goods and allowing unsanitary conditions in his shop, many readers anticipate that, like the rivalry between the Miller and the Knight and then between the Reeve and the Miller, the Cook will insult Harry Bailly by allegorically casting him as a character in his tale. During Chaucer's time, professional rivalries flared between cooks and innkeepers because London laws prohibited the latter from selling food; to evade these regulations, many innkeepers moved to the city's outskirts. Intriguingly, the Cook and the Host are the only pilgrims both named and based on Chaucer's contemporaries, which raises the possibility that Chaucer was encoding a real-life rivalry in his fictions. These characters are identified only by their occupations in the *General Prologue*, but in the *Cook's Prologue* the Cook refers to the Host as "Herry Bailly" (1.4358), and the Host calls the Cook "gentil Roger" (1.4353) and "Hogge of Ware" (1.4336).[5] Contemporary records verify that Harry Bailly served as a burgess representing Southwark in Parliament, and the 1380-81 Subsidy Roll for Southwark documents "Henricus Bailiff, Ostyler, Christian Uxor eius" (Henry Bailly, ostler, [and] his wife Christian).[6] Likewise, civic annals document that Roger of Ware lived in London and its environs: the De Banco Roll for 1384-85 names "Roger Knyght de War, Cook" as the plaintiff in a case of debt, with another record of 1377 mentioning "Roger Ware of London, Cook."[7] Harry Bailly apparently alludes to Roger's last name of *Knyght* when sarcastically dubbing him "gentil Roger." Also, when the Cook drunkenly falls off his horse in the *Manciple's Prologue*, Chaucer as narrator ironically comments, "This was a fair chyvachee [feat of horsemanship] of a cook!" (9.50), mocking the equestrian accomplishments expected of this degraded exemplar of knighthood.

Further pertinent to the issue of a potential rivalry between the Cook and the Host, although Roger promises that his tale will not insult Harry Bailly—"Though that my tale be of an hostileer. / But nathelees I wol nat telle it yit" (1.4360-61)—there is little reason to believe his words, for several pilgrims mischaracterize their tales over the course of their journey. The Man of Law declares that he will "speke in prose" (2.96) but builds his tale in stanzas featuring an intricate rhyme-royal pattern. The Clerk agrees to Harry Bailly's request for a "myrie tale" (4.9) or a "murie thyng of aventures" (4.15) but adds the essential caveat that he (the Clerk) will do so only "As fer as resoun axeth, hardily" (4.25); he then tells the quite unmerry tale of Griselda's patient suffering. The Merchant, alluding to his marital troubles, sighs that of his "owene soore, / For soory herte, I telle may namoore" (4.1243-44), yet he shares a tale of cuckoldry and uxorial duplicity. From the contextual evidence of the *Cook's Prologue* and the other *Canterbury Tales*, many readers anticipate that the *Cook's Tale* will allow Roger the opportunity to mercilessly satirize his financial and professional rival, Harry Bailly. At the very least, Roger's eagerness to tell his tale hints at his ulterior motive to lampoon the Host. Consistent with Chaucer the narrator's description of the *Miller's Tale* as a "cherles tale" (1.3169) and the Reeve's promise to echo its fabliau story line ("Right in his cherles termes wol I speke" [1.3917]), Roger the Cook promises to tell a "litel jape that fil in oure citee" (1.4343), with these words echoing his earlier mention of "a jape of malice in the derk" that befell a local miller (1.4338). For the most part, Chaucer uses *jape* when a character is joking with another, but in certain instances, it refers to a narrative form founded on a joke, such as when Dame Abstynence chastises Wicked-Tonge in the *Romaunt of the Rose* because "Thou spake a jape not longe ago" (7517). How much difference in theme and content should one expect between the Miller's and Reeve's churlish tales and Roger's "litel jape"? This background material to the *Cook's Tale* collectively suggests Chaucer's detailed attention to its structure and thematic connections to the *Canterbury Tales* as a whole, which then quickly peters out once the tale begins.

A mere fifty-eight lines, the *Cook's Tale* begins by introducing its protagonist, the apprentice Perkyn Revelour, who is "as ful of love and paramour / As is the hyve ful of hony sweete" (1.4372-73); he also enjoys such entertainments as dancing and gambling. Perkyn's master, wary of this young man's freewheeling ways, heeds the aphorism that bids, "Wel bet is [It is better that] roten appul out of hoord / Than that it rotie al the remenaunt" (1.4406-7), and relieves him of his duties. Perkyn leaves to reside with a friend, "a compeer of his owene sort, / That lovede dys [dice, gambling], and revel, and disport" (1.4419-20). This short tale ends by briefly mentioning the business pursuits of this man's wife, who "heeld for contenance / A shoppe, and swyved [fornicated] for hir sustenance" (1.4421-22). With this most intriguing of character introductions, the tale is apparently accelerating into a comic plotline featuring sex, adultery, and other shenanigans, yet it abruptly ends, leaving readers to wonder about the further escapades of this unrepentant reveler, his accommodating friend, and this man's entrepreneurial wife.

Chaucer's earliest readers and scribes found themselves perplexed by the tale's curt conclusion and struggled to explain this enigma. The scribe of the Hengwrt Manuscript appended to its final line, "Of this cokes tale maked Chaucer na moore," apparently to notify his readers that Chaucer left the tale unfinished.[8] While most readers interpret this marginal note as the scribe's statement of his own bewilderment (or disappointment, or resignation) at the tale's incompletion, lamenting that Chaucer wrote no more of it for him to copy, it is also plausible that he was attempting to alert his readers that the tale is indeed finished, that he realized readers might complain and therefore justified his work by asserting that "Of this cokes tale maked Chaucer na moore." Like the tale itself, the scribe's textual inscription provides insufficient evidence for definitive claims, and M. C. Seymour, acknowledging the vagaries of manuscript and copy-text circulation during the Middle Ages, asks rhetorically, "Did [this scribe] write from knowledge or assumption?"[9] What did this scribe know, and when did he know it? Jim Casey examines other manuscripts of the *Canterbury Tales*, including the Ellesmere, and posits, equally plausibly, that "the note may have been removed, rather than placed, under Chaucer's direction."[10] Seymour also proposes that a "simple bibliographical explanation . . . seems the most likely reason for the present defective state of the *Cook's Tale*" and posits that "the final quire of the booklet that contained the tales of Miller, Reeve, and Cook was lost very early in the manuscript tradition."[11] Moreover, the blank space following the *Cook's Tale* in many manuscripts generates debate about its intention, its role in the transmission of Chaucer's tales, and its relationship to manuscript production practices. Given the expense of manuscript production in the Middle Ages, blank spaces were often envisioned to be filled at a later date, which may indicate that scribes expected to receive more of the *Cook's Tale* for manuscripts other than Hengwrt. Further complicating matters, as David Lorenzo Boyd notes, all manuscripts that include the *Cook's Tale* present it in subtly (and sometimes not so subtly) different ways, each of which calls for a unique interpretation: "Each work of art called the *Cook's Tale* . . . supplies a different text for analysis, and from a recognition of this fact should follow a willingness to turn from the ideology of the text that editorial theory has constructed and toward a study of the particular and local."[12] While Boyd is surely correct that attention must be paid to the particular and local, these concerns are often overshadowed by the larger and subsuming question of whether the tale is finished.

From these curious narrative and scribal circumstances a swirl of theories has emerged. Many readers find it astounding that the tale concludes as it does and posit that Chaucer faced a devastating personal misfortune that derailed his work, as in J. M. Manly and Edith Rickert's assessment: "That Chaucer wrote thus far and stopped is difficult to believe. He seems not only master of a matchless technique but too thoroughly master of his story-material to stop. Only sudden illness or some other insurmountable interference could have prevented him from going on."[13] Douglas Gray summarizes three theories accounting for the tale's incompletion: "that more of it existed, but has been lost . . . ; that Chaucer was by some circumstance or other prevented from completing it, or that for some reason he decided not to do so."[14] Other readers propose Chaucer's self-censorship: that he abandoned the tale because, in accelerating the racy themes of the *Miller's Tale* and *Knight's Tale*, its humorous vulgarity would be too offensive for his audience. This theory is undercut by the anal kiss and thunderous fart of the *Miller's Tale*, for it is difficult to envision that an audience who enjoyed the *Miller's Tale* would then find a similar story offensive to its taste.

But is the tale incomplete? Even such an apparently simple question requires analysis and explication, as well as contextualizing the *Cook's Tale* within the framework of the *Canterbury Tales* as a whole. Most of the *Canterbury Tales* end with a prayer or blessing of some sort, with the narrator also recording the reaction of the tale-teller's fellow pilgrims. Odd exceptions to these patterns occur—for example, the pilgrims react neither to the *Summoner's Tale* nor to the *Canon Yeoman's Tale*—yet on the whole the rhetorical patterns of the *Canterbury Tales* would suggest a concluding prayer or a response from the Cook's fellow pilgrims to indicate its completion.[15] Without these features, the *Cook's Tale* appears unintegrated into the flow of the *Canterbury Tales*, despite the fact that its prologue clearly establishes its significance.

On the other hand, additional critics have posited that, even at its scant fifty-eight lines, the tale is complete. E. G. Stanley believes that the *Cook's Tale* condenses the expansive energies of the *Miller's Tale* and *Reeve's Tale* into a concentrated format that synthesizes their collective treatment of the *herbergage* theme. The humorous antics of the preceding tales, with their hundreds of lines of plot development, can be distilled into a pithy formula in which unlicensed sexual play can be indulged in without repercussions: "The last few lines of the *Cook's Tale* give the recipe for carefree *herbergage*: though the lodger be a thief, no loss if a thief in cahoots with him puts him up; though the lodger be a swiver, no danger if the landlady is a whore, and no honour to lose if the pimping landlord is her husband."[16] At the very least, a notable coincidence supports Stanley's thesis: if the *Cook's Tale* ended one line earlier, or if it ended on any line that failed to complete a couplet with the following line, or if it ended prior to the introduction of the friend's wife, readers would be able to argue more definitively that the tale is indeed unfinished.

While most critics presume that the beginning of the *Cook's Tale* lays the groundwork for a riotous fabliau, even this point has been disputed; instead, some readers theorize the likelihood of a moral exemplum. V. A. Kolve proposes that the *Cook's Tale* potentially belongs to the tradition of prodigal son narratives, in which Perkyn Revelour would transition from his "painful career as reveler into repentance and amendment, perhaps crowned by restitution to his former place in the master's household"

(257-85).[17] V. J. Scattergood, observing the similarities between Perkyn Revelour and the three young "riotoures" (6.661) of the *Pardoner's Tale*, suggests the *Cook's Tale* might have similarly concluded with an exemplary moral.[18] Providing contemporary evidence for these claims, medieval readers similarly argued for a moral reading of the *Cook's Tale*, notably the scribe of the Bodley 686 manuscript. This early editor interwove approximately forty-five more lines into the *Cook's Tale*, with lone words and phrases mixed in among Chaucer's text and an expanded conclusion outlining a moral lesson to be learned from Perkyn Revelour and his friend:

> And therfore, yonge men, lerne while ye may
> That with mony dyvers thoghtes beth prycked al the day.
> Remembre you what myschefe cometh of mysgovernaunce.
> Thus mowe [may] ye lerne worschep and come to substaunce.[19]

With this ending casting aside the fabliau hijinks of the *Miller's Tale* and *Reeve's Tale*, the *Cook's Tale* metamorphoses into an exemplum instructing an audience of young men to turn aside from "mysgovernaunce" for a life of probity and grace. As Daniel Pinti affirms, "The finished poem, with its decidedly 'new' verses at once linked to yet separate from the authoritative Chaucer's, dramatizes in itself the finisher's theme—the need for governance via the modeling of oneself after someone of high reputation."[20] While the possibility of a moral tale cannot be entirely discounted, the Cook's delighted response to the *Reeve's Tale*—"The Cook of Londoun, whil the Reve spak, / For joye him thoughte he clawed him on the bak" (1.4325-26)—does not bespeak the attitude of a man soon given to moralizing.

Further adding to the confusion surrounding the *Cook's Tale*, in the *Manciple's Prologue*, it seems that the Cook has not yet told his tale, as Harry Bailly abruptly takes notice of him, apparently for the first time: "Is that a cook of Londoun, with meschaunce? / Do hym come forth, he knoweth his penaunce; / For he shal telle a tale, by my fey, / Although it be nat worth a botel hey [bundle of hay]" (9.11-14). This passage apparently overlooks the *Cook's Prologue* in its entirety, although Harry's first line in this passage could be reasonably interpreted as dripping with sarcasm. Still, Harry demands that Roger tell *a* tale, not *another* tale, which confuses the exact significance of his meaning. Chaucer may have intended to cancel the *Cook's Prologue* after composing the *Manciple's Prologue*, but this possibility remains conjectural, and because the Cook is now too drunk to tell his tale, the Manciple volunteers to take his turn: "I wol as now excuse thee of thy tale. / For, in good feith, thy visage is ful pale" (9.29-30). Thus, without the *Cook's Tale*, the Cook would tell no tale at all, but then neither do several of the pilgrims, including the Yeoman, the Plowman, and the five guildsmen. Once again, contextual evidence about the *Cook's Tale* provides interesting material for consideration but little that could be considered evidence.

Instead of asking whether the *Cook's Tale* is complete or incomplete, it is a slightly different question to contemplate whether it achieves closure. While this may appear to offer a distinction without a difference, Chaucer's *Squire's Tale* and *Tale of Sir Thopas* exemplify the ways in which tales may be left incomplete yet nonetheless achieve closure within the overarching framework of the Canterbury pilgrimage. The Franklin cuts off the *Squire's Tale*, apparently fearing that this unwieldy narrative could prove virtually interminable, and Harry Bailly rudely interrupts Chaucer when telling his *Tale of Sir Thopas*: "Thy drasty rymyng is nat worth a toord [turd]!" (7.930). Deducing from these examples, Jim Casey hypothesizes that the *Cook's Tale* "can be understood within a larger framework, concluding in a manner wholly appropriate within the thematic framework" established as the stories proceed from the *Knight's Tale* to the completion of the *Reeve's Tale*; he proposes that "the accumulation of sins within it and the startling vulgarity of the final line may cause one to suspect that Chaucer intended to interrupt the tale of Perkyn's misadventures, as he does the *Tale of Sir Thopas*, the *Squire's Tale*, and the *Monk's Tale*. Thus, the tale may be complete for Chaucer, although not completed by the Cook."[21] One can readily imagine a disgruntled pilgrim halting the Cook before his story accelerates into vulgarity, but without even a trace of such an interruption, readers are again faced with conjecture rather than certitude.

In the end, the most frustrating aspect of the *Cook's Tale* as evidence of Chaucer's badness emerges in the likelihood that it points instead to a lost masterpiece testifying further to his genius. Its lightning-quick pacing conjures images of an ingeniously constructed tale that would tie together themes of the *Knight's*, *Miller's*, and *Reeve's Tale* in a tour de force narrative of comic brio and thematic brilliance. Left forever without a coherent conclusion, the *Cook's Tale* simply leaves one to wonder about the blanks of the archival record and to lament that which might never have existed at all. "Th'ende is every tales strengthe" (2.260), Pandarus tells Troilus in Chaucer's *Troilus and Criseyde*. For the *Cook's Tale*, a story with either a confused or absent conclusion, this irony speaks for itself.

CHAPTER 5

The Bounteous Boat and Prosperity Theology of the *Man of Law's Tale*

Few hypocrites rankle as infuriatingly as the rich sanctimoniously bemoaning the challenges of poverty and solicitously advising others of its harms. With his Man of Law, Chaucer puts such hypocrisy on display, yet he mostly refrains from satirizing its advocate and thus allows this hypocrisy to proceed unchallenged. Lamenting the tribulations of poverty, the Man of Law remains himself untouched by them, as does the protagonist of his tale, the saintly Custance. In this far-ranging narrative spanning the Mediterranean Sea and beyond, Chaucer weaves together elements of romance and hagiography, casting his suffering protagonist in story lines of courtship and marriage, conversion and revenge, and patience and reward. Notably absent from the tale, however, is the theme introduced in its prologue: poverty. As in so many cases, one may credit this failure to the pilgrim rather than to his creator and argue that Chaucer's satiric aim finds its target, yet if so, the Canterbury pilgrims do not recognize the Man of Law's hypocrisy, as he faces no comeuppance for his pretense of concern for the poor. In effect a medieval advocate of prosperity theology— the modern, mostly evangelical, belief that God rewards the faithful with earthly riches—the Man of Law grossly misrepresents central tenets of Christianity in his tale of Custance, a virtuous woman who travels the seas in a boat bounteously supplied to meet her needs, which thus sinks his theme of poverty's tribulations.

According to Ian McFarland, the hallmark of prosperity theology "is the belief that God intends prosperity . . . for believers and, correspondingly, that such prosperity is rightly interpreted as a sign of divine favour." Proponents of the prosperity gospel, as McFarland further notes, "have been criticized on a number of fronts, including captivity to a shallow materialism inconsistent with the poverty of Jesus and the apostles . . . and promoting an individualism that undermines Christian social responsibility."[1] Key biblical passages used to buttress prosperity theology include Malachi 3.10 ("Bring all the tithes into the storehouse, that there may be meat in my house, and try me in this, saith the Lord: if I open not unto you the flood-gates of heaven, and pour you out a blessing even to abundance"), 3 John 1.2 ("Dearly beloved, concerning all things I make it my prayer that thou mayest proceed prosperously"), and the parable of the talents (Matthew 25.14-30).[2] It should be acknowledged that applying the concept of prosperity theology to an author of the European Middle Ages is theologically anachronistic and geographically misplaced, as Kate Bowler identifies its distinctly American foundations.[3] Long before the tenets of the prosperity gospel coalesced into a branch theology of Christianity, however, such a shallow materialism corrupted countless individuals' understanding of biblical teachings. Thus, to posit the Man of Law as an early exemplar of this worldview provides an appropriate, if inexact, context for his rhetorical flourishes and thematic lapses.

As with many of the portraits in the *General Prologue*, Chaucer's naive introduction of the Man of Law subtly indicates his character flaws, particularly his hypocrisy and venality. Chaucer describes him in positive terms—"Discreet he was and of greet reverence"—but then undercuts this assessment as a facade: "He semed swich, his wordes weren so wise" (1.312-13). Further along these lines, the Man of Law indulges more in the pretense of his duties than in their execution: "Nowher so bisy a man as he ther nas, / And yet he semed bisier than he was" (1.321-22). Despite the artifice of his professional responsibilities, his clients pay him amply for his services, thus accentuating his interest in wealth (1.316-17). Furthermore, the Man of Law's work focuses on the acquisition of land and property, although it remains unspecified whether he expends these efforts on behalf of himself or of others: "So greet a purchasour was nowher noon: / Al was fee symple to hym in effect; / His purchasyng myghte nat been infect [invalidated, undone]" (1.318-20). As much as this portrait indicts the Man of Law for the conspicuous consumption evident in his many robes and the fees collected to purchase them, the final vision of him accentuates the modesty of his dress: "He rood but hoomly in a medlee cote" (1.328). Laura Hodges notes the absence encoded in this portrait's abrupt conclusion, arguing that "Chaucer declines to provide this character with costume signs that would testify to his professional and personal honor and to his social status."[4] As Hodges suggests, such an omission could be seen as a snub to the Man of Law's professional status, or it could contribute to the final vision of his "hoomly" outfit to indicate its simplicity, plainness, and lack of pretension. The ambiguity of the Man of Law's clothing undercuts efforts to draw firm conclusions about his character, yet the portrait as a whole depicts a man highly skilled in his profession, if ethically lax in its prosecution.

In the introduction to the *Man of Law's Tale*, Chaucer builds on the economic and legal themes introduced in the Man of Law's portrait. Harry Bailly, addressing the passage of time, employs a financial lexicon, including such words and phrases as "leseth," "wasteth," "steleth," "necligence," and "los of catel [chattel, property]" (2.19-27). His speech also carries legalistic phrasings when he alerts the Man of Law that he will stand as judge of his tale: "Ye been submytted, thurgh youre free assent, / To stonden in this cas at my juggement. / Acquiteth yow now of youre biheeste" (2.35-37). The Man of Law agrees to tell his story but claims that Chaucer has already told so many tales in his "Seintes Legende of Cupide" (2.61)— now known as the *Legend of Good Women*—that he has few left from which to choose: "I kan right now no thrifty tale seyn / That Chaucer . . . / Hath seyd hem in swich Englissh as he kan" (2.46-49). Significantly, the Middle English word *thrifty* denotes "prosperous; rich; of respectable social and economic position," in contrast to its modern meaning as economical, prudent, and parsimonious.[5] In effect, the Man of Law accuses Chaucer of claiming the richest tales for himself, leaving only the remnants—the unthrifty tales, the poor ones—for him. Assessing the rivalry between Chaucer and the Man of Law, Diane Cady posits that "the Man of Law's complaint about Chaucer's productivity becomes a deft form of advertising, making Chaucer a more prolific writer than Ovid,"[6] with his words also casting himself as narratively impoverished. Rich in money if not in tales, the Man of Law complains of a lack that could be discomfiting but hardly discomforting, in a key foreshadowing of his inability to develop his tale's themes.

Establishing a connection to the unthrifty tale left him by Chaucer, the Man of Law announces his theme of poverty, "O hateful harm, condicion of poverte! / With thurst, with coold, with hunger so confoundid!" (2.99-100). He envisions poor people blaming Jesus for their misfortunes, "Thow blamest Crist and seist ful bitterly / He mysdeparteth richesse temporal" (2.106-7), and alludes to the gospel account of Lazarus and the rich man, in which Lazarus ascends to heaven and the rich man, suffering in hell, begs Lazarus to allay his infernal torments (2.110-12). This gospel story concludes with the rich man learning an inversionary message: "Son, remember that thou didst receive good things in thy lifetime, and

likewise Lazarus evil things, but now he is comforted; and thou art tor-
mented" (Luke 16.25). In much Christian teaching, earthly poverty prefig-
ures heavenly riches, notably in the Beatitudes: "Blessed are ye poor, for
yours is the kingdom of God. Blessed are ye that hunger now: for you shall
be filled" (Luke 6.20-21). The Man of Law sees only the harms of poverty,
misreads the example of Lazarus and the rich man, and fails to recognize
the rewards promised to the poor in Christian thought.

Notably, the Man of Law's excursus on poverty is inspired by Pope
Innocent III's *De miseria condicionis humane* (On the Misery of the Human
Condition), in a section titled "Of the Misery of the Poor and the Rich."[7]
Instead of following Innocent III's lead and balancing his critique of pov-
erty with a critique of earthly riches, the Man of Law misreads his source
text and praises the wealthy, attributing to them the virtue of wisdom:
"Herkne what is the sentence of the wise: 'Bet is to dyen than have indi-
gence'" (2.113-14). These words are inspired by Innocent's, yet they lack
the context of his passage, in which he laments, "O shame! A person is
valued according to his wealth, when wealth should be valued according
to the person."[8] Ignoring Innocent's overarching message, the Man of
Law clearly envisions an audience comprised solely of wealthy auditors,
no matter the variety of social classes represented on the Canterbury pil-
grimage. He then apostrophizes, "O riche marchauntz, ful of wele been
yee," connecting their wealth to their innate virtue by lauding them: "O
noble, o prudent folk, as in this cas!" (2.122-23). In a passage extolling
rich merchants that, similar to the citation of Innocent III, misinterprets
its source, the Man of Law's words echo the Gospels: "Ye seken lond and
see [sea] for yowre wynnynges; / As wise folk ye knowen al th'estaat /
Of regnes" (2.127-29). These words likely allude to Jesus's curse of the
Pharisees: "Woe to you scribes and Pharisees, hypocrites; because you go
round about the sea and land to make one proselyte; and when he is made,
you make him the child of hell twofold more than yourselves" (Matthew
23.15). Jesus denounces an economics of spiritual degradation—the mul-
tiplying of children of hell—yet the Man of Law uses similar phrasings to
endorse merchants and their quest for earthly "wynnynges." As William
Quinn avows of the Man of Law's citation of Innocent III, "Though its first
sixteen lines offer a condensation of Pope Innocent III's *De miseria condi-
cionis humanae*, its concluding celebration of a financial *winning* (2.127)
posits a completely contradictory *moralitas*."[9] Thus, the virtuous rich that
the Man of Law imagines are set not merely in contrast to the poor but
in direct opposition to them. Also, he claims to have learned his tale of

Custance from a merchant (2.131-33). Earlier bemoaning that Chaucer left him only unthrifty tales from which to choose, the Man of Law now ironically reveals his source to be a wealthy, or (in its medieval sense) thrifty, merchant.

Continuing this paean to the wealthy, the opening stanza of the *Man of Law's Tale* extols rich merchants while also painting a picture of the many tradesmen eager to win their business:

> In Surrye [Syria] whilom dwelte a compaignye
> Of chapmen [merchants] riche, and therto sadde and trewe,
> That wyde-where senten hir spicerye,
> Clothes of gold, and satyns riche of hewe.
> Hir chaffare [merchandise] was so thrifty and so newe
> That every wight hath deyntee to chaffare [trade]
> With hem [them], and eek to sellen hem hire ware. (2.134-40)

The passage drips with praise for these purveyors of luxury merchandise, including spices, satin cloths, and other "thrifty" goods, such that everyone clamors to trade with them. The Man of Law directly aligns wealth with constancy and truth ("chapmen riche, and therto sadde and trewe"), despite the unlikelihood of riches uniformly corresponding with virtue. Ironically, these merchants play only a peripheral role in the Man of Law's story: in their travels across the Mediterranean they speak so highly of the Roman emperor's daughter Custance that the sultan of Syria immediately falls in love with her (2.186-89). These wealthy merchants commence the story's plot yet are soon rendered curiously unnecessary. The Man of Law (or Chaucer the author as his ventriloquist) could easily have devised another way for the sultan to learn of Custance's beauty, and so the opening stanzas prove more thematically than narratively significant. That is to say, the Man of Law appears invested in praising wealthy merchants, even when wealthy merchants are incidental to his tale.

For as much as the Man of Law proclaims his theme of poverty and contrasts it with the wealth of merchants, poverty never appears in his story, nor do rich merchants after this opening salvo. Rather, his tale focuses on Custance's patient suffering throughout a series of dramatic and traumatic events. Following her marriage to the Syrian sultan, Custance's mother-in-law slaughters her son and his courtiers for converting to Christianity and exiles Custance. After drifting on the seas for years, she finds refuge upon landing in Northumbria but is framed for the murder of kind Hermengild and then divinely rescued from prosecution. She marries King Alla but is again exiled through the machinations of her new mother-in-law Donegild. At long last, after years of turmoil and travel, she reunites with her family in Rome for a mostly "happy ever after" ending, in which, notwithstanding the death of Alla, "In vertu and in hooly almus-dede [charitable deeds] / They lyven alle, and nevere asonder wende [parted from one another]" (2.1156-57). At none of these points, however, is Custance's poverty—or the great wealth of her husbands—of much narrative or thematic significance.

Indeed, the Man of Law never portrays Custance as poor or otherwise deprived, even when he could credibly do so. When she is cast adrift on a boat, with the sultaness's henchmen taunting her to learn to sail home to Italy, the narrator stresses that her needs are abundantly met: "A certein tresor [treasure] that she thider ladde, / And, sooth to seyn, vitaille [food] greet plentee / They han hire yeven [given], and clothes eek she hadde, / And forth she sailleth in the salte see" (2.442-45). The Man of Law recognizes the inherent implausibility of abundance amid isolation, and as the "yeres and dayes" pass (2.463), Custance must endure "many a sory meel" (2.466). He concurrently indicates that she enjoys sufficient, if not plenteous, food through divine intervention:

> Where myghte this womman mete and drynke have
> Thre yeer and moore? How lasteth hire vitaille [food]?
> Who fedde the Egipcien Marie in the cave,
> Or in desert? No wight but Crist, sanz faille [without fail].
> Fyve thousand folk it was as greet mervaille
> With loves [loaves] fyve and fisshes two to feede.
> God sente his foyson [abundance] at hir grete nede. (2.498-504)

Like the biblical passages that inspired prosperity theology cited previously, the miracle of the loaves and fishes, as depicted in Matthew 14.13-21, Mark 6.30-44, Luke 9.10-17, and John 6.1-13, celebrates miraculous multiplication of earthly resources.

The Man of Law consistently depicts God multiplying economic and material plenty as Custance travels from one end of the Mediterranean to the other while winning converts to Christianity. In the parallel scene when she is exiled from Northumberland, the narrator again stresses that her ship is well supplied:

Vitailled was the ship, it is no drede,
Habundantly for hire ful longe space,
And othere necessaries that sholde nede
She hadde ynogh—heryed [praised] be Goddes grace!
For wynd and weder almyghty God purchace,
And brynge hire hoom! (2.869-74)

This scene defies both logic and thematic consistency: why would Done-gild, who despises Custance, abundantly stock her ship, thereby reenact-ing the unexpected mercies of the murderous sultaness? Again, the Man of Law passes the opportunity to connect Custance's plight to his excur-sus on poverty, instead portraying her as wealthy as one can be when cast adrift in the Mediterranean. Surely this is a paradox worth pondering—relative wealth amid absolute isolation—yet it is consistent with the Man of Law's repeated refusal to depict Custance as impoverished. Furthermore, God himself is implicated within an economic figuration of redemption, as he "purchases" the wind and weather that will direct her ship home. With this ironic word choice, God is depicted as the omnipotent purchaser, rather than bestower, of salvation for the faithful.

Whereas the Man of Law appears uninterested in pursuing his theme of poverty, he stresses the wealth of the monarchical families in his tale, thus further divorcing his proclaimed theme from his story line. When Custance travels to Syria, she is greeted with an opulent display: "riche was th'array / Of Surryens and Romayns met yfeere" (2.393-94). One could reasonably posit that the sultan's mother is condemned in her dis-sembling embrace of her daughter-in-law, "The mooder of the Sowdan, riche and gay, / Receyveth hire with also glad a cheeere" (2.395-96), yet this description does not indict her wealth as much as her hidden motives. In a later scene, the narrator calls on the wealthy to pity Custance after Hermengild's murder: "O queenes, lyvynge in prosperitee, / Duchesses, and ye ladyes everichone, / Haveth som routhe on hire adversitee!" (2.652-54). The image of royal women living in prosperity contrasts sharply with the image of Custance in the following line—"An Emperoures doghter stant [stands] alone" (2.655)—but the royal women are not censured for their riches, nor is Custance lionized for any sort of abstract yet never keenly felt poverty.

Whereas the wealthy merchants disappear from the *Man of Law's Tale* immediately after their introduction, the narrator introduces a spiritual theme that complements their pursuit of earthly riches, as Custance inspires multitudes to convert to Christianity. The sultan and his lieges embrace her religion when preparing for his marriage to Custance, and a similar mass conversion occurs when she travels to Northumbria: "And by Custances mediacioun, / The kyng—and many another in that place— / Converted was, thanked be Cristes grace!" (2.684-86). As a saintly protagonist, Custance succeeds in leading others to Christianity, and so within the narrative's spiritual themes, she is building their heavenly rewards through her works on earth. To juxtapose this image of saintly action with the rich merchants with whom the tale begins, however, is to corrupt with earthly prosperity the ostensibly selfless work of Custance's silent proselytizing.

Following the rhetorical patterns of the *Canterbury Tales*, the Man of Law ends his story with a prayer: "Now Jhesu Crist, that of his myght may sende / Joy after wo, governe us in his grace, / And kepe us alle that been in this place! Amen" (2.1160-62). As Chauncey Wood ably demonstrates, the happy ending with which the Man of Law concludes his tale differs remarkably from his source text, Nicholas Trevet's Anglo-Norman Chronicle of the early fourteenth century, which ends with the deaths of Custance's father and then Custance herself one year later.[10] Laurel Hendrix sees in the tale's conclusion a fitting end to its economic themes: "In the Man of Law's frame of reference, all accounts are settled: like the Logos sent into the world, the maiden which God prudently has circulated in the lands of the heathens has returned home, having accomplished the purpose for which she was sent."[11] Custance's life was racked by tribulations but never by poverty, rendering the disconnection between prologue and tale a likely source for Chaucer's satiric condemnation of the Man of Law—yet this condemnation never arrives.

For if Chaucer seeks to defame his Man of Law by associating him with a medieval version of prosperity theology, Harry Bailly's response to the tale indicates approval: "This was a thrifty tale for the nones!" (2.1165). The telling word *thrifty* appears again, and while one can imagine Harry satirically emphasizing this word and thus exposing its empty focus on wealth, it is equally, if not more, likely that he is simply voicing approval of it. The conversation then moves on, with Harry calling for the Parson to tell his tale, the Parson chastising Harry for swearing, and the Shipman interrupting and promising his own tale. It is particularly surprising that the Parson does not challenge the Man of Law's prosperity theology, for he scolds the wealthy in several passages of his own tale, such as when he declares, "Thus is an avaricious man, that loveth his tresor biforn God, an ydolastre [idolater], / thurgh this cursed synne of avarice" (10.750-51). In opting not to challenge the Man of Law's prosperity theology, Chaucer loses the satiric opportunity to upbraid the wealthy for their shallow understanding of poverty and its role in Christian traditions. Noting this satiric misfire in the depiction of the Man of Law, Jill Mann proposes that "by following a professional stereotype Chaucer, like other satirists, was led into inconsistences,"[12] and Roger Ladd similarly suggests that "Chaucer portrays merchants . . . as consistently failing to receive or produce the truth value of reliable discourse," such that his depiction of them appears to be "semi-satiric."[13] A "semi-satiric" satire, though, is a dart aimed for the bull's-eye that misses the mark. In the end, the Man of Law escapes censure for sidestepping his theme of poverty through his riveting tale of Custance and her travails. One of the deepest shared tropes of Christianity and comedy highlights the inversionary nature of life: the mighty brought low, the humble exalted, the wise made foolish. Without such a comic twist, Chaucer's Man of Law is never called to account, thus leaving his endorsement of a shallow prosperity theology unquestioned and the satiric potential of the story line unexploited for a richly comic payoff.

CHAPTER 6

The Forgotten Maiden and Phallic Renaissance of the *Wife of Bath's Tale*

Indefatigable and undefeatable: the Wife of Bath stands larger than life in the eyes of Chaucer's readers, boldly asserting a proto-feminist sensibility in medieval England, dauntlessly challenging patriarchal discourses of women's sinfulness and subordination, and obstinately affirming her desire for sexual pleasure without concern for any tut-tutting from her fellow Canterbury pilgrims. Surprisingly to many, the bawdy voice of the *Wife of Bath's Prologue* cedes to the rarefied romance of her tale, which complicates, productively but frustratingly, the gender politics she espouses. Indeed, her tale appears to undo her hard-fought struggles against patriarchal discourses, as notably recorded in her victory over her fifth husband, Jankyn, in which she regains control of her body and her household after ceding authority to him. Subverting masculine prerogatives in her prologue but buttressing them in her tale, the Wife of Bath reinstates patriarchal authority, as embodied in a renaissance of phallic male desire that she herself figuratively castrated. Appropriately enough, this wavering theme can be traced through the genitals, both masculine and feminine, that the Wife of Bath foregrounds throughout her narration, as well as through the figure of the raped maiden with whom her tale begins, who lies forgotten by its end. Among Chaucer's outmoded perspectives, his romanticizing of a rapist knight glaringly highlights the disjunctions between past and present views of women's sexual autonomy, which are further evident through the telling reversal of the tale's gender politics, in which Chaucer's proto-feminist heroine reinstates masculine prerogatives after insistently questioning them.

Within a psychoanalytic framework of sexual difference that views masculinity and femininity as opposed ends of a binary, women are conscripted as the gendered Other to bolster men's purported primacy. The penis symbolizes presence, the vagina symbolizes absence, and so the fantasy of phallic authority becomes collectively imagined as residing in the pendulous pudenda of men rather than in the internal genitals of women. A penis wields no cultural or ideological power in itself, but power is ascribed to it through the chimerical yet potent concept of the phallus. Within this heteronormative framework, men need women to reflect a narcissistic vision of themselves as culturally dominant, and so women are conscripted to endorse their purported inferiority by reflecting the lionized worth of men. Such are the dominant scripts of much of Western history and art, yet women, including fictional women such as the Wife of Bath, need not always succumb to the role they are assigned in this social drama.

Recognizing the stifling imbalance between the sexes in medieval England, the Wife of Bath arrogates phallic authority to herself throughout her prologue, rhetorically castrating men and demolishing any presumption of their authority to dictate the contour of women's lives. Her opening lines—"Experience, though noon auctoritee / Were in this world, is right ynogh for me / To speke of wo that is in mariage" (3.1-3)—sound a battle cry, trumpeting her personal experiences as sufficient grounds for overturning the viewpoints of learned men. As Jennifer Martin explains, Alison "creates her own hermeneutic system by incorporating both the 'male' realm of authority/text and the 'female' realm of experience."[1] In one of her most telling and repeated rhetorical moves, she dismissively envisions the genitals of male authorities, portraying them as impotent: "The clerk, whan he is oold, and may noght do / Of Venus werkes worth his olde sho, / Thanne sit he doun, and writ in his dotage / That wommen kan nat kepe hir mariage!" (3.707-10). The cultural presumption that men's phallic authority is tied to their penises—notably, their erect penises—is here ridiculed, as the Wife of Bath implicitly contrasts this man's flaccid appendage to her vagina ever ready to engage in "Venus werkes." Even the penises that provide sexual pleasure to women are mocked, such as when she asks of the marital debt, "Now wherwith sholde he make his paiement, / If he ne used his sely instrument?" (3.131-32). As the *Middle English Dictionary* attests, "sely" primarily means "spiritually favored, blessed; holy, virtuous," with secondary definitions as "innocent, harmless; good" and "weak, helpless, defenseless, hapless."[2] In any of these usages, a "sely" penis does not sound particularly impressive. She also laughs at the feeble erections of her first three husbands:

Unnethe [Hardly] myghte they the statut holde
In which that they were bounden unto me.

Ye woot [know] wel what I meene of this, pardee!
As help me God, I laughe whan I thynke
How pitously a-nyght I made hem swynke [work, copulate]!
(3.198-202)

Alison compels these three men to pay the marital debt, and then holds them up for public humiliation for their poor performance. In another jibe, she denies any enjoyment of sexual pleasure with these men: "For wynnyng [advantage, profit] wolde I al his lust endure, / And make me a feyned appetit; / And yet in bacon hadde I nevere delit" (3.416-18). Her derisive metaphor of bacon represents either these old men or their penises, or both simultaneously, and so as a symbol of men's power, the penis withers under Alison's scrutinizing gaze.

Further along these lines, the Wife of Bath creates fantasies about her husbands'—and their penises'—actions, thereby revealing her phallic authority over them. She accuses these men of infidelity to deflect attention from her own affairs: "I swoor that al my walkynge out by nyghte / Was for t'espye wenches that he dighte [fornicated with]; / Under that colour hadde I many a myrthe" (3.397-99). The juxtaposition between the earlier portrayal of these men and this later one is stark, with the former suggesting their near impotence and the latter suggesting their randy pursuits. In another twist, the Wife of Bath recalls that, when her husbands sought sexual pleasure with her, she would grant their desires only if they paid the appropriate toll: "I wolde no lenger in the bed abyde, / If that I felte his arm over my syde, / Til he had maad his raunson unto me" (3.409-11). In all of these scenarios, Alison wields ultimate control over the sex act, creating fantasies of desires sated or denied, as well as fantastic visions of penises engaging in or refused sexual activity according to her erotic agency. Extending this reasoning to spiritual matters, Alison spurns the authority of Paul and Jesus by citing their virginity. "I woot wel that th'apostel was a mayde" (3.79), she declares of Paul, and she likewise acknowledges, "Crist was a mayde and shapen as a man" (3.139). She therefore dismisses their spiritual advice: "I nyl [will not] envye no virginitee" (3.142). These virginal men are rejected as moral authorities, despite their preeminent positions in the Christian faith.

The Wife of Bath correspondingly aligns women's identity and agency with sexuality and the vagina, as evidenced in some of her more famous lines. "I wol bistowe the flour of al myn age / In the actes and in fruyt of mariage" (3.113-14), she crows, and further adds, "I wol persevere; I nam nat precius, / In wyfhod I wol use myn instrument" (3.148-49). She also declares euphemistically, "For if I wolde selle my *bele chose* [beautiful thing], / I koude walke as fressh as is a rose" (3.447-48), and she later divulges the praise her husbands bestowed upon her genitals: "And trewely, as myne housbondes tolde me, / I hadde the beste *quoniam* myghte be" (3.607-8). In her excurses on the pleasures of marriage, she views her husbands chiefly as a means to sexual satisfaction: "An housbonde I wol have—I wol nat lette [stop]— / Which shal be bothe my dettour and my thral, / And have his tribulacion withal / Upon his flessh, whil that I am his wyf" (3.154-57). Construing her husband as indebted and enslaved to her, Alison monitors and regulates his "propre body," which would surely include his penis as well. Through her narration of her sexual desires and the bodies necessary to achieve these pleasures, both her own and those of her husbands, the simplistic correlation of the phallus (as cultural authority) with the penis is undone. Although the Wife of Bath does not herself have a penis, she directs her husbands', and thus has access to and authority over them, and extends this uxorial control in her household well beyond its doors.

Within this marital economy in which she has seized control from her spouses, Alison admits her critical mistake in marrying Jankyn. Mary Carruthers pithily captures Jankyn's personality by contrasting him with Alison, stating that "Jankyn is all 'auctoritee' and no 'experience,' and such a combination is dangerous, as Alisoun discovers from his behavior."[3] Despite recognizing that she should never let her spouse "be maister of my body and of my good" (3.314), she ceded marital authority to him and gave him "al the lond and fee / That evere was me yeven [given] therbifoore" but soon repented this action because "He nolde suffre nothyng of my list [pleasure]" (3.630-31, 633). The argument between Jankyn and the Wife of Bath can be distilled to their differing views of women's control of their genitals, as evident in the litany of stories compiled in his Book of Wikked Wyves, which includes such legends as Pasiphaë's mating with a bull, Clytemnestra's adultery, Livia's fatal uxoriousness, and the lurid tale of the women who "han slayn hir housbondes in hir bed, / And lete hir lecchour dighte hire al the nyght, / Whan that the corps lay in the floor upright" (3.766-68). Jankyn taunts Alison with an aphorism prizing women's chastity—"A fair womman, but she be chaast also, / Is lyk a gold ryng in a sowes nose" (3.784-85)—a viewpoint that sharply rebukes her erotic worldview. The Wife of Bath violently rejects Jankyn's moralizing, and as Marilynn Desmond observes, his Book of Wykked Wyves inspires her to rebel because it "offers remarkable portraits of female agency and even sexual autonomy; these brief accounts of wicked wives actually authorize the agency the Wife of Bath herself exhibits when she becomes violent towards Jankyn's book and Jankyn himself."[4] Following this battle with Jankyn, Alison regains control of her marriage: "He yaf me al the bridel in myn hond, / To han the governance of hous and lond, / And of his tonge, and of his hond also" (3.813-15). Tongues are primarily used to symbolize gossip and talkativeness, yet they also connote the phallus.[5] Just as the Wife claimed control over the "propre body" of her previous husbands, she wins control over Jankyn's tongue and hand, as well as all the other body parts that they metonymically suggest. "After that day we hadden never debaat" (3.822), she triumphantly states, testifying to her successful co-optation of phallic authority throughout her many marriages.

Given the proto-feminist gender politics and symbolic castrations of the *Wife of Bath's Prologue*, Alison's *Tale* begins surprisingly. The opening lines comically foreground male desire, depicting the British countryside as populated with lecherous friars seeking sexual pleasure: "Wommen may go saufly up and doun. / In every bussh or under every tree / Ther is noon oother incubus but he, / And he ne wol doon hem but dishonour" (3.878-81). In this oddly disjointed image, women need not fear incubuses— demons legendarily associated with raping and impregnating their prey— but are the targets of friars, who "dishonour" them but presumably do not impregnate them. In this fictional world where men's erotic pleasures are elevated over women's sexual agency, the plot commences when one of King Arthur's knights rapes a maiden. A "lusty bacheler" espies a woman walking alone (3.883), and despite her pleas, "By verray force, he rafte hire maydenhed" (3.888). Following this assault against a woman's autonomy, the women of Arthur's court intercede—inexplicably, or at least unexplainedly—on this rapist's behalf, winning him the opportunity to redeem himself if he succeeds in his quest to answer the riddle of "What thyng is it that wommen moost desiren" (3.905). The rapist knight succeeds in his quest only after chancing upon a mysterious "olde wyf" (3.1000) who supplies him with the answer, which he shares with Arthur's court: "Wommen desiren to have sovereynetee / As wel over hir housbond as hir love, / And for to been in maistrie hym above" (3.1038-40). The stunning obviousness of his discovery—that women desire to control their erotic lives— would render rape an impossibility, tautologically demonstrating that the rapist knight need only have examined his own cruel actions to deduce the riddle's answer. Within the tale's phallic economy, the rapist knight must learn to disarm the violent threat of his penis. He, like the old clerks who cannot perform "Venus werkes," must be metaphorically castrated.

The rapist knight is compelled to confront the loss of his sexual autonomy when the old wife asserts her "sovereynetee" over him. Before learning the riddle's answer, he agreed to fulfill her subsequent wish (3.1010-12); after he escapes execution, she demands that he marry her. This scene accentuates the rapist's loss of erotic agency: he is "constreyned" and realizes that "he nedes moste hire wedde, / And taketh his olde wyf, and gooth to bedde" (3.1071-72). What unfolds is virtually a parody of a rape scene, in which the rapist knight now desperately hopes to resist what he previously took by force: sex with a woman. The narrator stresses the knight's discomfort and the old wife's delight as they jointly anticipate the consummation of their marriage: "He walweth and he turneth to and fro. / His olde wyf lay smylynge everemo" (3.1085-86). The man who physically forced a woman into intercourse is now expected to copulate with his spouse, but as Chelsea Skalak argues of the sexual politics of this scene, "On the one hand, it is clear that both spouses expect that sexual activity will follow marriage vows, so the knight cannot refuse his spouse, but on the other, the tale imagines no real possibility of how the wife might enforce her claims against her husband's will. Even in the case of magical loathly ladies, conjugal debt licenses only male, not female violence."[6] The rapist knight earlier employed sexual violence to satisfy his desires, but in contrast, his new wife employs social convention and gently teases him: "Is this the lawe of kyng Arthures hous? / Is every knyght of his so dangerous [standoffish]?" (3.1089-90). In response to these questions, the rapist knight again offends his wife, this time by insulting her as ugly, old, and lowborn.

In the following lines, the old wife patiently explains to the rapist knight his errors, detailing the shallow opinions of those who would denigrate others for their attractiveness, their age, or their birth status. In a learned exposition citing such sources as Dante, Valerius Maximus, Seneca, and Boethius, she gently upbraids him for his failings with an argument characterized by both logic and empathy. Certainly, when the wife explains to the rapist knight, "For, God it woot, men may wel often fynde / A lordes sone do shame and vileynye" (3.1150-51), her words should strike him to the core, for he must recognize himself as one of those ungentle scions of privileged families. As she further explains, people's actions bespeak their character: "Thanne am I gentil, whan that I bigynne / To lyven vertuously and weyve [avoid] synne" (3.1175-76). Finally, the old wife achieves her rhetorical victory, offering the rapist knight a choice: either she will transform into a young and beautiful woman who cuckolds him or she will remain an aged and less attractive woman who stays true to him. The rapist knight's phallic disarming appears complete when he cedes control of his body and his amatory affairs, as well as their marriage, to her: "My lady and my love, and wyf so deere, / I put me in youre wise governance" (3.1230-31), adding as well, "For as yow liketh, it suffiseth me" (3.1235). His final words in the tale, responding to her query of whether she has gained "maistrye" over him and may therefore govern both him and herself as she desires, ostensibly signify his complete subjugation: "Ye, certes, wyf . . . I holde it best" (3.1238).

If phallic authority has been undercut in the rapist knight's subjugation to his wife—a metaphorical castration—it is nonetheless apparent that his penis remains active within the erotic economy of the tale. The *Wife of Bath's Tale* concludes with the image of the old wife and the rapist knight in bed together, and one would need to be obstinately prudish to imagine that they do not consummate their marriage given the highly eroticized terms in which this scene is depicted. Foremost, the passage details the rapist knight's rising attraction to his new spouse: "And whan the knyght saugh verraily al this, / That she so fair was, and so yong therto, / For joye he hente hire in his armes two. / His herte bathed in a bath of blisse" (3.1250-53). Within the masculine economy of romance, male desire is sated whether it is expressed violently (as in the tale's opening rape scene) or consensually (as in the tale's concluding consummation scene); consequently, many readers find the tale's denouement disappointing, if not troubling. For instance, Susan Nakley notes the disjunction between the rapist knight's actions and his eventual reward, arguing that "the tale's happy ending seems a bit too happy for the Rapist Knight, no matter what he has learned."[7] For many readers, this rapist suffers insufficient punishment for his crime, and the victim of his attack simply falls forgotten into the story's background.

Yet in looking back at the prologue, readers must confront the possibility that rape plays a role in the Wife of Bath's fantasies, that she finds erections wielded by violent men sexually arousing. For instance, she romanticizes spousal abuse when describing her marriage to Jankyn: "And therwithal so wel koude he me glose [cajole], / Whan that he wolde han my *bele chose*; / That thogh he hadde me bete on every bon, / He koude wynne agayn my love anon" (3.509-12). Rather than viewing herself as controlling her sexual pleasure, Alison here accords erotic authority to

Jankyn's handling of her genitals, presumably through penetration. Also, in recalling her seduction of Jankyn, she reveals that she wooed him with a vision of spousal violence: "And eek I seyde I mette [dreamed] of hym al nyght, / He wolde han slayn me as I lay upright, / And al my bed was ful of verray blood" (3.577-79). Alison then denies that this image reflects her own fantasies—"And al was fals; I dremed of it right naught" (3.582)— yet it nonetheless speaks to the ways in which she feeds men's fantasies through visions of women's subjugation. In her metaphor of an abused cat, Alison casts herself as the victim of violence seeking refuge at her abuser's hands: "Thou seydest this, that I was lyk a cat; / For whoso wolde senge [singe, burn] a cattes skyn, / Thanne wolde the cat wel dwellen in his in [inn, abode]" (3.348-50). Even in less violent passages, Alison focuses on penises as the source of her pleasure, divulging that she selected her husbands for their physical attributes: "Of whiche I have pyked out the beste, / Both of here nether purs and of here cheste" (3.44a-b). As much as Chaucer allows the Wife of Bath to challenge gendered norms throughout her prologue, she ultimately remains a male creation: a male fantasy of a woman who speaks back against patriarchal authority while remaining enthralled by it and thus invested in refortifying its foundations, even as she repeatedly knocks some walls down. In a surprisingly poignant line, the Wife of Bath asks, "Who peyntede the leon, tel me who?" (3.692), alluding to the fable of a lion that, while gazing at an illustration of a lion slain by a human, points out that the slain beast would present the same events from a remarkably different perspective. A vision of a woman within a patriarchal medieval world, the Wife of Bath cannot free herself or her female characters of romance from the ideological world that denigrates women's agency. This is the essential paradox of the Wife of Bath and her fictions, and as Arthur Lindley rightly discerns, "Rather than trying to find the real Alisoun in this haystack of contradictions, we should see that the contradictions are the point."[8]

Many critics hypothesize that Chaucer originally intended the Wife of Bath to tell the *Shipman's Tale* because its narrator speaks self-referentially as a wife, talking about the "sely housbonde" who "moot us clothe, and he moot us arraye" (7.11-12). Chaucer's genius shines through in the realization that the *Shipman's Tale*, in its fabliau story line of an adulterous wife and her cuckolded husband, matches too obviously with the Wife of Bath's worldview. Yet in providing her with a romance in which a rapist knight is rewarded, which then foregrounds the violence of the sexual fantasies she shares in her prologue, Chaucer curtails her agency and provides for a phallic renaissance that constrains her yet again. In a keenly perceptive analysis of the gendered politics of romance, Angela Jane Weisl argues that "romance has a built-in 'glass ceiling.' Women may gain a measure of subjectivity and control, but they are ultimately controlled, either literally by the men (or male power structures) in the romance, or by the genre itself, while, oddly, controlling the genre, in the sense that without her, the romance cannot work as romance."[9] Romances need women characters, but most of these texts ultimately control and constrain their agency in the story of a knight triumphant or transformed. In the final images of the *Wife of Bath's Tale*, Alison shares a vision of phallic pleasure by implicitly envisioning a mass of erect penises in her fantasy of "Housbondes meeke, yonge, and fressh abedde" (3.1259), but in her final rhetorical contradiction, she then undercuts this image with her curse of "verray pestilence" (3.1264) on men who will not be governed by their wives. In this striking contrast between life and death, between sex in the bedroom and the Black Death ravaging England throughout the fourteenth century, women stand as the uncursed survivors of a gendered war between the sexes, brought about by a phallic renaissance that cannot fully subvert the cultural connection between the male body and ideological authority and one that they implicitly uphold through their own sexual desires. "Who peyntede the leon, tel me who?": Chaucer.

CHAPTER 7

The Damned Pan and Exemplary Inconsistencies of the *Friar's Tale*

Why would anyone damn a pan? The *Friar's Tale*, an ostensibly exemplary narrative, founders on this and other contradictions, thus blurring its ultimate meaning and its relevance to its narrator, the Friar, and his tale-telling battle with the Summoner. Owing to their professional rivalry that drips with mutual antagonism, the Friar and the Summoner exchange vicious insults under the guise of their fictional tales, following the pattern that Chaucer established with the Miller and Reeve. Within the parameters of Chaucer's estates satire, which details the failings of various members of English society to uphold the ideals represented by their occupations, it is fitting that these two men fall short of the spiritual standards expressed in their ecclesiastical occupations and wage a rhetorical battle against each other. By depicting a summoner carted off to hell for his unrepentant avarice, the Friar succeeds in his satiric jibe at the Summoner, but he undermines this objective by digressing into issues concerning anger and its spiritual expression. The *Friar's Tale* attempts to stage a moral lesson, but, ironically, it does so through the immoral actions of its most sympathetic character, the old woman harassed by the avaricious summoner. In so doing, the Friar succeeds in metaphorically damning the Summoner yet undercuts his message by digressing into the ethical dangers of righteous anger, as well as by depicting the old woman's surprising damnation of her cookware. An exemplum that struggles to exemplify a coherent message, the *Friar's Tale* stands as one of Chaucer's more intriguing specimens of genre trouble.

In introducing the Friar and the Summoner in the *General Prologue*, Chaucer stresses both men's dubious performance of their ecclesiastical duties and their respective sexual transgressions. The Friar, despite his vow of chastity, apparently engages in numerous heterosexual liaisons, whereas the Summoner enjoys a homosocial, and potentially homoerotic, friendship with the Pardoner. The Friar "hadde maad ful many a mariage / Of yonge wommen at his owene cost" (1.212-13), with these words hinting at his personal investment in finding husbands for these young women before any scandal erupts, for why else would he do so "at his owene cost"? Like the Friar, the Summoner surrounds himself with young women (1.663-65), yet it is his homosocial alliance with the Pardoner that carries undertones of eroticism. Chaucer reports of these traveling companions that when the androgynous Pardoner sings, "Com hider, love, to me," the Summoner would "bar to hym a stif burdoun" in reply (1.672-73). Indeed, even before the *Friar's Prologue*, Chaucer establishes the shared enmity between the two men. They squabble while the Wife of Bath concludes her prologue, as the Summoner denounces the Friar as a meddler. The Friar promises that he will "telle of a somonour swich a tale or two / That alle the folk shal laughen in this place" (3.842-43); the Summoner threatens to return such narrative fire. The Friar, opposed professionally to the Summoner in their joint pursuit of the Christian faithful's financial bounty and contrasted erotically with him in their respective liaisons, reveals his antipathy toward him in the opening lines of his prologue, as the narrator reports that "this noble Frere, / He made alwey a maner louryng chiere [angry face] / Upon the Somonour" (3.1265-67). The Friar then candidly announces his dislike of the Summoner: "Pardee, ye may wel knowe by the name / That of a somonour may no good be sayd" (3.1280-81).

With the *Friar's Tale*, Chaucer employs the generic structure of an exemplum, a narrative framework encoding a didactic lesson commonly used in the Middle Ages to illuminate the meaning of a sermon. In their connection to preaching, exempla elaborate on a moral that is illustrated by the narrative's action. As Katie Homar explains, "The medieval exemplum is an institutionally authorized set of established narrative and ecclesiastical conventions that create and reinforce the religious authority of its teller while communicating theological doctrine to a lay audience in an accessible form."[1] Given that didacticism is the overarching objective of an exemplum, the genre can assume numerous different forms, reflecting R. T. Lenaghan's proposition that "the exemplum is not easily identifiable as a literary genre, existing more in the narrator's intention and the application [made of this] narrative than in specifically identifiable features of that narrative."[2] Complicating these matters further, the Friar identifies his tale as a "game." "I wol yow of a somonour telle a game" (3.1279), he declares, which suggests his objective to entertain the Canterbury pilgrims with a story aligned more with humor than with moral instruction.

Ironically, the summoner depicted in the *Friar's Tale* advises his traveling companion to view his exploits as instructive—"taak heer ensample of me" (3.1580)—thereby metatextually alluding to the tale's interest in exemplary narratives. From these contrasting yet complementary statements, readers should expect the *Friar's Tale* to amuse and to entertain but also to instruct and to enlighten, and Nevill Coghill elucidates that the *Friar's Tale* is "a commonplace *exemplum* of the importance of Intention when invoking God, in this case specifically with regard to curses."[3]

In constructing its exemplary narrative, the *Friar's Tale* recounts the travels of a summoner seeking to extort money from parishioners by falsely accusing them of sins, in a story line that addresses the philosophical and theological issues surrounding exploitation, intention, and curses. The story begins with this summoner meeting a yeoman, with whom he immediately pledges a brotherhood oath. The summoner's new friend confesses that he is actually a devil from hell, a shocking revelation that pleases, rather than terrifies, the depraved summoner. As they travel together, the summoner and devil agree to share their winnings, with the summoner proposing: "Taak thou thy part, what that men wol thee yive [give], / And I shal myn; thus may we bothe lyve. / And if that any of us have moore than oother, / Lat hym be trewe and parte it with his brother" (3.1531-34). The complementary themes of ill-gotten gains, intention, and cursing come to fruition when they witness a carter damning his horse, cart, and hay that have become mired in mud. The summoner hopes to exploit his new friend's unexpected winnings; the devil, however, explains that the carter's words did not match his intentions and so they cannot commandeer his belongings. Traveling on, the summoner attempts to extort money from an old woman, threatening her with an ecclesiastical summons for the sin of adultery, until she loses patience and curses him to hell. Significantly for the tale's themes, the old woman offers the summoner the opportunity to repent his sins but he rudely refuses: "Nay, olde stot [slut], that is nat myn entente, / . . . for to repente me / For any thyng that I have had of thee" (3.1630-32). By reiterating his refusal to repent, the summoner, in effect, damns himself, and the devil, having won his prey, escorts him to his eternal perdition.

By damning the summoner of his tale, the Friar succeeds in his objective to narratively debase his rival, casting him as the narrative lead of an anti-exemplum that teaches a moral lesson through immoral actions. The Friar repeats the moral lesson of his exemplum, urging summoners to reform—"And leve this somonours goode men bicome!" (3.1644)—and concluding with a final admonition: "And prayeth that thise somonours hem [themselves] repente / Of hir mysdedes, er that the feend hem hente [captures]!" (3.1663-64). Yet as much as the summoner of the *Friar's Tale* merits his damnation, the punishment appears oddly anticlimactic, for as David Raybin points out, the summoner apparently desires to be damned and thus would not view his punishment as such: "Indeed, as is almost universal in the criticism, that the summoner does not really wish to go to hell, seems to me to deny the fundamental devilry of his character."[4] For instance, when the summoner learns the true identity of his traveling companion disguised as a yeoman, he peppers him with questions about hell (3.1456-60, 3.1469-70, 3.1473), wondering about the bodily forms of devils rather than reacting in fear and horror. Following his damnation, the devil promises that the summoner will now learn the answers to his many questions: "Thou shalt with me to helle yet tonyght, / Where thou shalt knowen of oure privetee / Moore than a maister of dyvynytee" (3.1636-38). An unjust man has met his just deserts, and so the tale appears to achieve the exemplary objectives that the Friar established for it, except that the punishment meted out to this unrepentant sinner seems poorly designed to achieve this purpose.

Beyond this disjunction between the summoner's punishment and his perception of it, the depiction of the old woman who damns the summoner is fraught with contradictions and inconsistencies, which calls into question her position as the tale's moral center and further fractures its exemplary aims. She initially appears as a model of Christian humility and forbearance. Despite the summoner's rude rapping on her gate, she answers mildly, "Who clappeth? . . . benedicitee! / God save you, sire, what is youre sweete wille?" (3.1584-85). After the summoner demands her appearance before an ecclesiastical court, she meekly prays for assistance, "Crist Jhesu, kyng of kynges, / So wisly helpe me, as I ne may" (3.1590-91). Even after the summoner demands twelve pence to acquit her of a crime that she did not commit, her language still resonates with Christian charity: "Twelf pens [pence]! . . . Now, lady Seinte Marie / So wisly help me out of care and synne" (3.1604-5). In their initial impression of this character, readers surely see her as a virtuous woman unjustly and unduly harassed by an avaricious man.

In this tale that challenges readers to peer beneath the facades that characters erect to deceive one another, primarily exemplified by the devil who travels the world under the guise of a yeoman, it should be noted that the old woman's financial circumstances are presented in conflicting terms and that readers must determine for themselves the truth of her initial appearance. The summoner states that she is simply miserly, denouncing her as "an old rebekke [crone] / That hadde almoost as lief to lese hire nekke / As for to yeve [give] a peny of hir good" (3.1573-75). In contrast, the old woman represents herself as impoverished: "This wyde world thogh that I sholde wynne, / Ne have I nat twelf pens withinne myn hoold. / Ye knowen wel that I am povre and oold" (3.1606-8). Apparently in dire financial straits, she pleads with the summoner to bestow his mercy and his money on her—"Kithe [show] youre almesse on me, povre wrecche" (3.1609)—which hints at her hopes of turning the tables on the summoner and winning a financial windfall from her adversary. Further along these lines, the three main characters of this tale announce poverty as the primary motivation of their actions, with the summoner declaring that he resorts to extortion due to his penury ("Nere [were it not for] myn extorcioun, I myghte nat lyven" [3.1439]) and the devil sounding a similar note: "My wages been ful streite and ful smale. / . . . / And therfore by extorcions I lyve" (3.1426-29). Within this fictional world where all characters openly claim their penury, the summoner and the devil ascribe their motivations to their unscrupulous superiors who underpay them. As Brantley Bryant proposes, the *Friar's Tale* incorporates within its extortionary themes "a contemporary idea of the official as a figure in danger of financial or spiritual damage [who is] constantly reconciling the financial demands of a superior with personal needs."[5] Surely the overarching tenor of the tale encourages readers to believe the old woman's self-description of her poverty rather than the summoner's self-serving assessment of her riches, yet at the very least readers must align their vision of her financial status with her strange damnation of her pan and its effect on the tale's genre of exemplum.

While threatening the old woman with accusations of adultery, the summoner mentions her pan as a potential payment: "Pay me . . . or by the sweete Seinte Anne, / As I wol bere awey thy newe panne / For dette which thou owest me of old" (3.1613-15). Christopher Dyer documents from mid-fourteenth-century peasant inventories the cost of a brass pot at two shillings and that of two pans and a tripod at one shilling,[6] yet even without a precise understanding of the financial value of medieval cooking utensils, the old woman's pan represents an object of sufficient worth that the summoner will accept it in his extortionary scheme. Extraordinarily and oddly, the old woman damns her pan along with the summoner: "Unto the devel blak and rough of hewe / Yeve I thy body and my panne also!" (3.1622-23).

Why would a poor woman curse her pan, which, according to the logic of the story, would be banished to hell along with the corrupt summoner? Moreover, how would an ostensibly poor woman afford a new pan to replace the lost one? When the devil asks her to clarify her intentions, she again damns both the summoner and her pan: "The devel . . . so fecche hym er he deye, / And panne and al, but he wol hym repente!" (3.1628-29). As mentioned previously, the summoner refuses to repent and is consequently damned to hell, which apparently provides an appropriate moral to this tale, yet this supposedly simple moral becomes theologically complex when considering the old woman's actions and motivations. Moreover, Chaucer stresses that the old woman does indeed lose her pan, as the devil claims ownership of the summoner's body and the old woman's pan, both of which he claims are "myne by right" (3.1635).

One could reasonably presume that, in her justified anger against the summoner, the old woman damns her pan in an initial spasm of anger, and thus that it was not her intention to do so, in a manner similar to the carter damning his horse, cart, and hay. While her anger may be viewed as justified within various strands of Christian thought, she sins by repeating her curse of the summoner and her pan, which taints her actions with malice aforethought. Significantly, the old woman positions herself as if in prayer for her curse, thus symbolically suggesting that she recognizes the gravity of her words, for "whan the devel herde hire cursen so," she rests "upon hir knees" (3.1624-25). This iconographic positioning appears in the analogues of the *Friar's Tale*, and John Scattergood notes the shared gesture of Chaucer's scene with that of Robert Rypon's sermon "A Greedy Bailiff," in which the old woman is referred to as a "poor widow" who curses her harasser "on bended knees with outstretched hands."[7] As the summoner's dogged pursuit of the old woman's money reveals the intentionality of his actions, so too does the old woman's prayer on bended knees underscore her persistent pursuit of revenge against him. Her initial burst of righteous anger boils over rather than cools down.

Chaucer understood such a distinction between justified and wicked anger, as evident from his *Parson's Tale* when the Parson, ruminating over the seven deadly sins, first explains that anger should not always be considered harmful. On the contrary, "The goode Ire is by jalousie of goodnesse, thurgh which a man is wrooth with wikkednesse and agayns wikkednesse; and therfore seith a wys man that Ire is bet [better] than pley" (10.537-38). According to the Parson, anger plays an important role in the development of Christian morality because it models an appropriate response to the sins of others. In contrast to righteous anger, the Parson identifies two species of "wikked Ire": "sodeyn ire," in which "the resoun of a man ne consente nat to thilke sodeyn Ire, and thanne is it venial" (10.541), and "ful wikked Ire," which "comth of felonie of herte avysed and cast biforn, with wikked wil to do vengeance, and therto his resoun consenteth; and soothly this is deedly synne" (10.542). One could reasonably debate whether the old woman's curse is the venial sin of "sodeyn ire" in her immediate, passionate outburst or the deadly sin of "ful wikked Ire" in her reasoned desire for vengeance, yet in either case it is apparent that the old woman sins in the repetition of her angry curse.

In an additional connection to the themes of the *Friar's Tale*, the Parson discusses the sinful nature of curses: "Malisoun [a curse] generally may be seyd every maner power of harm. Swich cursynge bireveth man fro the regne of God. . . . And ofte tyme swich cursynge wrongfully retorneth agayn to hym that curseth" (10.618-19). Christian scriptures repeatedly condemn curses, such as in the admonition, "Bless them that curse you, and pray for them that calumniate you" (Luke 6.26, cf. Romans 12.14). Yet as much as the Christian faith condemns curses in most circumstances, the medieval church held within its power the authority to curse sinners, as detailed in *Jacob's Well*, a treatise on the human conscience: "Ryght so, the swerd of holy cherche, that is, the sentence of the grete curs in ony of his artycles, smyteth & sleeth hem that ben gylty there-in; for it departyth god fro hem, that is the lyif of here soule, as a swerd departyth the body fro the soule of hem that he dedly woundyth."[8] Whether from an individual's sin of cursing or from the church's reaction to this sin through its own curse, medieval Christians confronted the severe repercussions for their oaths: as the Parson warns, a person's sin often redounds to one's own punishment. The old woman, while initially justified in her anger against the summoner, succumbs to a species of "wikked Ire" that would put the safety of her soul in jeopardy.

Beyond these matters of the old woman's anger, the tale also suffers from an inherent illogic, in which she damns the summoner to hell without any apparent right to do so. As T. A. Stroud rightly ponders, "How could the widow give the fiend something she did not legally own?"[9] The example of the carter damning his horse, cart, and hay is predicated upon his ownership of these objects, as is the old woman's damning of her pan. It is a small but telling point to consider, but caution is warranted as well, for as Przemyslaw Mroczkowski explains, it is not necessarily an illogical moment in the tale. Citing the fourteenth-century friar John

Bromyard, Mroczkowski outlines that many people of the Middle Ages believed that it was "dangerous to curse people" owing to the fear that "the malediction may turn on the speaker"—an apt warning for the old woman. Mroczkowski also cites Peraldus, who explains that "the Lord shall greatly punish the robbers" by heeding the "imprecations and curses spoken at them by widows and children whom they despoil."[10] Even without owning the summoner, the old woman may have suffi- cient authority to curse him, yet with the potential contradiction that in damning him, she may be damning herself.

Yet the most striking illogical moment of the *Friar's Tale* emerges in the Friar's statement of his moral: "Herketh this word! Beth war, as in this cas: / 'The leoun sit in his awayt [ambush] alway / To sle the innocent, if that he may'" (3.1656-58). His words echo Psalm 10.8-9 ("He sitteth in ambush with the rich in private places, that he may kill the innocent. His eyes are upon the poor man: he lieth in wait in secret like a lion in his den"), yet to which of his characters would they apply? One could hardly consider the summoner of the tale an innocent, and the devil corresponds with the lion, not the innocent person, of the passage. The old woman, despite her angry sins, remains unpunished in the tale's conclusion, thus eluding the logic of an innocent person slain by a lion. This lion, it would appear, must continue waiting to slay the innocent, for the Friar does not allow it the opportunity to do so in this tale. Joan Young Gregg explains that "despite its brevity, the exemplum had to appear as a complete rhetor- ical object; its structure had to convey a sense of closure leading logically to its moral."[11] With a damned pan, immoral anger, and illogical leaps, the *Friar's Tale* cannot achieve its exemplary objectives.

In the end, the old woman's anger taints the exemplum that the Friar employs to denigrate the Summoner. As with all interpretations that dis- place such narrative inconsistencies onto the pilgrims rather than onto Chaucer, one could reasonably posit that the theological contradictions of the *Friar's Tale* reflect his intention to place a morally dubious exemplum in the mouth of his morally dubious friar. Thus, one could see the Friar's inability to tell a theologically coherent exemplum as another stroke of Chaucer's artistic genius, in that this lapse fits with the Friar's depiction in the *General Prologue* as ethically unscrupulous. Yet it is then also odd that the Friar places in his summoner's mouth an insult to friars, when this avaricious character accuses the old woman of fornicating with friars: "Com out . . . thou olde virytrate [hag]! / I trowe thou hast som frere or preest with thee" (3.1582-83). Whether a small slip or a telling blunder, the Friar's allusion to sinful friars undercuts his attempts to smear the Summoner, which, rather than condemning his foe, hoists him on his own petard. The generic purpose of an exemplum is to teach its audience a clear moral lesson, one that does not confuse its message by a poor old woman's damnation of a pan expensive enough to be sought after by the most morally bankrupt of men.

CHAPTER 8

The Dead Children and Anti-carnivalesque Humor of the *Summoner's Tale*

Dark humor revels in testing taboos and breaking prohibitions, but few images elicit less laughter than those of dead children, and from this conflict arises the unbalanced comedy of the *Summoner's Tale*. Featuring two dead children as minor characters in his narrative, the Summoner infuses it with unexpected elements of pathos, despite aiming with his farcical and anal humor more for raucous laughter than for compassionate tears. Like the *Miller's Tale* and the *Reeve's Tale*, the *Summoner's Tale*, in its earthy, bawdy, sexual, excremental, and exaggerated humor, adheres to the generic structures of the fabliau, which features characters immorally pursuing the satisfaction of their selfish ambitions and comic climaxes sparking explosive laughter, all set in a landscape of inverted values. In his narrative of a greedy friar groping another man's anus in hopes of finding riches therein, Chaucer builds his tale to a riotously satisfying conclusion that locates rejuvenating humor through the carnivalesque potential of the anus and the logical puzzle of "ars-metrike" (otherwise known as "ass math," 3.2222), yet its dead children destabilize its many pleasures and trouble the comedy of its topsy-turvy imaginary. With dueling sensibilities evident throughout his tale—the carnivalesque humor that finds redemptive possibilities in excremental debasement and the anti-carnivalesque images of death and decay—Chaucer tacks back and forth between comic and anticomic modes, merging them to an uproarious but disjointed effect that subverts the full pleasures of the fabliau, thus demonstrating again the challenges of infusing genres with radically opposed sensibilities.

In his critical masterpiece *Rabelais and His World*, Mikhail Bakhtin proposes that much medieval humor is inspired by an inverted vision of the human form that elicits comedy from its degradations. According to various Christian traditions prevalent throughout the Middle Ages, the body is divided both between upper and lower and between front and back, with the upper and front privileged as the favored aspects of these binaries and the lower and back denigrated as corruptive and corrupting. As Bakhtin writes, "The upper part is the face or the head and the lower part is the genital organs, the belly, and the buttocks." He further observes the ironic comic potential in inverting these hierarchies: "In the literary sphere the entire medieval parody is based on the grotesque concept of the body."[1] Rejecting the typical schema of earthly existence, the carnivalesque revels in the humorous degradation of humanity, which for Bakhtin entails a process of "coming down to earth" so that characters must confront the outlandish repercussions of their "contact with earth as an element that swallows up and gives birth at the same time." Deepening his theories of the comic potential of degradation, Bakhtin explains, "To degrade also means to concern oneself with the lower stratum of the body, the life of the belly and the reproductive organs; it therefore relates to acts of defecation and copulation, conception, pregnancy, and birth."[2]

With words of particular relevance to Chaucer's corpus, Bakhtin argues that "carnivalesque humor is also reflected in the *fabliaux*," indicating the connections between medieval popular culture and Chaucer's literary art.[3] For the most part, Chaucer's carnivalesque fabliaux traffic in the debasements of the human body, thereby sparking conditions for hearty laughter that ultimately celebrate life. To reach such an affirming comedy, fabliaux employ images of humanity at our most exaggerated, earthy, and grotesque, which presents a formidable balancing act for authors to strike, yet in many instances this objective is achieved by depicting sexual shenanigans and exaggerated excremental humor rather than the trauma of death. Scenes of violence in the French fabliaux are more cartoonish than realistic, and fatalities appear rarely.[4] Among Chaucer's fabliaux—*Miller's Tale, Reeve's Tale, Summoner's Tale, Merchant's Tale*, and *Shipman's Tale*, with strong fabliau elements and themes evident in the *Cook's Tale* and the *Wife of Bath's Prologue*—the *Summoner's Tale* is the only one that encodes images of dead children, which opposes its efforts to maintain the air of rejuvenating humor so central to the genre's ethos.

As discussed in the previous chapter, the Friar and Summoner detest each other owing to their professional rivalries and possibly to their respective sexual predilections. Fuming over the Friar's story of a summoner damned to hell, the Summoner vows narrative revenge and, before beginning his tale, includes in his prologue the carnivalesque account of a friar who "ravysshed was to helle / In spirit ones [once] by a visioun" (3.1676-77). This friar espies none of his brethren among the infernal pits and inquires of his angelic guide whether men of his calling are so blessed by grace that none has ever faced damnation. The angel counters that "many a millioun" friars reside in hell (3.1685), and the prologue's anal humor is unleashed when he orders Satan to lift his tail: "Shewe forth thyn ers [ass], and lat the frere se / Where is the nest of freres in this place!" (3.1690-91). Twenty thousand friars teem out of Satan's anus, swarm around hell, and then return to their excremental nest: "And in his ers they crepten everychon" (3.1698). In this miniature narrative, the friar learns an appropriate moral lesson and reforms himself from his sinful ways because "so was the develes ers ay in his mynde" (3.1705). Within medieval thought, the *Summoner's Prologue* adheres to the formula of the fabula, which Giovanni Boccaccio identifies as "a form of discourse, which, under guise of invention, illustrates or proves an idea; and, as its superficial aspect is removed, the meaning of the author is clear."[5] Within this explosively anal vision of damnation, a spiritually affirming message is located within a grotesque and carnivalesque narrative: to enjoy the succors of eternal life in heaven, one must avoid sins that could result in perpetual damnation, and so a salvific theme emerges from this friar's unlikely visit to hell. Furthermore, the carnivalesque dynamics of the *Summoner's Prologue* illustrate the redemptive potential found in the most abject of entities and identities, for no location in the medieval Christian imaginary more signifies the lowness and the backwardness of the human form than Satan's anus.

Within narrative studies, it is both a vast oversimplification and a foundational axiom that tragic genres end in death while comic genres end in marriages thematically suggestive of rebirth and reproduction. Other than in comic subgenres specifically designed to elicit laughter from dark topics (e.g., gallows humor, black comedy), death is a force that most comedies seek to displace in favor of more refreshing pleasures. Death provokes haunting questions that no literary text can answer, despite the fact that humans crave to plumb its significance, as Simon Critchley explains: "If . . . death is not just going to have the character of a brute fact, then one's mortality is something in which one has to find a meaning."[6] The incomprehensibility yet irrevocableness of death has perpetually perplexed humankind, as we daily face its inexorable force and untold mysteries until each of us must ultimately confront our own dissolution. In contrast, while comedy may include a meaning—and satires by definition include some sort of meaning by ridiculing a human institution or foible—its pleasures are joyfully tautological: the purpose of comic literature is its very comedy, the laughter that it seeks to provoke. Within this overarching framework, comedy, typically viewed as a respite from the weariness of the world, would seem an inhospitable form for depicting the trauma of death. "Comedy has, understandably, been commonly held to be incompatible with the tragic experience of others' deaths or the awareness of one's own finitude," as Stephanie Bird avows.[7] In his prologue, the Summoner appears to recognize that a live and potentially repentant friar better serves the tone and timbre of his story than would a dead and eternally damned one.

In contrast, in this story of a greedy friar, John, who hopes to wheedle a financial windfall from ailing and angry Thomas, the Summoner introduces two dead children into his narrative: Thomas and his wife's recently deceased son and, in one of the friar's examples of the dangers of anger, the murdered son of Cambises's adviser. Readers encounter the first dead child when Thomas's wife greets the acquisitive friar visiting her household. "Now sire . . . but o word er I go. / My child is deed withinne thise wykes two," she tells him (3.1851-52), as he seizes upon her words to extol the efficacy of his prayers. Friar John claims to the child's mother, "His deeth saugh I by revelacioun" (3.1854), and states further that he witnessed his ascent to heaven: "After his deeth, I saugh hym born to blisse / In myn avision, so God me wisse!" (3.1857-58). For this unscrupulous man, the child's death serves as a means to wax eloquent on the blessed nature of friars, and he asserts the special grace granted to them as a consequence of their poverty: "That specially oure sweete Lord Jhesus / Spak this by freres, whan he seyde thus: / 'Blessed be they that povere in spirit been'" (3.1921-23). Along with developing the characterization of the friar as morally void, Thomas and his wife's dead child also hints at John's sexual improprieties, for it is implied that he, rather than Thomas, might be the boy's father. Certainly, the friar embraces Thomas's wife with surprising affection—"The frere ariseth up ful curteisly, / And hire embraceth in his armes narwe, / And kiste hire sweete" (3.1803-5)—and he speaks with the courtly phrasings of a chivalric lord when pledging himself as her "servant every deel" (3.1806). One of Chaucer's preferred euphemisms for sexual intercourse is *refresshed*, which the Wife of Bath uses to describe her active sex life, wishing "to be refresshed half so ofte" as King Solomon with his hundreds of wives (3.38). Employing a similar usage, the narrator describes Thomas's residence as "an hous ther [the friar] was wont to be / Refresshed moore than in an hundred placis" (3.1766-67). In reporting the status of her marital sex life, Thomas's wife recalls her nightly attempts to seduce her husband by wrapping her legs and arms around him but concludes resignedly, "Oother desport right noon of hym have I; / I may nat plese hym in no maner cas" (3.1830-31). Confronting the mother's memory not merely of a dead child but likely of his own dead child, John proceeds in his callous pursuit of Thomas's funds by crowing about the efficacy of his prayers.

This dead child, it must be acknowledged, contributes effectively to Chaucer's characterization of Friar John's moral failings, thus enhancing the fabliau's satiric objectives, yet it dissipates the carnivalesque energy so central to the genre's ambitions. As Patrick O'Neill explains, "Satire, though primarily an expression of derisive humour, . . . extends from what we might call benign satire, firmly and tolerantly anchored in its own value-system, through derisive satire in the narrower sense, where the emphasis begins to shift from the didactic to the punitive, until finally we reach black or entropic satire, where disorder is seen to triumph over order."[8] Chaucer unites satire and carnivalesque tropes in his *Summoner's Tale*, but at times the darkness of the satire overwhelms the life-affirming humor of the carnivalesque. As O'Neill further argues, "At the entropic end of the spectrum . . . we find an emphatic lack of belief in [satire's] efficacy as an agent of moral education, and didactic confidence gives way to a fascinated vision of maximum entropy, total disorder."[9] Few images better capture the concept of "maximum entropy" than those of dead children, young beings formerly representing life and promise but now merely the empty husks of their former potential.

The second dead child of the *Summoner's Tale* appears in John's series of exemplary narratives detailing the perils of anger. Diagnosing Thomas as afflicted with this sin, the friar cautions him that "Ire is, in sooth, executour of pryde" (3.2010) and recounts tales of anger and its repercussions, including Seneca's story of an unjust judge who condemns three blameless knights to death; an account of "Irous Cambises," who delights in casual depravity and drunkenness; and a legend of Cyrus the Elder, who avenges himself on a river that drowned his horse. J. Allan Mitchell explains the satiric aim of such stories for the *Summoner's Tale*. "The pilgrim Summoner . . . deploys the rhetoric of exemplarity for the purpose of satire," he asserts, as he also explores how this "satire is highly conventional" in "point[ing] up the usual vices of the itinerant preachers."[10] Within these satiric parameters, the story of "Irous Cambises" includes the second dead child of the *Summoner's Tale*. When one of his lords advises him to avoid drunkenness, Cambises takes umbrage and orders this man's son to be brought before them. To demonstrate that he retains control of his faculties despite his drunkenness, he drinks immoderately, takes up his bow, and "with an arwe he slow the child right there" (3.2068). The child's murder is thus all the more horrific, for Cambises executes his plan with awareness sufficient to halt any reasonable person from proceeding further. Cambises models the sins of anger and of gluttony, thus serving as an appropriate illustration of their dangers, yet the friar appears to realize that a dead child introduces a disconcerting and discordant note into his narrative, as he quickly concludes this portion of his lecture. "His sone was slayn; ther is namoore to seye" (3.2073), he declares, and the next "victim" recounted in his series of exempla is the river Gyndes, which Cyrus the Elder dams up to the extent that "wommen myghte wade it over al" (3.2084). The tonal shift between these two narratives is noticeable, from the pathos of a slain child to the ironic humor of Cyrus's ridiculous punishment of a river for a drowned horse. As a whole, as Marc Cels postulates, "These exempla . . . contribut[e] to the portrait of an inept preacher who ironically shows up his own shortcomings,"[11] and so it is again apparent that these dead children enhance the satiric objectives of the *Summoner's Tale* in calumniating friars but at the expense of its carnivalesque humor.

The drowned horse of the friar's exempla provides a more apt segue into the tale's remainder, which unleashes its carnivalesque climax. The friar requests that Thomas confess his sins solely to him ("But shewe to me al thy confessioun" [3.2093]), but Thomas replies that he will not do so (3.2094-95). The unctuous friar then attempts to persuade Thomas to bestow his generosity exclusively on his order, and Thomas appears to relent, instructing him where to find the treasures that John so desperately seeks: "Now thanne, put in thyn hand doun by my bak, / . . . and grope wel bihynde. / Bynethe my buttok there shaltow fynde / A thyng that I have hyd in pryvetee" (3.2140-43). The friar eagerly obeys Thomas's commands and excavates his anus, only to be met with a thunderous fart: "Ther nys no capul [horse], drawynge in a cart, / That myghte have lete a fart of swich a soun" (3.2150-51). Susan Crane captures the perfect synthesis of ironic humor achieved in this flatulent blast: "In a diegesis Bakhtin would have appreciated, the precise opposite of abstinent prayer is a sick man's fart, a supremely animal act."[12] At this moment the *Summoner's Tale* exhibits the bounteous and ultimately life-affirming humor of the carnivalesque anus, for Thomas's fart does not symbolize the victory of death and despair but rather the fecund possibilities of rebirth through the lower bodily order. Like the friar in the *Summoner's Prologue* after his encounter with Satan's anus, surely Friar John will reform himself after his anger cools and he mulls the meaning of his foray between Thomas's buttocks.

As much as the images of dead children trouble the carnivalesque humor of the *Summoner's Tale*, the figure of a child—or more accurately, of an adolescent—calms the disruptions to its humorous themes. After Thomas farts explosively in the friar's face, the friar is confounded by Thomas's condition that this "gift" must be shared with the other members of his fraternal order. Prior to humiliating the friar, Thomas advised him: "And in thyn hand thou shalt it have anon, / On this condicion, and oother noon, / That thou departe it so, my deere brother, / That every frere have also muche as oother" (3.2131-34). The friar turns to the lord of the village for help in resolving this conundrum, yet it is the lord's squire, Jankyn, who explains the proper method of dividing a fart among the friar and his brothers. Place the farter at the center of a cartwheel, he recommends, with the friars kneeling at the end of the spokes. Spin the wheel, and the spinning farter can then release his gas so that "equally the soun of it wol wende, / And eke the stynk, unto the spokes ende" (3.2273-74). The lord and lady of the village, as well as their guests, affirm the rightness of his proposal, and Jankyn wins a new gown for his ingenuity. In effect, the third child of the narrative triumphs in carnivalesque fashion, overturning hierarchies of senescence and juvenescence that follow Thomas's surprisingly generative fart. Indeed, as Bakhtin suggests, "Carnival celebrates the destruction of the old and the birth of the new world—the new year, the new spring, the new kingdom."[13] From this perspective, Jankyn represents the concluding triumph of youth against an adult culture portrayed as graspingly greedy in the friar and angrily ailing in Thomas. Moreover, as the friar preached against the sin of anger yet then becomes enraged after Thomas's fart—"He looked as it were a wilde boor; / He grynte with his teeth, so was he wrooth" (3.2160-61)—Jankyn silences his rage, proving his ironic solution to the fart riddle better soothes an angry man than the friar's many exempla that dispelled neither Thomas's anger nor his own.

Chaucer's rich fabliau humor is further evident in the surprising spiritual echoes to be found in this apparently trivial question of how best to divide a fart among the members of a fraternal order. Alan Levitan perceives the parodic similarities between the dispersal of a fart among twelve friars and Pentecost, which in Christian traditions commemorates the Holy Spirit's descent upon Jesus's apostles. "The *Summoner's Tale* is, in effect, a turning 'upsa-doun' of all the expected elements of Pentecost," he states.[14] In this foundational moment of the Christian faith, Jesus's apostles experience a miracle signaled by a mighty wind that sweeps across them: "suddenly there came a sound from heaven, as of a mighty wind coming, and it filled the whole house where they were sitting .... And they were all filled with the Holy Ghost, and they began to speak with divers tongues" (Acts of the Apostles 2.2-4). Glending Olson concurs with Levitan, observing that "the scatological substitution of Thomas's fart for the mighty wind accompanying the descent of the Holy Spirit in Acts 2 has religious significance as a satiric image of friars' false claims to apostolic stature."[15] With the outrageous image of a fart signifying the mighty wind that signaled the birth of Christianity, Chaucer marries the satiric and the carnivalesque effectively. As medieval Christians pondered the mysteries of their faith, they found humorous potential in the ways in which their bodies could not help but serve as models for understanding divinity, even as these earthly images contaminated divine ones through their very earthliness.

A more positive interpretation of the *Summoner's Tale*'s dead children would view them as ancillary tropes of the decaying order that the carnivalesque overthrows, for they are connected to Thomas's bitter anger and the friar's incessant efforts to win donations from him. In this light, these dead children represent the corrupt world that must be rejected in favor of the humorous world where Jankyn rules as the boy-king of unsurpassed wit and wisdom. At the same time, it must also be conceded that few entities less evoke laughter than images of dead children, and so their countervailing force cannot be wholly redeemed within the tale's carnivalesque humor. Speaking broadly of humor's ambitions, Patrick O'Neill declares, "All humour, and *a fortiori* all literary humour, black or otherwise, must ultimately be affirmative of life and a celebration of the victory of the embattled spirit over the void."[16] Much of the brilliance of the *Summoner's Tale* springs from its satiric jabs aimed at friars and its fabliau humor that debases their moneygrubbing ways, but comic genres, even in their shared focus on humor, do not always align smoothly and organically. Agnes Heller, considering the various effects of comic genres and voices, observes the challenge for authors to integrate disparate traditions: "Very heterogeneous attitudes or elements of the comic are frequently introduced in one single comic work, and authors do not usually make an effort to fit them tightly together, for they cultivate just this heterogeneity."[17] The heterogeneity of comic modes offers benefits and liabilities, yet as much as it is possible, if challenging, to imagine dead children as an effective comic trope, Chaucer's *Summoner's Tale* is bleached of some of its raucous pleasure after the blast of Thomas's explosive fart wafts away, leaving resonant images of lifeless youth for his audience to ponder. Farts easily belong in the generic range of fabliaux, dead children do not, and so this example of Chaucer's genre troubles leaves, with apologies for the mixed metaphor, a touch of bitter aftertaste after a gloriously smelly tale.

CHAPTER 9

The Wretched Smock and Gendered Theodicy of the *Clerk's Tale*

A simple rule of thumb: good husbands and fathers do not murder, or even to claim to murder, their children. Flagrantly defying this truism, the *Clerk's Tale* tells the brutal story of benevolent Griselda suffering for years at the hands of her tyrannous husband Walter, who cruelly tests her love and endurance by demanding complete submission to his desires, which extend to the apparent execution of their children. Griselda stoically withstands this unwarranted abuse and never utters a word of reprimand or reproach, even when Walter dismisses her to her father's home wearing only a "wrecched" smock (4.850). He then recalls her to attend to his new bride—who is actually their daughter. In the tale's climax, Walter finally relents, confesses that the supposed murders of their children were a ruse designed to test her, and allows the family's joyful reunion. The *Clerk's Tale* thus ends on a purportedly happy note, yet this conclusion has troubled readers for centuries, asking them to overlook Walter's cruelty now that Griselda's anguish has abated. To imagine a "happily ever after" ending for Griselda requires a suspension of disbelief beyond the willingness of many readers, for how can one view her marriage to a sadistic tyrant as the foundation for future happiness, even with her children restored to her? At its core, the *Clerk's Tale* can be understood as a secular reimagining of the theological concept of theodicy, which affirms the ultimate benevolence of an omnipotent deity who allows evil and suffering to exist. More so, as evident in Griselda's woe and the symbolism of her wretched smock, the *Clerk's Tale* reimagines the central questions of the theodicy as directly relevant to the gendered conditions of human existence but then sidesteps drawing any thematic conclusions about how readers should interpret Griselda's tormented narrative arc. In short, Chaucer's theodicy undercuts any likely theme, any moral lesson, that the tale might ostensibly uphold, leaving only the horror show of marital and paternal brutality.

The persistent conundrum between belief in divine goodness and the persistence of evil has long dogged humanity, and as Chad Schrock outlines, the theodicy "vindicate[es] divine justice" while acknowledging the "paradox of a creator god remaining just and good despite the existence of evil in the world he has created."[1] In attempting to reconcile God's goodness with daily suffering, many theologians optimistically propose that humanity cannot foresee the deity's grand design through an earthly perspective and that the necessity of human affliction will eventually be made clear. Various medieval theologians endorsed God's inherent goodness along these lines, discerning the utility of evil for a higher yet unfathomable objective. In his theological writings, Peter Abelard perceives God's inversionary logic for allowing evil: "For God uses even evil for a good purpose, and in a wonderful way turns perversity to good account, as one who employs both left and right hands as though they were both right hands."[2] Sounding a similar note, Julian of Norwich envisions the devil's chagrin when he is allowed to toy with humanity only then to be disappointed by the final outcome: "And that is the devil's sorrow, and he is put to terrible shame, for everything which God permits him to do turns to joy for us and to pain and shame for him."[3] Confronted by the everyday and greater evils that all humans witness, medieval Christians upheld their faith in God, espying a greater wisdom and a greater plan for their present suffering. The biblical book of Job serves as the paradigmatic narrative of the theodicy, in which Job, a righteous man, endures the loss of his livelihood, his children, and his health after God wagers with Satan that Job will not curse him despite these afflictions.

The theodicy recurs as a key theme in Chaucer's literature, addressed in such works as the *Knight's Tale* (1303-33), *Man of Law's Tale* (813-16), *Franklin's Tale* (865-93), *Troilus and Criseyde* (3.1016-22 and 4.958-1082), and *Legend of Philomela* (2228-37). From the *Friar's Tale*, it is evident that Chaucer's thematic treatment of the theodicy correlates with his understanding of the book of Job. This story's devil explains to his traveling companion that God constrains the power of evil: as "Goddes instrumentz," devils have no agency of their own but instead work through the divine will (3.1483-91). In Chaucer's *Tale of Melibee*, Prudence urges her husband Melibee to model himself after Job, quoting the biblical text: "Oure Lord hath yeve [given] it me; oure Lord hath biraft it me; right as oure Lord hath wold, right so it is doon" (7.1000, cf. Job 1.21). From the example of Job, medieval Christians learned to abide the pains they must endure and to accept God's eventual but undiscernible purpose while maintaining their faith, and diverse moments of Chaucer's fictions echo these view-points. Many readers and critics of the *Clerk's Tale* persuasively argue that, following the spiritual logic of the story of Job, the exemplary nature of Griselda's story should not be lost owing to its troubling treatment of her. As Charlotte Morse explains, Chaucer's heart-wrenching tale illustrates the challenges and triumphs of persevering in one's faith, a vision from which modern readers should not avert their eyes: "If Griselda's patience fails our tests, or if we believe it will, we will reject what was, for medieval translators, Griselda's most important function, her exemplary function."[4]

Although the theodicy, as a vindication of God's loving concern for humanity, provides a comforting lesson within a religious context—that the inscrutability of the divine plan will cede to perfect understanding in the afterlife—it loses its moorings when transposed to a secular tale of a virtuous woman married to a tyrant. Like Job, Griselda suffers unimaginable torments as her story unfolds, with Walter repeatedly testing her fidelity to him. The tale's opening, in which he first espies her and admires her virtuous morality, appears to be establishing a Cinderella-type story, in which a blameless young woman is rescued from poverty after a wealthy suitor recognizes her intrinsic worth. The story pivots when Walter demands Griselda's unquestioned fealty while negotiating their marriage: "I seye this: be ye redy with good herte / To al my lust [pleasure], and that I frely may, / As me best thynketh, do yow laughe or smerte, / And nevere ye to grucche it, nyght ne day?" (4.351-54). Similar to the ways in which humans will never apprehend God's justification for their earthly travails, Griselda cedes any right to question Walter's motivations for his inscrutable actions. Resigning herself to powerlessness, she agrees never to disagree, never to speak of any discontent that readers might expect her to feel. Walter first exhibits his appalling cruelty when he sends a sergeant to convince Griselda that he will execute their firstborn child, a daughter, soon after her birth. Following their son's birth, the pattern is repeated, with Griselda refusing to vent herself of the emotional pain of losing her children. Instead, she affirms her commitment to Walter: "I wol no thyng, ne nyl no thyng, certayn, / But as yow list. Naught greveth me at al, / Though that that my doughter and my sone be slayn" (4.646-48).

The loss of her children stands as Griselda's most torturous test, yet the Clerk extends the emotional horror behind his rags-to-riches plotline by emphasizing her thread-worn clothes, with her wretched smock further distorting the themes of this secular theodicy. When moving Griselda from her childhood home to his court, Walter delegates a company of

women to assist her in this transition, but they recoil at handling her rag-
ged attire: "thise ladyes were nat right glad / To handle hir clothes, where-
inne she was clad" (4.375-76). Later, when Walter dismisses Griselda from
his household, clothes again play a key thematic role in her suffering. He
grants her the right to take with her "thilke dowere [that dowry] that ye
broghten me" (4.807); she understands his words to mean only the "wrec-
ched clothes" she brought with her but "nothyng faire" that she received
during her tenure as his wife (4.850). So that she will not return home
naked, Griselda negotiates that she be allowed to wear "swich a smok as I
wont [accustomed] to were [wear]" (4.886) prior to their marriage. Leaving
Walter's court, Griselda's words echo Job's, deepening the tale's themes of
a secular theodicy. "Naked out of my fadres hous . . . / I cam, and naked
moot I turne agayn" (4.871-72), she declares, in comparison to Job's stoic
words: "Naked came I out of my mother's womb, and naked shall I return
thither" (Job 1.21). Notably, this gendered theodicy switches the site of
its speakers' origins: Griselda alludes to her father's house, in contrast
to Job's reference to his mother's womb. In scenes of gendered symmetry,
Griselda and Job envision their misery as facilitating the return to the
sanctity offered by their opposite-sex parents. Both locations metaphor-
ically suggest the comfort of their pasts and their resignation over their
futures, with Griselda's wretched smock covering her body yet indicat-
ing her naked despair. When she reaches her childhood home, Griselda's
father covers her "with hire olde coote" (4.913) that the narrator describes
as "rude was the clooth, and moore of age / By dayes fele [many] than at
hire mariage" (4.916-17). In his final cruelty, Walter conscripts Griselda to
return to his court to prepare the chambers of his new bride, their daughter
whom Griselda has long believed to be dead. This scene ironically com-
ments on Griselda's wretched smock, in that she who has been stripped
must participate in the sumptuous attiring of her replacement.

Beyond the thematic connections of Griselda's wretched smock, Job's
nakedness, and her daughter's dressing, the narrator of the *Clerk's Tale*
directly links Griselda's suffering to Job's. In so doing, the Clerk creates
a woman's theodicy, one in which gender ostensibly serves as a central
conduit for the text's creation of meaning:

Men speke of Job, and moost for his humblesse,
As clerkes, whan hem list [they prefer], konne wel endite,
Namely of men, but as in soothfastnesse,
Though clerkes preise wommen but a lite,

Ther kan no man in humblesse hym acquite
As womman kan, ne kan been half so trewe
As wommen been, but it be falle of newe [a recent event]. (4.932-38)

According to this narrator, women are spiritually stronger than men and thus better capable of modeling the humbleness and humility of Job in their patient suffering of life's adversities. As Shawn Normandin observes of the paradoxical quality of these lines, "The stanza takes away with one hand what it gives with the other. It enhances Griselda's moral authority by associating her with a biblical hero, but at the same time it undermines the authority of the biblical hero."[5] Because the narrator introduces gendered dynamics into the challenging issue of the theodicy and then prioritizes a woman's suffering, Job pales as a model of spiritual fortitude in comparison to Griselda. In effect, the narrator asks readers to assess the greater spiritual value of women's suffering over men's and to celebrate Griselda's intractable endurance of her husband's torments. All allegories involve slippage between their tenor and their vehicle, but most stories attempt to minimize, or at least gloss over, these differences. In contrast to this principle, the *Clerk's Tale* calls attention to these differences in the explicit contest it constructs between Griselda and Job, in which Griselda triumphs.

The *Clerk's Tale* and the book of Job converge again on their themes of silence. This may initially appear to be a surprising statement, given that the book of Job is comprised almost entirely of poetic dialogues, in which Job and his three friends discuss the cause of his agony for the majority of the book, and then a fourth friend pontificates on his understanding of God's wisdom. Finally, the Lord speaks and silences Job through his sharp questioning: "Where was thou when I laid the foundations of the earth? tell me if thou hast understanding" (38.4). More such pointed questioning follows, and Job learns his final lesson of accepting the Lord's wisdom without further questioning: "I have spoken unwisely, and things that above measure exceeded my knowledge. . . . Therefore I reprehend myself, and do penance in dust and ashes" (42.2-6). As Eric Carlton summarizes of Job's ordeal, "Job is silenced. And the lesson for all subsequent enquirers is simply that these matters are not for us and that we should be content with the assurance that omnipotence knows best."[6] In contrast to Job, who must learn to embrace silence after learning the futility of speech, Griselda remains silent throughout most of her narrative, accepting Walter's tyranny and thus stunning readers with her inviolate refusal to protest the meaningless murder of her children.

Related to this issue of speech and silence, the gendered theodicy of the *Clerk's Tale* is further apparent in the ways in which the narrator aligns Griselda's father, Janicula, with Job, with a woman's suffering and silence again surpassing that of a man's. In a telling juxtaposition, Janicula cannot match his daughter's ability to quietly endure. She abides patiently as he loudly laments her fate, and his words echo Job's: "Hir fader, that this tidynge herde anoon, / Curseth the day and tyme that Nature / Shoop hym to been a lyves creature" (4.901-3). These lines allude to Job's words cursing himself for being born only to be subjected to such grief: "Let the day perish wherein I was born" (3.3). Just as Walter cannot inflict any suffering upon Griselda that would cause her to cry out, thus proving women's better ability to suffer than men's, so too does Janicula's curse redound to heighten Griselda's ethical stature, for he curses agonies targeted at her, not him. With this theme of gendered silence, the narrator of the *Clerk's Tale* again stresses that women better model patient suffering than men, which elevates Griselda as a model of endurance for readers regardless of their gender.

Following the logic of the thematic connections between Griselda and Job, the story also aligns Walter with God, thus undercutting the theological and thematic message that it aspires to impart. Certainly, any connection between Walter and God undermines the allegorical nature of the *Clerk's Tale*, for Walter's actions first alienate him from his people and then lead them to despise him. He evinces little regard for their well-being in the story's opening, concerned more with his personal pleasures ("Thus in delit he lyveth" [4.68]) than with the sacrifices of governance. Later, learning that he has apparently ordered his children to be executed, his subjects react in horror: "For which, where as his peple therbifore / Hadde loved hym wel, the sclaundre of his diffame [infamy] / Made hem that they hym hatede therfore" (4.729-31). Even the narrator condemns Walter: "But as for me, I seye that yvele it sit / To assaye [test] a wyf whan that it is no nede" (4.460-61). From God to Walter represents a devolution from the unknowable to the simply unlikeable, and so any theme that the *Clerk's Tale* might aspire to impart becomes clouded to obscurity. A plausible counterargument to this reading might argue that Walter should be aligned not with God but with Satan because Satan torments Job, albeit with God's permission. While this point warrants consideration, it does not alleviate the challenges of interpreting either the book of Job or the *Clerk's Tale*, for the Lord approves of Satan's tests of Job in the former and Walter is accorded quasi-divine authority in the latter. And certainly,

Griselda employs the language of governance laden with religious over-
tones when speaking to Walter, such as when she states, "Ye been oure
lord; dooth with youre owene thyng / Right as yow list" (4.652-53), with
such words allegorically conflating Walter with God.

Further complicating the tale's allegorical constitution as a woman's
theodicy, Griselda is portrayed as so abundantly perfect that her suffering
registers as even less deserved than Job's, for she is explicitly compared to
Jesus. The narrator, detailing Janicula's modest home, casts Griselda as a
Christ figure owing to their shared roots in poverty: "Amonges this povre
[poor] folk ther dwelte a man / Which that was holden povrest of hem alle;
/ But hye God somtyme senden kan / His grace into a litel oxes stalle"
(4.204-7). Like Jesus in the manger, Griselda is born into a world of depri-
vation. Building on this Christological imagery, the narrator describes
Walter's subjects as so amazed by Griselda's wisdom that they view her as
a salvific figure: "So wise and rype wordes hadde she, / And juggementz of
so greet equitee, / That she from hevene sent was, as men wende [thought],
/ Peple to save and every wrong t'amende" (4.438-41). Griselda's wisdom,
judgment, and salvific mission establish her not merely as a good woman
but as a virtually perfect one. Returning to Griselda's smock, her humiliat-
ing disrobing further connects her to Jesus, who is stripped of his clothes
prior to his crucifixion. Within Christian thought, Jesus must be sacrificed
for the salvation of humanity, yet Griselda's torment precludes her from
pursuing her salvific mission on behalf of Walter's people.

As he winds down his gendered theodicy, the Clerk bestows upon it a
gendered moral that defies rational explication, crisscrossing the story's
meaning and its gendered themes in a manner that ultimately collapses:

> This storie is seyd nat for that wyves sholde
> Folwen Grisilde as in humylitee,
> For it were inportable [unbearable], though they wolde,
> But for that every wight, in his degree,
> Sholde be constant in adversitee
> As was Grisilde. (4.1142-47)

With these confounding words, the Clerk asserts that wives should not
view Griselda as a role model, yet he then declares that all people ("every
wight") should follow her example, which by necessity would include
wives among them. Even the Clerk appears to view his story as mean-
ingless, as he tacks to and fro to imbue it with a thematic depth liberated

from its horrific shell. Given these contradictory positions in the Clerk's depiction of Griselda, Leah Schwebel argues that "Chaucer explicitly rejects Griselda as a viable model for women, insisting that both she and her author represent obsolete models of authority."[7] Rejecting Griselda as a "viable model for women" calls into question the thematic meaning of the tale, for how could this protagonist's suffering thus be evacuated of any meaning? Lee Patterson sees in the *Clerk's Tale* its inherent thematic disintegration: "The Clerk has managed to take an already difficult narrative and render it not just enigmatic but virtually uninterpretable."[8] Within the conflicting levels of narrative, source texts, allegory, and allusion, Chaucer, or Chaucer's Clerk, cannot distill a coherent theme from the troubling story of a woman forced to endure scarring but wholly unwarranted torments.

Toward the conclusion of this confused tale, a cacophony of voices chimes up, thus modeling the interpretive disarray that confronts its readers. The Clerk apparently dismisses the relevance of his story to contemporary circumstances: "It were ful hard to fynde now-a-dayes / In al a toun Grisildis thre or two" (4.1164-65). The passage subtitled "L'Envoy de Chaucer"—which could represent either the continued speech of the Clerk or Chaucer's interruption—jokingly bemoans the dearth of patient women. This voice sings, "Grisilde is deed, and eek hire pacience" (4.1177), and then ironically implores women, "Ne lat no clerk have cause or diligence / To write of yow a storie of swich mervaille / As of Grisildis pacient and kynde" (4.1185-87). In effect, he encourages women not to model the sort of patience and suffering that has just served as his theme, not to create conditions to allow him to tell the very story he just told. Harry Bailly and the Merchant regretfully see in their wives the wholesale rejection of Griselda as a model of uxorial forbearance, with the former wishing that "My wyf at hoom had herd this legende ones!" (4.1212d) and the latter sighing, "Ther is a long and large difference / Bitwix Grisildis grete pacience / And of my wyf the passyng crueltee" (4.1223-25). Harry Bailly and the Merchant lament their wives' astute ability not to misread this text and emulate Griselda's patient suffering; in effect, these men would prefer their wives to misinterpret the themes of the *Clerk's Tale*, for a misreading would bolster their withered masculinity. Readers have long attempted to distill a coherent theme from this story that refuses to grant one, with Harry Bailly's and the Merchant's efforts highlighting the greater likelihood of desiring a misreading in order to control women rather than distilling the story's essence from its byzantine treatment of theodicy.

In sum, the concept of the theodicy is sufficiently challenging when considering the Divine, for it confronts believers with the inscrutability of God's actions in earthly terms. When the theodicy is translated into a secular tale of a tormented wife and her tyrannous husband, its scope is diminished to the domestic realm while its vexing questions remain as frustrating. As Helen Cooney argues in her reading of the *Parliament of Fowls* as a theodicy, "Chaucer's poem ultimately prompts the reflection that allegory confounds different kinds of evil, and so implies the inadequacy of the allegorical mode as a basis for a theodicy of any kind."[9] With Walter representing God and Griselda representing both Job and Jesus, the *Clerk's Tale* devolves into a theodicy in which two entities of the Christian Trinity—the Father and the Son—are respectively imagined as testing the other and as abiding this torment as it is meted out. Allegories crumble when their tenors and vehicles carry too many contradictory and self-collapsing themes, and such is the case with the *Clerk's Tale*, a gendered theodicy that, like Griselda's wretched smock, attempts to cover a body from prying eyes. Readers, however, cannot help but to look at the pain on display ostensibly for our (literary) pleasure, and thus to see the holes in meaning from which Chaucer attempts to divert our attention.

CHAPTER 10

The Apologetic Narrator and Fragmented Perspectives of the *Merchant's Tale*

Teller and tale, speaker and spoken: for the most part, Chaucer vibrantly aligns his pilgrims and their stories, thereby deepening the character portraits of the former and strengthening the themes of the latter. Because his characters express themselves through their tale-telling, it is virtually inconceivable to imagine transpositions between most tellers and their tales, such as the Knight narrating the *Miller's Tale* or the Squire recounting the *Reeve's Tale*. Moreover, most of the *Canterbury Tales* evince a consistent voice in their narration, and so just as it is difficult to imagine the Knight telling the *Miller's Tale*, it is equally unlikely that he would introduce the scurrilous humor of the fabliau into his narrative indebted to traditions of romance and epic. With the *Merchant's Tale*, however, contrasting voices speak at different moments, and they react in divergent ways to its ironic treatment of the joys and pains of marriage. As Robert Jordan observes, "Structural and stylistic evidence seems to indicate conclusively that there is no single viewpoint governing the narrative."[1] Without a unified and focalizing perspective for the story's account of the old knight January's mismatched marriage to young May, readers are left to discern among a cacophony of voices the tale's overarching assessment of marriage, cuckoldry, and desire, including a particularly perplexing and unexpectedly apologetic voice who regrets his fabliau's sexual shenanigans, despite their centrality to its meaning and humor. The narrator of the *Merchant's Tale* thereby proves mischaracterized, if not wholly uncharacterizable, by the perplexing plenitude of contradictory opinions expressed.

Given the thematic congruency between tellers and tales established in the previous episodes of the *Canterbury Tales*, readers are conditioned to expect the portrait of the Merchant in the *General Prologue* to hint at the type of story he will tell. This depiction satirizes him for the successful facade he presents to his fellow pilgrims, as he consistently inflates his earnings ("Sownynge [announcing] alwey th'encrees of his wynnyng" [1.275]) and hides his losses ("Ther wiste [knew] no wight that he was in dette" [1.280]). No mention is made of the Merchant's family life in the brief portrait of the *General Prologue*, but in the prologue of his tale, he introduces himself as a miserably married man. "I have a wyf, the worste that may be" (4.1218), he laments, as he then continues, "She is a shrewe at al" (4.1222). In an early sign of the fragmented perspectives forthcoming, the Merchant declares that his tale will not address his personal marital pains—"of my owene soore, / For soory herte, I telle may namoore" (4.1243-44)—yet he then tells the story of a *senex amans* cuckolded by his young bride. A wife who cuckolds her husband need not necessarily be a shrew—as exemplified by Alison in the *Miller's Tale* and the merchant's wife in the *Shipman's Tale*, who betray their marital vows in a winsome, never hectoring, manner—and so there need be no inherent contradiction in the Merchant's words. It is nonetheless a disjointed introduction to the ensuing narrative: a tale of an unsatisfying marriage from a man who has just stated that he will not tell a tale of an unsatisfying marriage. As Holly Crocker explains of this prologue and its inconsistencies, "The Merchant attempts to establish a position of masculine authority for himself," yet, as becomes apparent as his story proceeds, he cannot uphold the "claims to masculine authority within the tale itself."[2] In other words, he cannot be the character he proclaims himself to be.

In the opening lines of the *Merchant's Tale*, the narrator introduces the broad outlines of his story: a sixty-year-old knight, January, decides to marry, and the character sketch accompanying his introduction points to fabliau themes of unrestrained carnality and erotic deception. The narrator ascribes January's motives arising either "for hoolynesse or for dotage / I kan nat seye" (4.1253-54), in a jocose tone congruent with the tale's humor. Then in a puzzling line the narrator alludes to January's lusty appetite, declaring that he "folwed ay his bodily delyt / On wommen, ther as was his appetyt, / As doon thise fooles that been seculeer" (4.1249-51). If the narrator is indeed the Merchant, why would he, a secular man of trade, insult men such as himself as fools? Several critics propose that this line indicates Chaucer's original intention for the *Merchant's Tale* to be told by one of the religious members of the pilgrimage, perhaps the Friar or the Monk.[3] In contrast, Donald Howard interprets these lines as appropriate for the Merchant, proposing that they indicate "the Merchant would willingly disavow the whole of the secular estate in which the norm is marriage."[4] It is also plausible that Chaucer wrote this tale before envisioning it in the voice of one of his Canterbury pilgrims, and so any subsequent assignment of it would likely result in some disjunction between its subject matter and its speaker. At the very least, this opening reference to "fooles that been seculeer" notifies readers that the ascription of the tale to the Merchant may not accord with Chaucer's original vision, as it also foreshadows the surprising shifts in this character's perspective throughout the ensuing tale.

A few lines later, another crux appears in a passage commonly referred to as the marriage encomium (4.1267-392), in which the speaker opines in such dissimilar voices that he cannot be conclusively identified. Immediately preceding the encomium, January praises the joys of marriage, thus establishing his hopeless naivete: "Noon oother lyf . . . is worth a bene [bean], / For wedlok is so esy and so clene, / That in this world it is a paradys" (4.1263-65). Surely this is an exaggerated view of marriage's pleasures, and the narrator ironically assesses January's viewpoint: "Thus seyde this olde knyght, that was so wys" (4.1266). The marriage encomium then begins with the declaration, "And certeinly, as sooth as God is kyng, / To take a wyf it is a glorious thyng" (4.1267-68). Manuscripts of the *Canterbury Tales* lack common punctuation such as quotation marks, and so the source texts do not indicate which character Chaucer envisioned as speaking these words. Some lines appear written for naive January, such as the optimistic rhetorical questions about a wife's uxorial devotion that the remainder of the story disproves: "For who kan be so buxom [obedient] as a wyf? / Who is so trewe, and eek so ententyf [diligent] / To kepe hym, syk and hool, as is his make [mate]?" (4.1287-89). In contrast, some opinions sound appropriate for an omniscient and benevolent narrator, such as in the heartfelt comparison between spousal and spiritual love: "Love wel thy wyf, as Crist loved his chirche. / If thou lovest thyself, thou lovest thy wyf" (4.1384-85). Some lines appear to belong to an ironic narrator, possibly Chaucer himself or his unhappily married Merchant, such as in this grim warning: "A wyf wol laste, and in thyn hous endure, / Wel lenger than thee list, paraventure" (4.1317-18).

Notably as well, some passages, depending on how they are intoned, could be credibly attributed to any of these voices, such as the following rhetorical question: "A wyf! a, Seinte Marie, benedicite! / How myghte a man han any adversitee / That hath a wyf? Certes, I kan nat seye" (4.1337-39). In a subsequent passage, this unidentified and unidentifiable speaker cites four biblical women—Rebecca, Judith, Abigail, and Esther—as examples of good wives (4.1362-74), but Judith is a widow, Abigail insults her husband and then marries King David, and Rebecca and Esther willfully disobey their spouses. Should these lines be construed as evidence of January's ignorance, of a benevolent narrator's citation of biblical authority, or of Chaucer's or the Merchant's pointed irony? As Donald Benson concludes of the marriage encomium, "None of the proposed assignments of the passage—to the Merchant, to January, to Chaucer—resolves all of its seriously problematical aspects. None of the major modes of interpreting the context of the passage—narrative, dramatic, rhetorical—accounts for these aspects in a convincing way."[5] Throughout the marriage encomium, the grounds of interpretation shift unexpectedly, destabilizing readers' ability to gauge the tale's conflicting accounts of marriage and its discontents. The marriage encomium ends when the omniscient narrator's voice can be clearly discerned again: he mentions "this Januarie, of whom I tolde" (4.1393) and thus returns the narrative to surer footing, if only momentarily.

The plot recommences as January seeks counsel from his advisers Placebo and Justinus about his plans to select a young bride, yet this scene further clouds the relationship between teller and tale. Placebo sycophantically echoes January's belief in marriage's pleasures, whereas Justinus cautions him of its pains. Their exchanges participate in the traditions of medieval debate literature, in which allegorical figures argue their cases between a neutral authority who selects the victor at the story's close. January, as the arbiter of his companions' debate, allows Placebo to have the final word. "I seye it is a cursed man . . . / That letteth [hinders] matrimoigne, sikerly [certainly]" (4.1572-73), he avows, with the promarriage voice triumphing despite the antimarital views expressed by the Merchant in his prologue. This promarriage perspective is bolstered as the narrative stresses the pleasures of erotic desire, and January clearly states his preference for a young woman because he would likely "han no plesaunce" (4.1434) in an "oold wyf" (4.1432) and thus would "lede my lyf in avoutrye [adultery] / And go streight to the devel whan I dye" (4.1435-36). Noting January's desire for a young and beautiful wife, the narrator assesses May's attractiveness, channeling for the reader his eroticized gaze reveling in her beauty:

> Mayus, that sit with so benyngne a chiere [face],
> Hire to biholde it semed fayerye [an enchantment].
> . . . .
> I may yow nat devyse al hir beautee.

But thus muche of hire beautee telle I may,
That she was lyk the brighte morwe of May,
Fulfild of alle beautee and plesaunce.
This Januarie is ravysshed in a traunce
At every tyme he looked on hir face. (4.1742-43, 46-51)

Readers are encouraged to envision May's erotic attractiveness in these lines, yet it is also a curiously distracted passage that quickly redirects readers' attention from May to January gazing at May. As Jacob McDonie points out, "The Merchant skips the details of her beauty to focus once again on January's erotic desires," which constructs May as the object of January's desire while also deflecting attention away from her.[6] Yet again the narrator's focalizing perspective is bifurcated. Readers are positioned to enjoy May's beauty and the comedy of January's amatory appetite, but the concluding lines compel them to watch January rather than May, and thus the visual pleasure of the scene is corrupted.

Further along these lines, if the unhappily married Merchant is assumed to be the character telling this tale, it appears inconsistent that he would present January satirically and May sympathetically, yet readers are explicitly encouraged to laugh at January on numerous occasions. As the narrator reports, Venus ridicules January's unrestrained desires: "And Venus laugheth upon every wight, / For Januarie was bicome hir knyght" (4.1723-24). In a similar moment, the narrator's account of January and May's wedding night—and more specifically, the graphic depiction of their marriage's consummation—clearly elicits sympathy for the disenchanted bride. According to John Finlayson, this scene shifts the tale's generic debts, thus again revealing a fractured perspective: "The narrative changes its mode from verbal and intellectual satiric irony to the comedy of action," with this latter perspective characterized by "sexual directness or prurience and intrigue which is the stuff of fabliau."[7] Building the comic excess of fabliau, the narrator emphasizes January's advanced years by hinting at his impotence and revealing his plans to sustain his erection, mentioning that he imbibes various wines in order "t'encreessen his corage" (4.1808) and citing Constantinus Africanus's *De coitu* for the recipes of these performance enhancers (4.1811-12). As "the slakke skyn aboute his nekke shaketh" (4.1849), January promises May a long, arduous night of lovemaking (4.1828-41) and cautions her that his erotic attentions may prove tiring, if not fatal ("Al my corage, it is so sharp and keene! / I am agast ye shul it nat susteene" [4.1759-60]).

Her reaction captures her disgust: "Whan she hym saugh up sittynge in his sherte, / In his nyght-cappe, and with his nekke lene; / She preyseth nat his pleyyng worth a bene" (4.1852-54). As mentioned previously, January previously extolled marriage with similar terms to her dismissal of it—"'Noon oother lyf . . . is worth a bene'" (4.1263)—again widening the chasm between the tale's sympathies for May and the Merchant's unhappy marriage to his shrewish wife.

Surprisingly, the narrator who so graphically describes the consummation of January and May's marriage assumes an unexpected air of modesty as the tale continues. Reporting another instance when May must fulfill her conjugal obligations, he candidly discloses but then discreetly cloaks the scene's sexual activity:

> Adoun by olde Januarie she lay,
> That sleep til that the coughe hath hym awaked.
> Anon he preyde hire strepen hire al naked;
> He wolde of hire, he seyde, han som plesance;
> He seyde hir clothes dide hym encombraunce,
> And she obeyeth, be hire lief or looth.
> But lest that precious folk be with me wrooth,
> How that he wroghte, I dar not to yow telle,
> Or wheither hire thoughte it paradys or helle. (4.1956-64)

This passage is rife with ironies and contradictions that undercut the narrator's voice. The scene mirrors that of their wedding night, with May again in bed with ancient January, whose elderly body is now suggested by his hacking cough instead of his neck's slack skin. Immediately aroused, he demands that she undress, and so the audience must envision May in the nude, and, more so, they must envision the couple copulating, for from what other purpose might her nightclothes "encumber" January? The narrator then imagines his listeners as comprised of "precious folk" who could not bear to hear these erotic escapades recounted in detail, yet why would he now see them as too "precious" to hear for a second time events virtually identical to those previously described? He then refuses to divulge whether May viewed their sexual activity as "paradys or helle," but in the previous scene, he stated that "She preyseth nat his pleyyng worth a bene." It is unlikely that May has reconsidered her views of ardent January, and so the narrator's shift in his storytelling perspective undercuts the consistency of his viewpoint. As this scene concludes, May decides to take Damian as her lover: "Certeyn . . . whom that this thyng displese / I rekke noght, for heere I hym assure / To love hym best of any creature" (4.1982-84). Christine Rose espies in this passage "a slippage [that] signals a disjunction of the narrative voice in the tale, which provides us a space where we glimpse the narrator retooling the character of May, transforming her from silent raped young girl to shrewish adulterous wife."[8] Of course, characters evolve as a story progresses, yet the slippage that Rose perceives arises from the fact that the Merchant's antagonistic stance toward wives should ostensibly preclude her development into a character capable of defending her extramarital erotic desires.

Although the narrator alters his stance on January and May's sexual activities, announcing his hesitance to paint too vivid a picture, he repeatedly returns to this topic. After Fortune blinds January, his jealousy increases such that he keeps his "hond on [May] alway" (4.2091) and hungrily pursues intercourse with her again. "Januarie hath caught so greet a wil, / Thurgh eggyng of his wyf, hym for to pleye / In his gardyn" (4.2134-36), the narrator reports, while also repeating this *senex amans*'s suggestive words: "Com forth now, with thyne eyen columbyn [demure, dovelike]! / How fairer been thy brestes than is wyn [wine]" (4.2141-42). As J. A. Burrow and other critics attest, January's words allude to imagery in the Song of Songs, and he then repeats his demand for intercourse: "Com forth, and lat us taken oure disport" (4.2147).[9] The narrator ends this section of the tale with an apologetic note of moral disapproval— "Swich olde lewed wordes used he" (4.2149)—which again results in a discordant voice. If we envision his distaste as deriving from the combination of fabliau humor and biblical allusions evident in January's words, it is noteworthy that Chaucer applies similar humor to achieve a more unified effect in the *Miller's Tale*. When Absolon woos Alison, he refers to her as a "hony-comb," a "faire bryd," and "my sweete cynamome" (1.3698-99), employing a lexicon likewise inspired by the Song of Songs. The narrator of the *Miller's Tale* does not moralize over Absolon's words, and so it is apparent that Chaucer envisioned these narrators as speaking in different voices to enhance the themes of the respective tales.

As the *Merchant's Tale* approaches its comic climax, with May escaping January's grip purportedly to pick a pear from a tree but actually to fornicate with Damian, the narrator apologizes to the women in his audience for the crudity of his subject matter: "Ladyes, I prey yow that ye be nat wrooth; / I kan not glose [euphemize], I am a rude man— / And sodeynly anon this Damyan / Gan pullen up the smok, and in he throng [thrust]"

(4.2350-53). It is, of course, a ridiculous enterprise to hector a fictional construction, but surely this character should realize that, if one is going to apologize for a fabliau, one should not tell a fabliau in the first place. Such an insincere apology would appear congruent with the aims of an ironic narrator, but a few lines later Chaucer again modulates this narrator's voice to conceal the sexual activity that he so recently revealed. Pluto restores January's sight, and the old man sees that "Damyan his wyf had dressed / In swich manere it may nat been expressed, / But if I wolde speke uncurteisly" (4.2361-63). The phrase "in he throng" clearly indicated the sexual activity the narrator now modestly avoids, claiming his desire not to speak "uncurteisly." In a keen reading of these conflicting voices, Karla Taylor sees the narrator as "pseudo-reticent" in his attempts to "appeal to our polite sensibilities [and] suggest that 'curteisie' is only the phony covering for a most 'uncurteis' mind."[10] Such a reading bears great merit, as does Emerson Brown's assessment of the tale's conflicting voices: "The Merchant['s contempt] for Januarie almost leads him to sympathize with May. Contempt for May almost leads him to sympathize with Januarie. His contempt rather easily triumphs over his sympathy, but these tensions break the calm, ironic restraint he would like to impose on his feelings and distort the tale he tells."[11] Whether with a pseudo-reticent narrator or with a multiply conflicted Merchant lashing out at his characters and himself or with some other construction of a polyvocal narrating perspective, the *Merchant's Tale* resists any effort to pin down its dominant voice and thus its dominant comic ethos. The narrator's steady stream of apologies and the divergent viewpoints expressed on similar issues undermine the tale's ability to create an organic whole.

Finally, as much as the narrative voice of the *Merchant's Tale* frequently shifts in confusing ways, January's adviser Justinus similarly breaks its frame. When Justinus advises January not to marry, he refers to the Wife of Bath in a confusing passage where text and metatext collide: "The Wyf of Bathe, if ye han understonde, / Of mariage, which we have on hond, / Declared hath ful wel in litel space" (4.1685-87). As the *Wife of Bath's Prologue* is the longest prologue of the *Canterbury Tales*, and is also far longer than many of the tales, Justinus's irony is apparent, yet his motivation in this jest becomes confused in the layers of text and metatext. Chaucer has not depicted any friction between the Merchant and the Wife of Bath, and so the jibe does not contribute much to the overarching view of the fractious pilgrims, nor does it confront the puzzling issue of why a fictional character in one text would know of a fictional character in another.

In its debts to the debate tradition, the *Merchant's Tale* features a series of sharp exchanges, notably those between Placebo and Justinus over the desirability of marriage, between Pluto and Proserpina over their respective support for cuckolded husbands and cuckolding wives, and between May and January over the events that transpired in the pear tree. Within this tale of hearty fabliau humor and pointed debate, the voices of these six characters remain distinct, with each demarcated by clear objectives and a consistent tone.[12] The tale's narrator, in contrast, speaks in the same yet different voices, both sincerely and ironically, both reveling in and apologizing for the erotic humor at the heart of a fabliau, both reflective of the Merchant and his distaste for marriage and distanced from him. Without a clear understanding of why the Merchant, a man who promises not to speak of the woes of marriage, would do so and then apologize for the sexual comedy of a *senex amans* and his unfaithful wife, Chaucer's *Merchant's Tale* spins out tantalizing threads of tale-telling and interpretation that fail to unite into a seamless narrative tapestry. The triumphs of the *Merchant's Tale* notwithstanding, such slips might indeed be something worth regretting, if only we could pinpoint which character should offer the apology.

CHAPTER 11

The Nurse of Digestion and Camp Pleasures of the *Squire's Tale*

"Ista fabula est valde absurda" (This story is exceedingly absurd), declared Jean of Angoulême, a fifteenth-century reader of Chaucer.[1] With due respect to Jean of Angoulême, to accuse the *Squire's Tale* of absurdity, and more so, to accuse it of lacking eloquence, structure, and sense, is to state the purposefully and painfully obvious. Chaucer's Squire, imagined as a "lovyere and a lusty bachelor" in the *General Prologue* (1.80), one who "koude songes make and wel endite, / Juste [joust] and eek daunce, and weel purtreye [draw] and write" (1.95-96), represents a devolution of the masculine military ideal represented by his father, the Knight. The father tells an adventurous tale of romance and epic; in contrast, the Squire can only begin, but not finish, an unwieldly romance that threatens to drag on for lines and lines of verse and for hours and hours of the pilgrimage until the Franklin politely intercedes. "As to my doom [judgment], ther is noon that is heere / Of eloquence that shal be thy peere" (5.677-78), he interjects, with words kindly offered but blatantly untrue. In light of the Franklin's interruption that cuts short a story seemingly without end, it is evident that Chaucer offers his *Squire's Tale* as an exercise in the failures of literary art and that he intends its very badness as its raison d'être. Given these conditions, the *Squire's Tale* approximates a medieval vision of camp, an artistic perspective on the creation and consumption of cultural artifacts that transforms their jaw-dropping flaws into their beloved virtues. In the *Squire's Tale*, Chaucer pens a masterpiece of bad art, one whose delights can be best enjoyed by reveling in, rather than lamenting, the Squire's many rhetorical failures.[2]

Writing in the 1960s, Susan Sontag established herself as the foundational authority on camp and its pleasures, raising it from an underground, queer art form to a widely acknowledged cultural phenomenon. As she hypothesizes, "Camp is a vision of the world in terms of style—but a particular kind of style. It is the love of the exaggerated, the 'off,' of things-being-what-they-are-not."[3] With his exaggerated romance, the Squire plays the Canterbury game believing himself to be a worthy contender for Harry Bailly's prize, but as the story unfolds, what appears to be a romance devolves into virtually a parody of the form. Sontag further speculates, "Camp is art that proposes itself seriously, but cannot be taken altogether seriously because it is 'too much.'"[4] Certainly, readers are initially encouraged to take the Squire and his tale seriously, for Chaucer includes nothing in its brief prologue to indicate the travesty that will soon unfold, and the portrait in the *General Prologue* suggests more his proficiency with festive pastimes than his startling deficiencies. Among her numerous theses concerning camp and its consumption, Sontag defines it with succinct precision: "Camp sees everything in quotation marks. It's not a lamp, but a 'lamp'; not a woman, but a 'woman.'"[5] With the *Squire's Tale* Chaucer gives readers not a romance but a "romance," one that adheres to the standard story lines and tropes of the genre but, through its inherent excess, renders them both tediously exhausting yet richly humorous—in essence, so bad that it's good.

Before beginning his tale, the Squire apologizes for his rhetorical shortcomings, in a pointed sign of the debacle to come. "Have me excused if I speke amys; / My wyl is good, and lo, my tale is this" (5.7-8), he states, with his words establishing his ethos as a speaker who modestly refrains from trumpeting his skills. He apologizes again after beginning his tale, finding himself tongue-tied at the prospect of describing his heroine:

> But for to tell yow al [of Canacee's] beautee,
> It lyth nat in my tonge, n'yn my konnyng;
> I dar not undertake so heigh a thyng.
> Myn Englissh eek is insufficient.
> It moste been a rethor excellent
> That koude his colours longynge for that art,
> If he sholde hire discryven every part.
> I am noon swich, I moot speke as I kan. (5.34-41)

Incapable of capturing his protagonist's beauty, the Squire flounders in this dilatory passage, neither advancing his narrative nor contributing to its thematic development. His words, like those of his prologue, might initially appear a flourish of oratorical modesty, a tactic that numerous rhetoricians of the classical and medieval eras endorsed. For instance, Cicero advised rhetoricians to avoid self-serving speeches, lest they alienate their audiences: "We shall win good-will from our own person if we refer to our own acts and services without arrogance."[6] Yet the modesty trope suffers from internal contradictions, and in contrast to Cicero's words, the author of *Rhetorica ad Herennium* notes its inherent paradox: "For if modesty consists in saying nothing or writing nothing, why do they write or speak at all? But if they do write something of their own, why does modesty keep them from composing, themselves, everything they write?"[7] Truly modest people might not speak at all, this author posits, while recognizing the implausibility of expecting modest people not to speak simply owing to their modesty. In light of these rhetorical traditions, whereas one might first view the Squire's words as an attempt to proclaim his virtue as a speaker by foregrounding his modesty, as his tale unfolds they appear more like an unheeded warning.

Despite his rhetorical lapses, the Squire successfully deploys a key trope of chivalric romance when commencing his tale. A mysterious knight on a brass steed interrupts Cambyuskan's feast, and similar exciting moments spark the narrative action of a range of medieval romances, including Chrétien de Troyes's *Lancelot* and the anonymously penned *Sir Gawain and the Green Knight*. As much as the Squire succeeds in this moment of his story, his lack of rhetorical skills becomes further evident when he admits that he cannot properly capture the eloquent dialogue of the genre. He first states that this mysterious knight equals the legendary Gawain "as wel in speche as in contenaunce" (5.94), yet he does not yet allow his character to speak, and so readers cannot judge the character's— and thus the tale-teller's—eloquence. The Squire again relies on the modesty trope to apologize for his rhetorical deficiencies: "Al be that I kan nat sowne his stile [style], / Ne kan nat clymben over so heigh a style [stile, fence], / Yet seye I this, as to commune entente: / Thus muche amounteth al that evere he mente" (5.105-8). The Squire must, in effect, translate the words of his character who speaks more eloquently than he but who cannot speak in any voice other than the one that the Squire grants him. Within this mishmash, the Squire rhymes "stile" with "style," in a hint of further poetic infelicities forthcoming.

With a rhetorical tic that repeatedly frustrates his tale's progress, the Squire interrupts himself to alert his auditors of the many plot points that he will not share with them. He will not speak of the riches of Cambyuskan's feast (5.63-66), nor of the birds, swans, and herons that are enjoyed as delicacies in his land (5.67-74). He refuses to elaborate on the celebrations of Cambyuskan's court, dismissing any attempt to do so with a rhetorical question: "Who koude telle yow the forme of daunces / So unkouthe, and swiche fresshe contenaunces, / Swich subtil lookyng and dissymulynges / For drede of jalouse mennes aperceyvynges?" (5.283-86). One might reasonably imagine a Canterbury pilgrim interrupting to point out that the answer to this question is the Squire himself, but the Squire then supplies his own answer: "No man but Launcelot, and he is deed" (5.287). Lancelot, if he lived, could portray the festivities of Cambyuskan's court, but the Squire, who has allotted himself the challenge of telling this tale, admits he cannot. Soon after, the Squire asks, "What nedeth yow rehercen hire array [clothing, finery]?" (5.298) and then dismisses the relevance of this material: "Ech man woot [knows] wel that a kynges feeste / Hath plentee to the meeste and to the leeste, / And deyntees mo than been in my knowyng" (5.299-302). This contradiction in the Squire's words undercuts any vision of him as an accomplished storyteller, for he declares that everyone knows the bounteous foodstuffs available at a king's feast, except himself, for they are beyond his "knowyng." In a grating aside, the Squire notes that a tale-teller should not digress in the middle of a story owing to the "fulsomnesse of his prolixitee" (5.405); he then concludes, "And by the same resoun, thynketh me, / I sholde to the knotte condescende, / And maken of hir walkyng soone an ende" (5.406-8). The better way to move the story forward, the Squire realizes, is simply to move the story forward, not to dillydally in halting digressions, particularly when the narrative action at hand simply notes the fact that his heroine is walking. Per Sontag's words, the Squire represents not a tale-teller but an ironic, exaggerated, and campy exemplar of a "tale-teller," one whose narrative lapses highlight his failure to speak engagingly, which thus alerts readers to search for comic pleasures other than the literary ones initially expected from this fanciful story.

Romances delight in wonders and marvels that aid or sabotage their questing protagonists, and the Squire acknowledges this tradition while rendering it ridiculous in his tedious account of the magical horse, mirror, ring, and sword that the mysterious knight brings to Cambyuskan's court. Scholars have noted the ways in which these wondrous items deepen the *Squire's Tale*'s investment in the tropes of romance and the rhetorics of narrative. As Michelle Karnes argues, "The *Squire's Tale* . . . link[s] marvels to storytelling, showing how misleading appearances enliven imagination much like literature itself."[8] Offering rich readings of the tale's interest in the marvelous, Karnes limns the ways in which magic enhances the story's themes, yet from a camp perspective, these marvels simply provide another opportunity for the Squire to derail his story. Instead of simply marveling at these marvels, the Squire both excuses his ignorance and explicates their functioning with overly detailed but ultimately meaningless babble. Of the magic sword, the Squire says: "They speken of sondry hardyng of metal, / And speke of medicynes therwithal, / And how and whanne it sholde yharded be, / Whiche is unknowe, algates unto me" (5.243-46). Speaking of that which he knows too little about to speak, the Squire once more proves himself incapable of telling his tale, thereby winning his audience's amused pity.

In a similar yet distinct moment, Cambyuskan's courtiers voice their suspicions concerning the brass steed that can magically travel vast distances: "But everemoore hir mooste wonder was / How that it koude gon, and was of bras" (5.199-200). A quick answer is supplied—"It was a fairye, as the peple semed" (5.201)—with the mysterious knight then explicating in a lengthy passage how it works, detailing which pins to turn to cause which effect (5.312-34). Yet again, though, this passage provides evidence of the Squire's striking ineloquence, as the answer to this question was already succinctly supplied—"It was a fairye"—that should obviate any further questions. As an imaginary construct, magic is the quintessential tautology of fantastic literature, in that magical items function simply because they are magical, and any further explanation risks exchanging the supernatural for the tediously pseudoscientific. In a further frustrating moment, the brass steed then disappears—"The hors vanysshed, I noot [do not know] in what manere, / Out of hir sighte"—yet instead of following the disappearing horse into an exciting adventure, the Squire concludes this section of his romance with a terse dismissal: "ye gete namoore of me" (5.342-43). As Shirley Sharon-Zisser explains, the disappearance of this magic steed "leads the reader to expect to next see this horse actually perform and help the plot advance," yet it instead contributes to the tale's "almost total absence of plot."[9] Tellingly, after the Franklin interrupts the Squire and commences his own tale, he too confronts the challenge of explaining magic yet accomplishes this objective much more expeditiously. His heroine, Dorigen, convinces her unwelcome suitor, Aurelius, that she will accept his affections if he succeeds in the impossible task of removing the black rocks that line the coast and that threaten her husband Arveragus's safe return. The Franklin mentions briefly "swiche illusiouns and swiche meschaunces / As hethen folk useden in thilke dayes" (5.1292-93) and then succinctly summarizes the efficacy of this magician's spells:

"But thurgh his magik, for a wyke or tweye, / It semed that alle the rokkes were aweye" (5.1295-96). Authors of medieval romances and of modern fantasy fiction face the inherent challenge of explaining how magic functions in their narratives, but in most instances, a silence that evades the subject offers a more satisfying explanation than a lengthy discourse on its inexplicable mysteries.

In the second part of his tale, the Squire depicts the trials and tribulations of love—another common trope of medieval romance—but in this instance the love affair involves a weepy falcon lamenting to Canacee of her betrayal, and so once again his unwieldy narration derails his narrative into camp. A handsome tercelet, who "semed welle of alle gentillesse," cloaked his true motivations of "treson and falsnesse" (5.505-6) and abandons her for a kite: "And sodeynly he loved this kyte so / That al his love is clene fro me ago" (5.625-26). Throughout this lengthy speech of approximately 150 lines, the Squire accentuates the falcon's suffering in love, imbuing her story with tropes of courtly love and betrayal. In an omen that the Squire's storytelling will soon run amok, Canacee has an enclosure built for her new bird friend that "is peynted grene," in which is "peynted alle thise false fowles, / As ben thise tidyves [small birds], tercelettes, and owles; / Right for despit were peynted hem bisyde, / Pyes [magpies], on hem for to crie and chyde" (5.646-50). It is a bizarre moment in the tale—who, having suffered the pains of amatory betrayal, would want their walls decorated with images of infidelity?—and also another certain sign of the Squire's excess, in that he continually weighs down his primary story line with narrative threads unworthy of further pursuit. The bathos of this miniature bird romance highlights the failures of the Squire's Tale as a whole, in the comic disjunction between ambition and execution that highlights its comic infelicities.

In another campy twist, the Franklin and the other pilgrims rightly fear that the Squire's story could prove nearly interminable, as he outlines a plot that would necessitate hundreds, likely thousands, more lines of poetry to reach completion. With a brass steed that can cross the globe, a mirror that can reflect the future and a lover's duplicity, a ring that allows one to communicate with birds, and a sword of invincible strength that can both hurt and heal, the Squire has introduced so many plot points that any unified resolution appears difficult to foresee. A common principle of narrative proposes that authors should introduce only elements essential for a story's development and resolution and that they should excise anything ultimately inconsequential. If the Squire adhered to this principle, each of these items and characters would by necessity receive due attention as the plot proceeded—or more likely, ambled—to its conclusion. Furthermore, one can virtually hear the breathlessness of his voice as he lists his characters' ensuing adventures:

> First wol I telle yow of Cambyuskan,
> That in his tyme many a citee wan [won, defeated];
> And after wol I speke of Algarsif,
> How that he wan Theodora to his wif,
> For whom ful ofte in greet peril he was,
> Ne hadde he ben holpen by the steede of bras;
> And after wol I speke of Cambalo,
> That faught in lystes with the bretheren two
> For Canacee er that he myghte hire wynne.
> And ther I lefte I wol ayeyn bigynne. (5.661-70)

As with so many matters of literary interpretation, these lines can be read in sharply contrasting ways. They could be enunciated augustly, as the Squire gravely announces the forthcoming episodes of his romance, but it seems more appropriate to this unwieldy tale to read them excitedly, almost frenetically, as if a little boy had piqued the momentary attention of the grown-ups and eagerly seized his moment in the limelight. At the very least, the Squire, sketching out so many directions for his plot, displays little control of his story, and thus better serves as a specimen of camp humor than merely of rhetorical ineptitude.

These lines contain another possible justification for the Franklin's abrupt interruption of the Squire's romance, in that he alludes to Canacee's incestuous relationship with her brother. In classical mythology, Canacee falls in love with her brother and bears their child, who is then executed by their father Aeolus.[10] In the introduction to his tale, the Man of Law speaks of the "wikke ensample of Canacee, / That loved hir owene brother synfully" (2.78-79), and so the pilgrims have already been alerted to the controversial aspects of this legend.[11] John P. McCall proposes that the Squire's allusion to Canacee further indicates his failings as a storyteller— "Perhaps the gentle Squire did not realize what he would have been letting himself in for if he had continued"[12]—and Elizabeth Scala documents how readers have struggled to preserve Chaucer's reputation despite the unseemliness of this reference: "Besides the possibility of incest, the battle for Canacee proposed in the poem's final lines likewise gives cause for moral alarm to critics concerned for Chaucer's 'good name.'"[13] Whether as a sign of the Squire's or of Chaucer's rhetorical failures, the turn to incest in the *Squire's Tale* represents the limits of its narration, as its untimely termination occurs quickly after.

The great authors of medieval romance wax poetic when penning their tales, employing evocative language to describe the beauty of the beloved lady, the bravery of the chivalric knight, and the treachery of the villain. The Squire, however, lacks the ability to elevate the eloquence of his romance through figurative and metaphoric language, and some of the tale's campiest moments appear as sparkling grace notes of humor that interject moments of meta-ridiculousness into an already ridiculous narrative. In an odd and excessively corporeal metaphor, the Squire refers to sleep as the "norice [nurse] of digestioun" (5.347) and then personifies Sleep as approaching Cambyuskan and his courtiers "with a galpyng [gaping] mouth" (5.350), kissing them, and advising them to lie down. In Robert Miller's words, this scene creates "a deliberate comic fracture of the atmosphere of romance."[14] With a particularly apt but visually empty adjective, the Squire describes the mysterious knight's brass horse as "so horsly" (5.194). Lest any of his auditors be simpletons, he defines the length of a day for them: "the space of o day natureel— / This is to seyn, in foure and twenty houres" (5.116-17). Chaucer gives no sense of the pilgrims' reactions before the Franklin ends the Squire's tale, yet surely one should imagine many of them exasperated by this unnecessary explication. Finally, while Chaucer's mastery of rhyme, meter, and poetic form are unrivaled, the Squire's rhymes more undermine than enhance his art. Lindsey Jones observes couplets rhyming in quick succession on such words as "telle / helle," "above / love," "two / wo," "speke / wreke," "drede / dede," "chace / grace," and "est / beest" (5.447-60) and states, "The repetition of these simple rhymes creates the impression of a sing-song pattern which mars much of the tale."[15] On the narrative, thematic, structural, poetic, and metrical levels of his tale, the Squire fails to achieve sustained artistry, instead falling flat in each of these registers and rendering his tale a failure that nonetheless demands the readers' engagement, as we wonder what amusing travesty of style or description will next occur. How might the laughably bad description of a "horsely" horse ever be outdone?

With undaunted enthusiasm the Squire commences the third part of his tale—"Appollo whirleth up his chaar [chariot] so hye / Til that the god Mercurius hous, the slye—" (5.671-72); however, the Franklin abruptly cuts off the story, saving his fellow pilgrims from a meandering tale that threatens to stretch endlessly. Chaucer slips in a final irony at the Squire's expense in the references to Apollo and Mercury, with A. C. Spearing affirming that it is "delightfully appropriate that [the tale] should be terminated by the shooting down in mid-sentence of Apollo, the god of poetic inspiration, on his way into the mansion of Mercury, the god of eloquence."[16] On the narrative level of the Canterbury game, this solution saves the pilgrims from a poor contribution by a poor tale-teller; on a metanarrative level, one in which readers are attuned to the camp humor arising from the excesses of rapturous badness, it is unfortunate that the Franklin ends prematurely a story that would likely have only worsened as it proceeded, and thus paradoxically proved immeasurably more entertaining. Bad storytelling is not always to be lamented but sometimes to be reveled in for its campy fun, in which its very badness elevates it into an oft-overlooked art form. Not a romance but a "romance," the *Squire's Tale* represents Chaucer simultaneously at his very worst and his very best, distilling rich humor from an unbelievably inept, inapt, and inelegant tale. And so, although one need not laugh at the image of a "nurse of digestion" or the other specimens of badness examined in this chapter, the *Squire's Tale* becomes immensely more pleasurable when one revels in the humor of a tale-teller so gloriously awful in his chosen pastime. The poor dear, he really does mean well.

CHAPTER 12

The Stony Lady and Lovely
Contradictions of the *Franklin's Tale*

With apologies for the redundancy, one might simply call Chaucer's *Franklin's Tale* a lovely tale of love. Following the comic cuckoldry of the *Miller's Tale* and the *Merchant's Tale*, the raucous spousal battle of the *Wife of Bath's Prologue*, and the tyrannous husband of the *Clerk's Tale*, the *Franklin's Tale*, in its vision of a companionate and compassionate union, restores optimism about the possibility of a marriage grounded in mutual respect, affection, and fidelity. Notwithstanding these central aspects of its appeal, the *Franklin's Tale* attempts to but ultimately cannot unify competing medieval visions of love and affection—*fin' amor* and courtly love—which culminate in the oddly unsettling figure of the protagonist Dorigen. Both the romantic ideal of *fin' amor* and the imperious beloved of the courtly love tradition, Dorigen's character is bifurcated by these opposed but overlapping traditions, resulting in a figure whose actions belie her own reasoning. With a heroine both emotional and emotionless, both passionate and stony, the *Franklin's Tale* denies readers a stable sense of Dorigen's motivations and desires, thereby questioning the meaning of love that serves as its key theme. Among Chaucer's mischaracterized characters, Dorigen stands out as particularly enigmatic and unknowable owing to his confused depiction of her understanding of love.

Few concepts of medieval life are as confused and confusing as those constellations of amatory discourse referred to as *fin' amor* and courtly love, which coincide and intertwine but can be distinguished by their conceptions of romance, marriage, and adultery. Mark Taylor locates *fin' amor* as "abid[ing] where a man and woman experience mutual erotic passion (one of the 'two desires') which is controlled by the emotion of love guided by right reason or whole thinking (the second desire). In this love relationship the passion fuels the will in the exercise of virtue which expands from the personal into all aspects of secular society."[1] E. Jane Burns, building from the foundational scholarship of Gaston Paris, defines courtly love "as an illicit, furtive, and extraconjugal liaison that placed the [male] lover in the service of and at the mercy of a haughty and capricious lady, a state that inspired courageous feats and refined behavior, and an art governed by highly codified rules of proper conduct."[2] According to these brief definitions that by necessity simplify complex social, amatory, and literary phenomena, *fin' amor* is envisioned as the mutual affection of aristocratic lovers that fosters virtue in all who witness it, whereas courtly love is conceived as an unequal relationship in which the woman, in the role of the imperious beloved, assumes absolute and arbitrary power over her chivalric suitor. As much as one may attempt to demarcate firm boundaries between them, slippage inevitably results, for whether as a social performance or as a literary convention, love rarely influences any two people—or any two characters—uniformly.

The opening lines of the *Franklin's Tale*, which recount Arveragus and Dorigen's journey from courtship to marriage, repeatedly conflate the tropes of *fin' amor* and courtly love, with these divergent views of love tying the narrator in rhetorical knots. He attempts to explain the nature of their relationship but is repeatedly ensnared by love's inherent contradictions. At first, the tale adheres to the tropes of courtly love, with Arveragus described as "a knyght that loved and dide his payne / To serve a lady in his beste wise" (5.730-31); these lines place him in a subservient position to Dorigen, his imperious beloved. More so, her beauty and lineage intimidate him, to the extent that he fears to confess his affections: "That wel unnethes [hardly] dorste this knyght, for drede, / Telle hire his wo, his peyne, and his distresse" (5.736-37). In her role as the imperious beloved, Dorigen finally notices Arveragus, pities him, and agrees to marry him, although she then cedes the authority of this role when she promises that she "wol be youre humble trewe wyf" (5.758). Leah Otis-Cour argues that Dorigen's words reveal her intention to abdicate her role as the imperious beloved: "In pledging to be humble rather than promising to obey, Dorigen is forswearing 'ladying' it over Arveragus as a courtly lady might her lover, or as a social superior might his or her inferior."[3] Notably, the narrator shifts his amatory discourse and endorses their marriage with terms suggestive of the *fin' amor* tradition of mutuality: "For o thyng, sires, saufly dar I seye, / That freendes everych oother moot obeye, / If they wol longe holden compaignye. / Love wol nat been constreyned by maistrye" (5.761-64). The narrator then attempts to meld *fin' amor* and courtly love in his depiction of Arveragus and Dorigen's marriage:

Heere may men seen an humble, wys accord;
Thus hath she take hir servant and hir lord—
Servant in love, and lord in mariage.
Thanne was he bothe in lordshipe and servage.
Servage? Nay, but in lordshipe above,
Sith he hath bothe his lady and his love. (5.791-96)

The amatory contradictions accumulate: Dorigen has accepted Arveragus as her servant in love and lord in marriage, and the narrator confirms Arveragus's oxymoronic status of lordship and servanthood. In a dramatic reversal, the narrator then rejects the image of Arveragus as Dorigen's servant and emphasizes his position "in lordshipe above" because he has "bothe his lady and his love." As Wan-Chuan Kao posits, "The Franklin glosses Dorigen and Arveragus's marriage agreement as a utopic fusion of courtly love and marriage," pointing out as well that such an arrangement "is more complicated than it appears."[4] Throughout the *Franklin's Tale*, issues of mutuality versus mastery percolate, with Arveragus and Dorigen's mostly mutual and companionate marriage threatened by the potential that one might seek mastery over the other, whether by Dorigen returning to the role of the imperious beloved or by Arveragus asserting patriarchal authority over his wife.

As much as the narrator seeks to liberate Arveragus and Dorigen from the traditions of courtly love after they marry, the shadow of the imperious beloved haunts aspects of her character and at times overrides her more central role as his loving wife, casting her as an unfathomable figure whose actions do not align with her purported objectives. Within the traditions of chivalric romance, the imperious beloved demands her lover follow her every whim, no matter how unreasonable or painful. Illustrated by Guinevere in Chrétien de Troyes's *Lancelot*, the imperious beloved is a haughty and potentially cruel figure, such as when Guinevere compels Lancelot to "do his worst" in chivalric tournaments, and thus to suffer mightily for his perceived transgressions. In Jacques Lacan's formulation, the Lady represents the object of the knightly lover's desire, although her desirability is simply presumed rather than delineated: "The Lady is never characterized for any of her real, concrete virtues, for her wisdom, her prudence, or even her competence. . . . On the contrary, she is as arbitrary as possible in the tests she imposes on her servant."[5] Building on Lacan's work, Slavoj Žižek similarly outlines the ways in which the Lady functions to delay, rather than to facilitate, the consummation of desire: "What the paradox of the Lady in courtly love ultimately amounts to is thus the paradox of *detour*: our 'official' desire is that we want to sleep with the Lady; whereas in truth, there is nothing we fear more than a Lady who might generously yield to this wish of ours—what we truly expect and want from the Lady is simply yet another new ordeal, yet one more postponement."[6] In line with Lacan's observations, Arveragus pursues Dorigen not for her "real, concrete virtues" but simply for her status as a beautiful and highborn women (6.734-35). In line with Žižek's observations, Dorigen, despite her marriage to Arveragus early in the tale, introduces obstacles that frustrate the consummation of his desire for mutuality in marriage. In sum, Dorigen is caught between two amatory discourses, and the traces of the courtly love tradition of the imperious beloved result in the odd unknowability and stoniness of her character, the disconcerting moments in the story when her actions appear inexplicable.

After little more than a year of enjoying the bliss of marriage, Arveragus departs for England to seek adventure and prestige in accord with his knightly occupation, and Dorigen sinks into a spiral of despair, mourning his absence so excessively that her friends worry. The imperious beloved of the courtly love tradition is recognized for her lack of humanity, and the *Franklin's Tale* aptly captures this aspect of Dorigen's character by likening her to rocks and stones. In an extended metaphor, the narrator compares the lengthy process of engraving a stone to Dorigen's friends' attempts to comfort her:

> By proces, as ye knowen everichoon,
> Men may so longe graven [engrave] in a stoon
> Til some figure therinne emprented be.
> So longe han they conforted hire til she
> Recyved hath, by hope and by resoun,
> The emprentyng of hire consolacioun,
> Thurgh which hire grete sorwe gan aswage [assuage, lessen].
>   (5.829-35)

More than simply a metaphor for Dorigen's torpor, stones represent the impenetrability of the imperious beloved and thus of women's mostly static role in courtly romance. Andrea Rossi-Reder contrasts the activity of the tale's male characters with Dorigen's more stationary role, noting the stony qualities she embodies: "Masculine agency in Chaucer's *Franklin's Tale* involves physical mobility while female agency entails intel-

lectual movement, which serves as a remedy for limited physical move-
ment and rock-like fixity."[7] This metaphor for Dorigen's character is then
extended from abstraction to reality because stones also represent the
physical barrier separating her from Arveragus: the "grisly rokkes blake
[black]" that line the Brittany coastline (5.859), upon which Dorigen fears
that Arveragus's ship will founder when he returns home. This stonelike
woman prays for these stones to disappear: "But wolde God that alle thise
rokkes blake / Were sonken into helle for his sake! / Thise rokkes sleen
[slay] myn herte for the feere" (5.891-93). Within psychoanalytic terms,
Dorigen appears to be engaging in projection, discerning in these rocks
an intentionality that she overlooks in herself. As Emily Houlik-Ritchey
argues of this paradox, "Dorigen's . . . relationship with rock emerges in
the dual dynamic that she does not like them, and yet she is like them."[8]

Unhappily awaiting Arveragus's return, Dorigen is wooed by an
unwanted suitor, Aurelius, and as she pines for Arveragus, so does Aure-
lius pine for her for over two years until finally declaring his love. Dorigen
is shocked by any imputation of adulterous desire: "Ne shal I nevere been
untrewe wyf / In word ne werk, as fer as I have wit" (5.984-85). First
rejecting the adulterous potential of courtly love for the mutuality of *fin'
amor*, Dorigen then, in a moment of vulnerability, again assumes the role
of the imperious beloved and offers Aurelius the slightest hope to win her
favor in a variation of Guinevere's "Do your worst" command to Lancelot.
She orders him to "remoeve alle the rokkes, stoon by stoon" that line the
coast (5.993) and then repeats herself: "I seye, whan ye had maad the coost
so clene / Of rokkes that ther nys no stoon ysene, / Thanne wol I love yow
best of any man" (5.995-97). Dorigen's words evoke the folkloric tradi-
tion of the rash promise, in which characters speak too hastily and thus
commit themselves to future actions that they would never reasonably
undertake. This literary tradition is illustrated in the Hebrew and Chris-
tian scriptures in Jephthah's vow to slay whoever first exits his home if the
Lord grants him a military victory, as recounted in the book of Judges and
alluded to in Chaucer's *Physician's Tale*. It also commonly appears in folk
and fairy tales, such as when the miller's daughter promises to give her
firstborn child to Rumpelstiltskin if he teaches her to spin straw into gold.
Within the amatory and literary traditions of the *Franklin's Tale*, Dorigen's
words adhere to the protocols both of the rash promise and of the imperi-
ous beloved, establishing a test for her lover that will challenge his ability
to suffer on her behalf while also binding her to a promise that she should
never make as a devoted wife. Moreover, as Bonnie Wheeler acknowledges,

the imperious beloved of courtly romance often faces an ultimate limit to her authority, stating that the "woman who is chosen as a beloved is allowed myriad delaying techniques, but postponement is as close as she can come to a final *no*."[9] In returning to the character position of the imperious beloved, this stony woman has spoken and now must live with the consequences of her words that trap her in an overdetermined social role.

Initially paralyzed by the impossible quest that Dorigen has set for him, Aurelius seeks the assistance of a magician and pays him a thousand pounds to remove the black rocks. With this miraculous feat achieved, he returns to Dorigen and employs the language of courtly love to remind her both of his subservience and of her promise, addressing her as the imperious beloved of romance:

> "My righte lady," quod this woful man,
> "Whom I moost drede and love as I best kan,
> And lothest were of al this worlde displese,
> Nere it that I for yow have swich disese
> That I moste dyen heere at youre foot anon,
> Noght wolde I telle how me is wo bigon." (4.1311-16)

Assuming the role of the courtly lover, Aurelius asserts his love for Dorigen, beseeches her to pity him, and confesses his fear of dying at her feet. Yet by adhering to the terms of Dorigen's rash promise, Aurelius wields unexpected power in this encounter, and when he tells her that he has removed the rocks, Dorigen is virtually petrified: "He taketh his leve [departure], and she astoned stood; / On al hir face nas a drope of blood" (5.1339-40). With the pun on "astoned" and her bloodless face, Dorigen is again conceived as nearly inhuman, as a stonelike monument of her love for Arveragus. In this ironic image, the imperious beloved of the courtly love tradition is shocked back into the emotionless realm from which her marriage to Arveragus allowed her respite. In effect, Dorigen's narrative arc can be traced as a series of episodes in which she is portrayed as stony, or as "astoned," rather than as fully human. Men continually view her as the imperious beloved of courtly love rather than allowing her to inhabit the mutuality of *fin' amor*.

As much as the narrator stresses Dorigen's stony nature, he concurrently depicts her as emotionally distraught to the point of suicide, thus further complicating her character and motivations. First, when Dorigen mourns Arveragus's departure, her friends worry, if not precisely that she will commit suicide, that her actions will bring about her premature death: "They prechen hire, they telle hire nyght and day / That causelees she sleeth hirself, allas!" (5.824-25). They finally convince her "awey to dryve hire derke fantasye" (5.844), with this "derke fantasye" never precisely defined but provocatively suggestive of suicide. The possibility of suicide returns when Dorigen contemplates death as an escape from her rash promise to Aurelius: "'Allas,' quod she, 'on thee, Fortune, I pleyne, / That unwar [unaware] wrapped hast me in thy cheyne, / Fro which t'escape woot I no socour, / Save oonly deeth or elles dishonour'" (5.1355-58). Dorigen cites numerous examples of virtuous women who killed themselves rather than facing disgrace and decides that she should follow their example: "I wol conclude that it is bet for me / To sleen myself than been defouled thus. / I wol be trewe unto Arveragus, / Or rather sleen myself in som manere" (5.1422-25). Confronting herself with the many women of classical legend who chose death over dishonor, Dorigen appears to be steeling herself to act, but, stonelike, she does not: "Thus pleyned Dorigen a day or tweye, / Purposynge evere that she wolde deye" (5.1457-58). As Susan Crane explains of this rejection of suicide exempla, Dorigen "begins to become [a] 'resisting' reader as the speech's rote quality and disproportionate length imply her refusal of the clerical version of her identity and duty. She resists only passively, by reciting the models long enough to elude their instruction to kill herself, but the double process of assent and postponement makes a small place for self-assertion under the sign of acquiescence."[10] We can further see the legacy of the courtly lady in Dorigen's ruminations over suicide, for chivalric romances frequently feature knights contemplating suicide at the prospect of losing their lady's love. In Chrétien de Troyes's *Lancelot*, Lancelot prepares to kill himself after hearing a rumor of Guinevere's death, following the example she set after hearing a similar rumor concerning him: "She is so beside herself that she repeatedly grasps her throat with the desire to kill herself."[11] Romances often treat suicide as a viable option for the grieving knight who fears himself expelled from his lady's good graces, and in the *Franklin's Tale*, the courtly lady contemplates suicide yet remains such an inviolate character that she cannot act upon herself.

As Dorigen delays her suicide, Arveragus returns home—"But nathelees, upon the thridde nyght, / Hoom cam Arveragus, this worthy knyght" (5.1459-60)—which thus shifts her relationships to courtly love and *fin' amor* yet again. Dorigen confesses her obligation to Aurelius, which Arveragus initially accepts with surprising grace: "This housbonde, with glad chiere, in freendly wyse / Answerde and seyde as I shal yow devyse: / 'Is ther oght elles, Dorigen, but this?'" (5.1467-69). Continuing the suicide theme of Dorigen's lament, Arveragus declares his willingness to die for her, thereby modeling himself after the sacrificial lover of courtly romance: "I hadde wel levere ystiked [stabbed] for to be / For verray love which that I to yow have, / But if ye sholde youre trouthe kepe and save" (5.1476-78). With these moving words that celebrate the mutuality of his love for Dorigen, Arveragus ironically alludes to suicide to signal his devotion, yet in a closing contradiction in the tale's depiction of love, Arveragus asserts his *maistrye* over their marriage. He tells her that she must keep her promise to Aurelius—"Ye shul youre trouthe holden, by my fay!" (5.1474)—and threatens her with murder: "I yow forbede, up peyne of deeth, / That nevere, whil thee lasteth lyf ne breeth, / To no wight telle thou of this aventure" (5.1481-83). With the amatory discourse shifting from *fin' amor* to patriarchal marriage, in which the husband's reputation stands as more significant than his wife's life, the *Franklin's Tale* renders not only Dorigen but Arveragus strangely unknowable characters, whose motivations shift according to the model of marriage currently in effect during a given scene.

The tale reaches its climax as Dorigen encounters Aurelius on the street and informs him that she will maintain her pledge to him: "Unto the gardyn, as myn housbonde bad [commanded], / My trouthe for to holde—allas, allas!" (5.1512-13). Surprisingly, he releases her from the obligation. Dorigen and Arveragus's marriage, which has teetered between *fin' amor* and courtly love, now appears grounded on mutuality: "Arveragus and Dorigen his wyf / In sovereyn blisse leden forth hir lyf. / Nevere eft ne was ther angre hem bitwene" (5.1551-53). Aurelius returns to the magician to repay his debt, but upon learning of his generosity to Dorigen, the magician releases him from this obligation. In this conclusion, as Mary Bowman notes, Arveragus and Aurelius are confronted with the necessity of sacrifice: "Arveragus and Aurelius are both able to give up their claims to Dorigen willingly, if not happily, in exchange for the moral satisfaction of fulfilling certain ideals."[12] In a sense, loving Dorigen entails embracing sacrifice: Arveragus suffered to win her love at the story's opening, with Aurelius's suffering soon following. Wooing the courtly lady, however, is a challenge akin to "emprentyng" stone, as Alastair Bennett explains of the ways in which Dorigen and Aurelius have each persistently pursued their desires: "While Dorigen . . . discover[s] the rewards and satisfactions of complaint even as she recognizes the difficulty of 'emprentyng' stone, Aurelius is never able to abandon the fantasy of 'emprentyng' his desires on Dorigen, and goes to elaborate lengths to sustain it, against the evidence of his own experience."[13] As a stonelike figure, Dorigen resists Aurelius's efforts to mold her to his desires, yet her momentary acquiescence and her suicidal musings complementarily posit the implausibility, if not impossibility, of a woman remaining in the status of the imperious beloved, despite the desire of her lover to position her as such.

As the narrator brings his tale to a close, he asks his auditors to contemplate its meaning with a *demande d'amour*: "Lordynges, this question, thanne, wol I aske now, / Which was the mooste fre, as thynketh yow?" (4.1621-22). On the surface, all characters in the story stand as potential candidates for the designation as "mooste fre," although some critics debar Dorigen from contention owing to her stony passivity. Arveragus, Aurelius, and the magician each forgive a debt or a promise—respectively, Dorigen's wedding vow of fidelity, her rash promise, and Aurelius's financial obligation—whereas Dorigen's actions are forgiven but she herself does not forgive another character. Janemarie Luecke argues that the tale "cannot include Dorigen" among the possible candidates "in the closing *demande d'amour* . . . since she is not an active agent."[14] Throughout much of the *Franklin's Tale*, Dorigen's behavior casts her as stony and stonelike, which blurs her motivations and desires, as well as readers' interpretations of her. In this lovely tale of love, Chaucer has created a world where mutual affection stands as the highest objective and most ennobling force, yet the untamed contradictions of *fin' amor and courtly love* render Dorigen a strangely uncanny, oddly unknowable character: a lovable rock, if one can love a rock at all.

CHAPTER 13

The Executed Governess and Errant Themes of the *Physician's Tale*

A child's death before her father's dishonor: in the moral economy of Chaucer's *Physician's Tale*, Virginius prefers executing his daughter Virginia to maintain her perpetual virginity rather than embracing her as living and deflowered. On one level this paradigm is hardly noteworthy: throughout the classical and medieval eras many narratives celebrate virgins and virtuous women who esteem chastity as a cultural ideal worth dying for. The *Physician's Tale* endorses this viewpoint while concurrently positing a less dire end for Virginia, thereby undercutting the coherency of its themes. In his digression on governesses and in his off-key allusion to the biblical story of Jephthah's daughter, the Physician identifies alternate and resistant paths for his heroine, only then to override these options for the standard ending of a virtuous woman murdered to preserve her flawless character—and more so, to preserve the patriarchal stature of her father. With this thematic binary of virtue and vice undermined but then reinstated, the narrator's concluding moral to forsake sin loses any sort of interpretive ballast, for Virginia remains blameless throughout the tale yet is executed nonetheless. Without any sort of coherent theme, the *Physician's Tale* has long been denigrated as one of Chaucer's worst tales.

The portrait of the Physician in the *General Prologue* paints the picture of a mercenary, not a merciful, practitioner of the healing arts, and so the thematic inconsistencies of his tale can readily be attributed to his shallow understanding of morality. Chaucer introduces him with typical hyperbole—"In al this world ne was ther noon [no one] hym lik" (1.412)— and soon reiterates such praise: "He was a verray, parfit praktisour" (1.422). Following this paean to the Physician's medical skills, Chaucer paints the character's more sordid side, divulging his chicanery and graft with the local apothecaries (1.425-28). After documenting this man's extensive medical education, Chaucer discloses the shallowness of his moral edu-

cation: "His studie was but litel on the Bible" (1.438). As Samantha Katz
Seal observes, this short line encapsulates Chaucer's ironic critique of the
Physician: "What better way to emphasize the gratuitous folly of a life
spent learning secular (often pagan) knowledge than to expand at length
upon the vastness of erudite ambitions before puncturing the very proj-
ect with a reminder of its limitations? Chaucer's Physician is a man who
reads with skill, but without understanding."[1] From this perspective, an
inaptly thematized tale would be consistent with the Physician's unethical
character, and so the slips of the *Physician's Tale* can be attributed to him
rather than to Chaucer. Such a viewpoint, while bearing merit, opens up
an interpretive paradox: if the line "His studie was but litel on the Bible"
reflects the Physician's moral failures, then any failure in his tale becomes
subsumed by this character flaw. His unsavory character and stunted bib-
lical education predict an ethically suspect and underdeveloped tale, and
so Chaucer, no matter the infelicities of his story, remains above the fray.

The Physician commences his tale by introducing the worthy knight
Virginius and his daughter Virginia and then quickly sketches her immac-
ulate character. First praising her beauty, the narrator segues into a paean
to women's chastity:

And if that excellent was hire beautee,
A thousand foold moore vertuous was she.
In hire ne lakked no condicioun
That is to preyse, as by discrecioun.
As wel in goost [spirit] as body chast was she,
For which she floured in virginitee
With alle humylitee and abstinence. (6.39-45)

This passage, while elevating Virginia as a feminine ideal, concurrently
establishes a model of women's virtue dependent on chastity and sexual
innocence that curtails their agency. As R. Howard Bloch explains: "The
discourse of praise, which culminates in the figure of the apparently per-
fect woman, the virgin, is neither the antidote to nor the opposite of the
medieval discourse of misogyny."[2] Laudations of virginity in the Mid-
dle Ages, although ostensibly praising virtuous women, create such a
rigid model of identity that they cannot be divorced from misogynistic
discourses because both ideologies constrain women's activity, and thus
women themselves, according to unyielding norms.

Following his celebration of virtuous Virginia, the narrator expresses anxiety about the sexual maturation of young girls and the likelihood that they will succumb to seduction, but he also advocates an important social function for such women. Whereas Virginia feigns illness to avoid "feestes, revels, and . . . daunces, / That been occasions of daliaunces" (6.65-66), other young maidens, according to the narrator, face their moral downfalls at these events: "Swich thynges maken children for to be / To soon rype and boold, as men may se, / Which is ful perilous and hath been yoore" (6.67-69). As much as the narrator frets over young women falling into sexual temptation, he identifies a compensating benefit in that they may protect future generations of girls from similar fates. In a digression addressed to "maistresses . . . / That lordes doghtres han in governaunace" (6.72-73), or in another word, governesses, the narrator distinguishes between two types of women holding this position:

Outher for ye han kept youre honestee,
Or elles ye han falle in freletee [frailty],
And knowen wel ynough the olde daunce,
And han forsaken fully swich meschaunce
For everemo; therfore, for Cristes sake,
To teche hem vertu looke that ye ne slake. (6.77-82)

According to this moral logic, a woman's virginity stands as her preeminent virtue, yet if she fails to withstand the rigors of chastity, she can continue to serve a crucial societal role in employing her knowledge of love's stratagems to protect her charges. The Physician builds this theme by comparing such governesses to poachers who, having reformed themselves from criminality, are now better situated to work as game wardens (6.83-85). While modern readers may rightly bristle at the gendered biases encoded in such terminology as the "fallen woman" and at the *Physician's Tale*'s overweening interest in monitoring women's sexuality, its moral compass extends beyond the simplistic binary of virgin and whore to locate virtue arising from prior sexual transgressions, only then to lose these moorings as the tale proceeds.

With these prefatory materials completed, the narrative action of the *Physician's Tale* commences: Virginia and her mother travel to town, and Apius, a judge, is so entranced by the adolescent girl's beauty that "his herte chaunged and his mood" (6.126). He resolves to possess her—"This mayde shal be myn, for any man!" (6.129)—and conscripts the "cherl" Claudius, under the threat of death, to claim that Virginius kidnapped Virginia from him when she was a young child. In the sham trial that ensues, Apius rules in Claudius's favor, and Virginius realizes Apius's objective "in lecherie to lyven" (6.206) with his daughter. To preserve her honor, Virginius urges Virginia to accept death at his hands. Perceptively reading this scene, Glenn Burger underscores that it focuses less on feminine virtue than on male pride: "When the perverse gaze of Apius threatens to sully first the body of purity (Virginia) and then its essence (Virginius's reputation), the 'natural' order must be inscribed on the physical and social body in ever more extreme ways. At whatever cost, true masculinity must maintain itself as subject not object of the gaze of the other."[3] In a moment relevant to Burger's reading, Virginius admits that Virginia does not merit the imminent execution that he is planning. "For nevere thou deservedest wherfore / To dyen with a swerd or with a knyf" (6.216-17), he proclaims, as he then, in a sharp irony, refers to her as his "deere doghter, endere of my lyf" (6.218), although it is he who seeks to end her life. Virginius then urges Virginia to accept her unwarranted fate: "O gemme of chastitee, in pacience / Take thou thy deeth, for this is my sentence. / For love, and nat for hate, thou most be deed: / My pitous hand moot smyten of thyn heed" (6.223-26). Imposing this judgment on his daughter, Virginius arrogates for himself the role of judge, a position that Apius has already perverted in his lusty pursuit of her. Whether through rape or execution, both Apius and Virginius demand that Virginia accede to their desires to exploit women's sexuality, whether for one's unlawful pleasure or the other's patriarchal pride. Within this tale, misogyny offers an inescapable double bind.

Despite the grim circumstances confronting Virginia, one can envision an ending to this story—the one ostensibly foreshadowed in its opening discussion of governesses—in which either as Apius's former conscripted mistress or as Virginius's chaste daughter, her ultimate destiny would be to serve as a governess to a young girl, thus to protect her ward from such corrupt judges as Apius and her father. Instead, Virginius sees greater moral utility in murdering a potential governess than in pardoning his blameless daughter. Realizing her dire situation, Virginia beseeches him for clemency—"O mercy, deere fader" she pleads (6.231)—as she then asks both fearfully and hopefully, "Goode fader, shal I dye? / Is ther no grace, is ther no remedye?" (6.235-36). No mercy is granted, and as Anne Laskaya posits, such a display of "moral absolutism . . . elicits our outrage at the death of an innocent woman," stating further that "the narrative condemns Virginius's detached absolutism as well as Apius's lust."[4]

Indeed, rather than confronting Apius over his corrupt prosecution of his duties, Virginius confronts his daughter over this man's lust and her faultless actions. As several critics have noted, Virginius's concern over Virginia's sexuality carries incestuous undertones, notably in the pun on her *maidenhead*: Apius lusts for Virginia, and so would deprive her of her maidenhead both in its symbolic form as her virginity and in its physical form as her hymen. In this misogynistic battle between men in which Virginia is conscripted as a pawn, Virginius decapitates her, cutting off this maiden's head and then delivering it to Apius: "Hir heed of smoot [cut off], and by the top it hente [seized], / And to the juge he gan it to presente" (6.255-56). Linda Lomperis exposes the gender politics metaphorically at hand, pointing to the phallic posturing behind Virginius's barely disguised cruelty: "In short, this entire scene can be said to expose the sexual basis of Virginius's own actions, to pull down the pants, so to speak, of the male-dominated forces that rule the social order."[5] With this semantic play on *maidenhead* and with Virginius assuming the role of a judge deciding his daughter's fate, the *Physician's Tale* encodes troubling parallels between Apius and Virginius that imply their moral and ethical equivalence. Quite simply, Virginia is unsafe with either of them.

As the *Physician's Tale* broaches the theme of fallen governesses only to override it with Virginia's execution, so too does it introduce a biblical allusion to Jephthah's daughter only to dismiss its deeper relevance. The account of Jephthah's daughter, recounted in the book of Judges, employs the folkloric trope of the rash promise, in which characters speak too quickly and soon regret their words. In this story's opening, Jephthah vows to the Lord, "If thou wilt deliver the children of Ammon into my hands, whosoever shall first come forth out of the doors of my house . . . the same will I offer a holocaust to the Lord" (Judges 11.30-31). Jephthah is granted his victory, and upon returning home, his only child, a daughter, rushes out to greet him. He regrets his promise, but his daughter accepts her fate, requesting only a reprieve of two months to "bewail my virginity with my companions" (Judges 11.37). Virginia compares herself to this biblical figure, pleading that her father treat her similarly: "'Thanne yif [give] me leyser [leisure, respite], fader myn,' quod she, / 'My deeth for to compleyne a litel space; / For, pardee, Jepte yaf his doghter grace / For to compleyne, er he hir slow [slew], allas!'" (6.238-41). Rather than passively accepting her father's death sentence, Virginia requests a reprieve, and as Daniel Kline argues, "Virginia's reference to Jephthah's daughter in the *Physician's Tale* establishes a subject position resistant to the discourses that have so violently subjugated her, especially those articulated by her father Virginius."[6] In aligning herself with Jephthah's daughter, Virginia seeks a reprieve that is not granted; in her petition, she nonetheless proves herself a perceptive textual interpreter, one who finds relevant precedents to her dire circumstances and employs them to resist her fate. Moreover, many medieval exegetes sharply criticized readings of this narrative that endorsed Jephthah's actions. Judson Boyce Allen and Theresa Anne Moritz, in examining a variety of medieval voices responding to the tale of Jephthah's daughter, conclude, "Glosses on the story of Jephthah's daughter are generally disapproving, and generally because human sacrifice is not considered the thing to do." They cite Hugh of Saint-Cher as one of their sources, quoting his words: "And so it is clear that [Jephthah] vowed with bad intention, therefore his vow was bad."[7] Comparing Virginius and Virginia as readers, it is apparent that the former forces interpretations that align with his patriarchal and misogynistic worldview, whereas Virginia devises interpretations that allow a space of women's agency despite the strictures of binary gender roles.

In a further irony indicative that relevant biblical sources are misapplied to the themes of the *Physician's Tale*, the account of Jephthah identifies his mother as a "harlot" (Judges 11.1), with this reference to a "fallen woman" tacitly endorsing sexual transgressions for their unexpectedly beneficial consequences. Like the governesses that the Physician mentions in his tale's opening, Jephthah's mother illustrates a narrative option not allowed to Virginia yet central to the tale's construction of feminine virtue as arising from former vice. And certainly, although many medieval Christian traditions prized women's chastity as a preeminent virtue, it is acknowledged in the opening genealogy of the Gospel of Matthew that Jesus descended from Rahab, another prostitute from Christianity's Old Testament: "And Salmon begot Boaz of Rahab. And Boaz begot Obed of Ruth. Obed begot Jesse," with this family tree culminating in Jesus's birth (Matthew 1.5). In the book of Joshua, Joshua sends two men to spy out the Promised Land; Rahab protects them from the king of Jericho by allowing them to hide in her home. In return, Joshua orders the Israelites to spare her: "Let only Rahab the harlot live, with all that are with her in the house: for she hid the messengers whom we sent" (Joshua 6.17). From the examples of Jephthah's mother and of Rahab, medieval Christians would recognize the ways in which a woman's vice could lead to salvific benefits for society as a whole, whether as the mother of a military hero in an Old Testament episode or as an early ancestor of Jesus cited by name in the opening lines of the first Gospel. Furthermore, as Sandra Pierson Prior posits, the Catholic Bible offers a more apt analogy through which the Physician might filter Virginia's story: "If Virginia were to invoke a biblical type, Susannah would seem the more appropriate predecessor. Susannah's story, like Virginia's, involves lust, perjury, and a corrupt justice system, over which God's justice ultimately triumphs through the brilliant legal defense of the prophet Daniel."[8] Rather than a story of divine providence defending the unjustly accused, the *Physician's Tale* can only envision a depraved world in which a guiltless woman is executed owing to the lust, pride, and misogyny of others.

Notwithstanding Virginia's innocence and its sharp contrast with Apius's guilt, Virginius executes his daughter and the tale rushes to its conclusion. He delivers her head to Apius, but when Apius orders Virginius to be hanged for Virginia's death, "right anon a thousand peple in thraste, / To save the knyght, for routhe and for pitee, / For knowen was the false iniquitee" (6.260-62). Justice, in the form of this angry mob, was absent for Virginia but miraculously emerges for her murderous father. The concluding lines of the *Physician's Tale* admonish readers to learn from its befuddled moral lesson:

> Heere may men seen how synne hath his merite.
> Beth war [aware, wary], for no man woot [knows] whom God wol
>   smyte
> In no degree, ne in which manere wyse;
> The worm of conscience may agryse [shudder]
> Of wikked lyf, though it so pryvee be
> That no man woot therof but God and he.
> For be he lewed man, or ellis lered [learned],
> He noot how soone that he shal been afered [frightened].
> Therfore I rede [advise] yow this conseil take:
> Forsaketh synne, er synne yow forsake. (6.277-86)

But to whom do these words apply? As Anne Middleton succinctly points out, "What the story is 'about,' it seems, depends entirely on *whom* it is about,"[9] yet even this apparently simple question muddies interpretive clarity. None of the primary characters stand as appropriate candidates for this moral: Apius, the unjust judge, does not fall to God's punishment but to his own, hanging himself in his prison cell. Virginius suffers no reprisal for executing his daughter, and he forgives Claudius for his role in the plot, choosing to exile rather than to execute him. Clearly, these lines cannot apply to Virginia, the tale's dead woman who was refused a future as a governess and who was blameless throughout her life. The tale's themes collapse at this moment, particularly because Virginia is earlier described as so perfectly virtuous that young girls should model themselves after her: "This mayde, of which I wol this tale expresse, / So kepte hirself hir neded no maistresse, / For in hir lyvying maydens myghten rede, / As in a book, every good worde or dede" (6.105-8). But what young girl reader could take comfort from this tale of feminine virtue ending in the woman's execution at her father's hands? Thomas Hanson summarizes of this themeless theme, this moral-less moral, that "the Physician has told the Virginia story in such a way as to suggest not that virtue will be rewarded in Heaven but that virtue leads inexorably to death."[10] In effect, the tale demonstrates that no amount of virtue is sufficient to save oneself from the desires of others, and in a further irony, the narrator reiterates his theme of governesses in these lines, stating that Virginia exemplified such virtue that she had no need of one. On the contrary, a governess experienced in the duplicities, double-dealing, and lusts of men might have provided the only lifeline available to Virginia once Apius succumbed to his immoderate desire.

The *Physician's Tale*, which continually teeters between its purported themes and its narrative action, fails as well to deliver a coherent theme for parents. The narrator earlier warned parents that their example could lead to their children's untimely demise, but following the passage concerning governesses, this voice exhorts them:

> Ye fadres and ye moodres eek also,
> Though ye han children, be it oon or mo,
> Youre is the charge of al hir surveiaunce,
> Whil that they been under youre governaunce.
> Beth war, if by ensample of youre lyvynge,
> Or by youre necligence in chastisynge,
> That they ne perisse [perish]; for I dar wel seye
> If that they doon, ye shul it deere abeye [pay the penalty]. (6.93-100)

But Virginia does not suffer from her parents' neglect: her mother accompanied her when Apius lustfully espied her, and she does not perish because she follows their example but because her father's governance is precisely the mechanism of her death. John Pitcher assesses this cruel irony:

"Virginia's death at the hand of her father serves to locate the primary threat to the safety of girls within the family, rather than outside it."[11] Moreover, the cautionary exhortation that parents "shul it deer abeye" if their children fall into temptation, sin, and death withers when compared to the tale's ending, for Virginius does not appear to face any repercussions for executing his daughter.

The critical consensus on the *Physician's Tale* denounces it as one of Chaucer's weakest efforts in the *Canterbury Tales*. Placing it within long-standing critical traditions, Richard Hoffman alludes to a desire among certain readers to jettison it altogether: "Chaucerians traditionally have considered the tale sufficiently inferior to their author's best and most mature work as not really to merit inclusion in the *Canterbury Tales*."[12] Sandra Pierson Prior evaluates it harshly: "By virtually any critical judgment, a badly told story: inconsistent in tone, inept in story line, incoherent in sentence, and devoid of *solas*."[13] As a specimen of Chaucer's forays in bad writing, the *Physician's Tale* rules supreme. Yet in a final irony, Harry Bailly, perhaps modeling Chaucer's vision of the tale's ideal reader, rails against Apius's injustice but then rhapsodizes over the emotional power of Virginia's death: "Algate this sely mayde is slayn, allas! / Allas, to deere boughte she beautee!" he cries (6.292-93). He soon concludes, "Myn herte is lost for pitee of this mayde" (6.317). With Harry Bailly enacting the role of a reader ravished by the tale's cruel injustice, Chaucer proleptically batted away criticisms of his tale, highlighting its raw power against any petty readers who might notice its many thematic inconsistencies, which is to say, its striking badness.

And on a final note, although I have concentrated on its thematic lapses in this chapter, the *Physician's Tale* also stands as a striking example of Chaucer's outmoded perspectives, in its creation of a fictional world structured by virulent misogyny. As Kate Manne argues, "We should think of misogyny as serving to uphold patriarchal order, understood as one strand among various similar systems of domination (including racisms, xenophobia, classism, ageism, ableism, homophobia, transphobia, and so on). Misogyny does this by visiting hostile or adverse social consequences on a certain . . . class of girls or women to enforce and police social norms."[14] Misogyny suffuses the landscape of the *Physician's Tale*, denying women agency and even mercy, defining their lives via their instrumentality for men. Along with his conflicted themes, Chaucer envisions a bleak world where misogyny suffocates women while their fathers murder them.

CHAPTER 14

The Old Man Walking and Pseudo-crux of the *Pardoner's Tale*

A moral tale told by the most immoral of men, the *Pardoner's Tale* stands as one of Chaucer's crowning achievements as he balances the irony of an unrepentant sinner preaching a particularly fitting and effective sermon—and then using it as the opportunity to sin yet again. Following the depravities displayed in his portrait in the *General Prologue* and in his tale's introduction and prologue, the tale itself is surprising in its refusal to shock as brazenly as readers might expect. Rather, it adheres to standard structures of medieval sermonizing, details with steady precision the sins of gluttony, gambling, and swearing, and then illustrates their baleful repercussions through an apt exemplum of three rioters eternally punished for indulging in their pleasures. In this otherwise paradigmatic exemplum, Chaucer incorporates a crux of a character who has puzzled readers for centuries but who contributes little to its themes. On their journey from raucous sinning to rightful punishment, these three men encounter an enigmatic old man who directs them to their deaths, but this figure has steadfastly resisted all efforts to pinpoint his identify. He has been variously viewed as an allegorical representation of Death, as a descendant of such figures as Noah, Odin, the Wandering Jew, and Judas, and as the metaphorical enactment of another such allegory or legendary forebear, but readers' attempts invariably fall short of a wholly convincing and cogent identification. This old man is, in effect, a pseudo-crux—an interpretive puzzle that is ultimately puzzling for its refusal to puzzle—which thus represents the triumph of the text's surface over any subtext. Through his tantalizing yet overdetermined characterization of this old man, Chaucer leads his readers astray from the Pardoner's morally sound exemplum into the uncharted territory of a character crux without the need of a solution.

Cruxes differ from other matters of literary interpretation in that they presume the possibility of a correct answer, whereas the latter, in all their variety, may generate conflicting yet nonetheless coherent readings. "A crux is not much of a crux, after all, if there's no doubt about how it should be understood," states William Frost, as he points to the perplexing challenge of cruxes that require but resist definitive answers.[1] Famous Chaucerian cruxes include such questions as the speaker of the marriage encomium in the *Merchant's Tale* and the identity of the "man of gret auctorite" (2158) whose arrival heralds the abrupt ending of the *House of Fame*. Presumably Chaucer envisioned specific identities for these inscrutable figures, yet they remain unnamed and unnamable. Another variety of Chaucerian crux circulates around the manuscripts of his writings and the words thereon, as various physical conditions—including blurred ink, crabbed handwriting, and variant spellings—generate a host of contradictory transliterations, yet with the presumption that Chaucer and his scribes likely intended specific words, not multiple and contradictory possibilities. In contrast to cruxes, literary interpretations admit a wide range of compelling meanings, and the open significations of a text are often praised as reflecting its sophisticated treatment of its characters, morals, and themes. Consider, for example, the controversial question of whether, in Chaucer's *Troilus and Criseyde*, Criseyde sleeps with her uncle Pandarus after her night of passion with Troilus. Many readers vehemently reject this claim, yet the narrator presents their time together with a disclaimer—"I passe al that which chargeth nought to seye" (3.1576)—and then broaches the subject of divine mercy: "God foryaf [forgave] his deth, and she al so / Foryaf, and with here uncle gan to pleye" (3.1577-78). *Pley* frequently suggests sexual intercourse in Chaucer's lexicon, and this stanza intriguingly concludes, "And Pandarus hath fully his entente" (3.1582). The narrator's nod to the necessity of discretion, the allusion to divine forgiveness, the sexually charged connotations of the word *pley*, and the ambiguity of Pandarus's full intentions accumulate to pique the suspicion of some readers about what precisely transpires in this scene. As much as readers may feel passionately about the correctness of their unique interpretations, and equally passionately about the incorrectness of others', most would also grant their openness to contrasting, if perhaps not fully conflicting, interpretations, for there can be no definitive analysis of a polyvalent text. A crux, on the other hand, typically addresses a more technical matter on which all readers could ostensibly agree, if a convincing solution were discovered.

On the issue of a crux as opposed to a literary interpretation, readers could also consider the Pardoner himself, for this character invites varied and conflicting readings of his gender, his sex, his body, and his erotic desires, thus collectively evincing many of the characteristics that today fall under the umbrella category of queerness. As narrator of the *General Prologue*, Chaucer describes a strong homosocial friendship between the Pardoner and the Summoner, and because the Pardoner sings "Com hider, love, to me!" as the Summoner "bar to hym a stif burdoun [strong bass voice]" (1.672–73), a homoerotic reading of their friendship is adumbrated as well. Chaucer's depiction of the Pardoner's voice and body abounds in ambiguity: "A voys he hadde as smal as hath a goot. / No berd hadde he, ne nevere sholde have; / As smothe it was as it were late shave. / I trowe he were a geldyng or a mare" (1.688–91). Whereas the metaphorical comparison of the Pardoner to a gelding or a mare would suggest that he does not have testicles, Harry Bailly later threatens this part of the Pardoner's anatomy: "I wolde I hadde thy coillons in myn hond" (6.952). By drawing attention to the indeterminacy of the Pardoner's body, Chaucer introduces an interpretive riddle that refuses a definitive answer, and critics have posited numerous potential identities and explanations for the Pardoner and his gendered and erotic ambiguity, including that he is a eunuch, a crossdresser, a gay man, or a woman. Yet as much as the Pardoner appears to represent a queer figure, he also proclaims his heteroerotic interests, mentioning to his fellow pilgrims that he has "a joly wenche in every toun" (6.453) and inquiring of the Wife of Bath for marital advice: "I was aboute to wedde a wyf; allas! / What sholde I bye [pay for] it on my flessh so deere? / Yet hadde I levere wedde no wyf to-yeere [this year]!" (3.166–68). As Robert Sturges points out, "The problem . . . is not that Chaucer provides too little information. . . . Rather, he provides too much: the Pardoner's gender identity signifies in too many ways."[2] The unknowability of the Pardoner's body and erotic desires transcends the technicality of a crux to become one of the defining mysteries of the *Canterbury Tales*, which highlights by contrast the problematic nature of the pseudo-crux of the old man's characterization in his tale. The *Pardoner's Tale* is not noticeably enhanced through this enigmatic figure, whereas the indecipherability of the Pardoner himself productively complicates readers' understanding of his character, his desires, and his strange motivation to confess his sins, and then to indulge in them again.

Following the prefatory materials that allow readers to contemplate the enigma of his identity, and after confessing his scams for defrauding the faithful, the Pardoner concludes his prologue with a compelling statement of his rhetorical skills: "For though myself be a ful vicious man, / A moral tale yet I yow telle kan" (6.459-60). The tale that follows proves his words true. Robert Merrix assesses the *Pardoner's Tale* as "a representative example of late medieval sermons," for it adheres to this genre's standard structures.[3] The Pardoner states his theme of *"Radix malorum est Cupiditas"* (The root of evil is greed; 6.334), expounds on and discusses this theme, illustrates it with an exemplum, and then recapitulates and applies his theme for his audience. In the exposition portion of the sermon, he introduces subthemes of gluttony ("O glotonye, ful of cursednesse!" [6.498]), gambling ("Hasard is verray mooder [mother] of lesynges [lies]" [6.591]), and swearing ("Gret sweryng is a thyng abhominable" [6.631]). He commences his exemplum to illustrate the dangers of these sins, as brazenly indulged in by a "compaignye / Of yonge folk that haunteden folye, / As riot, hasard, stywes [brothels], and tavernes" (6.463-65). A passing boy reports that one of their friends was slain by Death, and, not understanding the common trope of personification, the three rioters vow to avenge themselves by tackling the impossible task of killing Death. As these revelers begin their journey, they encounter an old man:

> Whan they han goon nat fully half a mile,
> Right as they wolde han troden over a stile,
> An oold man and a povre with hem mette.
> This olde man ful mekely hem grette [greeted them],
> And seyde thus, "Now, lordes, God yow see!" (6.711-15)

This initial depiction of the old man contains no hint of a supernatural encounter, and he is painted simply as old in body, poor in social class, and meek in manner. His greeting to the three rioters evinces concern for their spiritual well-being, an appropriate gesture given this sermon's moral themes. In light of these men's depraved lifestyles, his words are charged with an ironic yet beneficent undertone, reminding them that God witnesses all their sinful acts.

For many readers, the character of the old man shifts notably when the "proudeste of thise riotoures three" (6.716) insults him by asking, "Why artow al forwrapped [wrapped up, clothed head to toe] save thy face? / Why lyvestow so longe in so greet age?" (6.718-19). In response to these rude questions, the old man cryptically replies:

> For I ne kan nat fynde
> A man, though that I walked into Ynde [India],

Neither in citee ne in no village,
That wolde chaunge his youthe for myn age;
And therfore moot I han myn age stille,
As longe tyme as it is Goddes wille.
Ne Deeth, allas, ne wol nat han my lyf.
Thus walke I, lyk a restelees kaityf,
And on the ground, which is my moodres [mother's] gate,
I knokke with my staf, bothe erly and late,
And seye "Leeve mooder, leet me in!" (6.721-31)

The old man's words broach, but do not confirm, numerous supernatural possibilities. Could he—did he—walk to India on a quest to find another man who would exchange youth for senescence? Most likely the old man speaks ironically with these words, pointing out the implausibility that a person would trade the relative health of youth for the bodily infirmities of advanced age, but his reply hints at the eerie possibility that, if he found such a person agreeable to the trade, such a change could have been effected. Furthermore, the old man appears to have supernatural foreknowledge of the three rioters' fate, for he directs them to the Death that they so foolishly seek: "Now sires . . . if that yow be so leef / To fynde Deeth, turne up this croked wey, / For in that grove I lafte hym, by my fey, / Under a tree, and there he wole abyde" (6.760-63). In his final words, the old man urges the three rioters to repent their sins: "God save yow, that boghte agayn [redeemed] mankynde, / And yow amende!" (6.766-67). The rioters follow his directions to the tree, find bushels of gold coins, and then murder one another in hopes of winning a larger share of the fortune. As Steven F. Kruger argues, the death of these men can be traced to their failure to understand symbolism: "The rioters' brotherhood is formed out of a misunderstanding of the personification of Death, and their quest is thoroughly informed by this misunderstanding. Their ultimate error, the inability to recognize the gold treasure as itself equivalent to death, also represents a failure of allegorical reading."[4] Within the allegorical economy of the *Pardoner's Tale*, the failure to decode symbolism leads the three rioters to their demise, and so they serve as a cautionary tale not only against gluttony, gambling, and swearing but also against a mindless literalism.

Given his elliptical words and the tale's supernatural aura, scholars have proposed various solutions to the crux of the old man's identity, primarily by interpreting him as an allegory, personification, or allusion. Owing to his quest for death and his advanced years, he has long been viewed as a symbolic representation either of Death or of Old Age. As George Lyman Kittredge writes in *Chaucer and His Poetry*, "The aged wayfarer whom the three rioters encounter . . . is undoubtedly Death in person."[5] While initially appealing, this interpretation fails to withstand scrutiny, for it remains unexplained why Death should be seeking his own death; the paradox collapses inward, negating its possibility. Yet if not Death, the old man may be Death's spy, a theory put forth by Marie Padgett Hamilton,[6] or the theological concept of the *secunda mors*, or second death, a theory put forth by L. O. Purdon.[7] He might represent Old Age and time's inexorable passage, with Takami Matsuda espying such a metaphoric cast to the old man: "His age is a message for youth, insomuch as it points out the common fate of all men and functions as a mirror of self-knowledge to the young."[8] Robert Miller sees in the old man the Pauline concept of the *vetus homo* who represents "any human being, [in] the image of fallen Adam, unregenerate in accepted grace and unredeemed by Christ," noting further that "the Old Man of whom Paul wrote cannot die, and will not die so long as human nature does not change."[9] While these compelling readings offer insight into the old man's multiple levels of meaning, it should be noted that not every old man symbolizes Old Age and that the assumption of a deeper allegorical interpretation is not necessarily warranted. For example, few readers correspondingly argue that the three rioters, although they are young, represent Youth.

Additional theories concerning the old man's identity abound, with several scholars viewing him as an unnamed avatar of well-known mythological, biblical, or legendary figures. Robert Barakat proposes that the Norse god Odin "appears to be the ultimate prototype of the old man," noting that "Chaucer's old man and Odin go among the people as the Wanderer, wearing a cloak that almost completely covers their bodies, and each carries a staff, meting out rewards or punishment."[10] Peter Beidler places the story within its historical and geographical context of fourteenth-century England suffering repeated outbreaks of the plague and links the old man to Noah, for both men survive the devastating catastrophes that befall their contemporaries. Beidler thinks that Chaucer's audience "would have thought of the Pardoner's old man as a kind of contemporary Noah who reminded them that sin does not go unpunished."[11] Some scholars espy similarities between the old man and apocryphal accounts of the Wandering Jew cursed to roam the world until the Second Coming, whose legend arose from Jesus's words in the Gospel of Matthew: "Amen I say to you, there are some of them that stand here, that shall not taste death, till they see the Son of man coming in his kingdom" (Matthew 16.28). Nelson Sherwin Bushnell connects the old man to the Wandering Jew: "One of the most striking features of the Jew which Chaucer seems to have imitated is that he is a wanderer, just as he is immortal, by divine compulsion."[12] Mary Flowers Braswell theorizes that the old man "contains vestiges of the biblical tale" of Judas.[13] With Odin, Noah, the Wandering Jew, and Judas, readers see thematic connections to Chaucer's old man, but little evidence that they provided direct inspiration.

Beyond these attempted identifications of the old man as an allegory, personification, or allusion, scholars cannot agree whether he represents a positive or negative force in the tale's figuration of divine, or simply poetic, justice. In a paean to the character's goodness, Alfred Kellogg sees him as simultaneously signifying divine justice and earthly humility: "The Old Man possesses dignity because he possesses humility. He is at once the symbol of the unassailable might of divine government and the symbol of obedience and humility, of the soul angelic or human which subjects its own will to the will of God."[14] In stark contrast, Alexandra Hennessey Olsen argues that the old man represents a devilish figure,[15] and Elizabeth Hatcher discerns his ironic reflection of the rioters' desire for eternal life: "The Old Man thus embodies a *reductio ad absurdum* of the revelers' aspiration, their 'rash wish.' He *is* what they seek: endless physical life."[16] A notable subset of interpretations identifies the old man as the Pardoner himself, such as in Alfred David's proposition, "Through the old man Chaucer reveals the Pardoner's real secret, the joylessness of the life he professes to relish so much."[17] More specifically, Gudrun Richardson sees the old man not as the Pardoner but as "the soul of the Pardoner condemned to suffer a living hell for having turned away from God."[18]

In contrast to these voices who assert a thematic resonance for the old man, several scholars reject these claims and advise readers to remain on the surface of the text rather than to seek subterranean meanings. If too liberally applied, the principle of Occam's razor—that the simplest explanation is most likely the correct one—would denude literary criticism of much of its sophistication and pleasure, yet at times it provides a necessary countercurrent to the critical tide. Resisting interpretations of the old man based on allegory, personification, and allusion, these critics advise readers to accept the old man simply as an old man. John Steadman concludes, "Chaucer's *senex* is quite intelligible on the literal level without resort to allegorical explanations. His chief significance is to be found in the ethical contrast he provides to Chaucer's characterization of the rioters."[19] Helen Cooper, in her definitive *Oxford Guides to Chaucer: The "Canterbury Tales,"* avows succinctly, "He is what the text says he is: an old man seeking death," although she also acknowledges the "extensive implications" of this assessment.[20] Why insist on an allegorical crux when the simplest explanation—the old man is who he presents himself to be—resolves any interpretive conundrums?

Despite the merits of this argument for simplicity, it should be conceded that, at this point in the *Canterbury Tales*, readers are accustomed to characters encountering mysterious, otherworldly figures when they travel throughout the countryside. In scenes similar to the three rioters meeting the old man, the rapist knight of the *Wife of Bath's Tale* happens upon the mysterious old woman who divulges the answer to the riddle of his quest and then magically transforms into a youthful beauty at the story's end, and the corrupt summoner of the *Friar's Tale*, on his journey to defraud the old woman, chances upon a devil who leads him to hell following her damning words. Through these previous scenes of the *Canterbury Tales*, Chaucer has, in effect, conditioned his readers to expect such encounters to broach the realm of the supernatural. Roy Pearcy examines the discussion between the old man and the three rioters through the logical and rhetorical device of *amphibologia*, which he defines as "an exchange between two characters, one of whom, by virtue of some superhuman insight into the future, is alert to the correct interpretations of a statement while the other is not," with the character granted this insight into the future usually "a supernatural being, not necessarily a god but possibly also a devil."[21] The patterns of the *amphibologia* hold in the *Wife of Bath's Tale* and the *Friar's Tale*, which lead readers to suspect this old man of similar supernatural capabilities.

Yet if this old man might wield any such unworldly powers, he never demonstrates them, nor does he guide the three rioters to a new understanding of their moral fallacies (as does the old woman of the *Wife of Bath's Tale*), nor does he escort them to their eternal damnation (as does the devil of the *Friar's Tale*). He is an old man, not an Old Man, but with this cruxless crux, many of Chaucer's readers have generated interpretations, no matter how sound or otherwise convincing, that do little to enhance our understanding of this character or of his tale. Other scholars have simply—and wisely—given up, which Lisa Lampert-Weissig (tentatively) admits in her touchstone study of the ways in which antisemitism influences Chaucer's depiction of the Pardoner and the *Pardoner's Tale*: "I have given up (for now at least) on attempting to solve definitively the mystery of the Old Man's identity."[22] With his mischaracterized old man distracting readers from more pressing themes, Chaucer diverts attention away from where it belongs: on a morally sound sermon, told by the most immoral and enigmatic of men.

CHAPTER 15

The Groanworthy Puns and Semantic Enigmas of the *Shipman's Tale*

Long pilloried as the lowest form of humor, puns frequently elicit groans rather than laughs, and many detractors of this comic genre simply yawn in response to their wearying obviousness. On the whole, knock-knock jokes are not heralded for their sophisticated wit. More generously, one could counterargue that puns garner reactions ranging the gamut from clenched chuckles for their banality to roaring laughter for their éclat. But this is true of virtually all subgenres of humor: some jokes land, some fall flat, and comic authors, while aspiring for their jokes to hit their marks, face the concomitant risk that they will fall flat. The *Canterbury Tales*, and particularly the *Shipman's Tale*, employs a punning humor that accentuates the inherent playfulness of language arising from the multiple connotations of countless words. With two of his most famous puns occurring in this story, Chaucer riffs on the double (if not multiple) meanings of *cosyn* and *taillynge*, and in so doing reveals the vagaries of a punning narrator who appears unable to restrain himself from repeating his favorite jokes. In an otherwise peerless fabliau of sexual economics and erotic double-dealing, the *Shipman's Tale* shifts its humorous style into the realm of puns, insisting its auditors hear repeated (and thus increasingly stale) jokes that some might prefer to miss the second and third, or even the first, time around. When these conditions are paired with the semantic fog surrounding the meanings of Middle English slang, Chaucer's puns become more challenging to identify and to decode, and thus the humor at their heart less steady. Chaucer's puns clearly belong to the realm of his purposefully bad humor, with any potential comic pleasures sparking concomitant questions of readers' individual tastes.

As is well known, puns entail a play on the multiple meanings of a given word or a pair of homophones. In a formulation that hints at his dismissive attitude toward puns, W. W. Skeat writes, "To *pun* is to pound words, to beat them into new senses, to hammer at forced similes," with his verb choices construing this form of wordplay as lexical violence.[1] Paull F. Baum offers a more optimistic assessment: "In the true pun . . . there is first a recognition of two or more possibilities, and a rapid balancing between them; then the pleasure of finding that either will fit; and finally the increased pleasure of seeing that both will fit. The two meanings remain distinct; there was no real choice between them because neither is absorbed in the other."[2] This well-known grammatical example illustrates Skeat's and Baum's observations: "The past, the present, and the future walk into a bar. It was tense!" The past, present, and future represent temporalities but also verb tenses, with the punchline relying on the additional meaning of *tense* as "anxious" or "anxiety-producing." And thus the question: to groan or not to groan? Either way individuals respond, their reactions to puns offer insights into their view of humor. As Jonathan Culler theorizes, some auditors grumbling in response to puns are attempting to maintain the stability of language in the face of a meaningless lexical coincidence: "To groan at puns . . . is viscerally to reaffirm a distinction between essence and accident, between meaningful relations and coincidence, that has seemed fundamental to our thinking."[3] Yet where some see an inconsequential accident of language in puns, others see a felicity of possibility, with defenders of puns, such as John Pollack, countering that, if it were indeed true that they represent comedy's nadir, "it would make punning the foundation of all humor."[4]

But was Chaucer a punster? The critical tradition has long downplayed or even outright denied this possibility.[5] In *Studies in Chaucer* (1892), Thomas R. Lounsbury states that Chaucer was "free from these verbal quibbles,"[6] and John S. P. Tatlock, while regretfully acknowledging Chaucer's use of "casual jingles," defends them as typical of "poets of humor."[7] Helge Kökeritz opened the critical floodgates of Chaucerian pun scholarship by exploring his debts to classical and medieval rhetorical traditions involving wordplay, particularly *traductio* ("using the same word over and over again without offending good taste"), *adnominatio* ("reproducing almost the same word or name by changing only its quantity or, alternatively, one or two of its letters, so that two similar words express different ideas"), and *significatio* ("when a word can be taken in two or more senses but has the one the speaker wishes to give it").[8] Appearing in 1958, Baum's essay "Chaucer's Puns" offers a detailed, if at times speculative, account of the author's lexical humor, with his subsequent essay, "Chaucer's Puns: A Supplementary List," published soon after.[9] In subsequent decades scholarship on Chaucer's puns proliferated, but in a 1984 article Larry Benson forcefully attempted to swing back this interpretive pendulum by cataloging instances of contemporary critics discerning modern meanings in medieval words. He urges "those who have the modern obscenity constantly on their minds [to] stop allowing it to interfere with their reading of Chaucer," while also conceding that "in all charity we must tolerate the punsters as best we can."[10] Archibald Hill similarly argues against many of Chaucer's supposed puns, pointing out that "meaning is maximally derived from context and only minimally from individual lexical items."[11] What seems clear from these critical conversations is that some readers appear to think that any vision of a punning Chaucer would diminish his poetic accomplishments—in short, to sully his literary reputation with a patina of badness. At any rate, Benson's and Hill's admonitions did not curtail critical interest in Chaucer's puns, which continues as a steady stream of inquiry in studies of his literature.

A quick, and by necessity somewhat scattershot, overview of Chaucer's puns testifies to the potential of the form, as well as to its pitfalls. In the *Summoner's Tale*, the unctuous friar preaches to ailing Thomas with a masterful pun: "Fro Paradys first, if I shal nat lye, / Was man out chaced for his glotonye; / And chaast was man in Paradys, certeyn" (3.1915-17). With the pun on *chaced* and *chaast*, the friar links Adam's blissful state of chastity to the baleful consequences of the Fall, in which he is chased out of Eden; such wordplay testifies to this friar's rhetorical gifts, which surly Thomas resists. The *Summoner's Tale* includes as well Chaucer's stunningly apt pun—"In ars-metrike shal ther no man fynde, / Biforn this day, of swich a question" (3.2222-23)—which turns *arithmetic* into "ass-math," an appropriate academic discipline for answering the question of how to divide a fart among the members of a fraternal order. In the *Franklin's Tale*, the narrator recounts Dorigen's emotional reaction upon Arveragus's return—"O blisful artow now, thou Dorigen, / That hast thy lusty housbonde in thyne armes, / The fresshe knyght, the worthy man of armes" (5.1090-92)—with the second use of *armes* signifying both the weapons of a warrior and the welcoming arms of his lady, as adumbrated in the preceding line. Similarly playing on the multiple meaning of a single word in the *Miller's Tale*, Chaucer describes Nicholas's graphic "seduction" of Alison in punning terms: "As clerkes ben ful subtile and ful queynte; / And prively he caughte hire by the queynte" (1.3275-76). The shift in the meaning of *queynte* from the adjective *cunning* to the noun *vagina* causes readers to reflect upon this duality, thus productively complicating the scene's humor and its characterization of Nicholas. As these examples attest, many of Chaucer's puns relate intimately to his rhymes, and Joseph Dane notes the poet's use of rime riche, which includes "homophonic rimes (*hear/here*), rimes of simple and compound forms (*form/inform*), rimes of different grammatical forms (*delight* as noun and verb), and identical rimes (where two words with the same meaning and grammatical form rime)."[12] Despite so many instances of their vibrancy and delight, some of Chaucer's puns fail to match up to their fellows. In the *Wife of Bath's Tale*, Chaucer puns on *heed* as advice and *maydenhed* as hymen in detailing the rapist knight's assault, resulting in a grim mismatch between the tone of the scene and its verbal humor: "maugree hir heed, / By verray force, he rafte hire maydenhed" (3.887-88). The pun on Calkas's name in *Troilus and Criseyde*—"So whan this Calkas knew by calkulynge [calculating]" (1.71)—surely stands as one of Chaucer's most noted groaners.

On the continuum between gems and groaners, the puns of the *Shipman's Tale* resist easy assessment, yet it is clear that they serve a structuring, not solely ornamental, purpose for its humor, particularly in the overuse of *cosyn* and *taillynge*. As Ruth Fisher argues of the first of these words, "Chaucer, whether punning or not, is using and deliberately overusing *cosyn* with mocking irony."[13] For instance, the narrator, speaking from the perspective of the merchant, refers to the monk in adulatory and familial terms: "Who was so welcome as my lord daun John, / Oure deere cosyn, ful of curteisye?" (7.69). The characters repeatedly refer to one another as cousins, such as when the merchant's wife warmly greets their guest, "O deere cosyn myn, daun John" (7.98). She then denies to him that on the previous evening she enjoyed sexual intercourse with her husband: "Nay, cosyn myn, it stant nat so with me" (7.114). Additionally, the relationship between the merchant and the monk is described as cousinly. "Cosyn, it standeth so" (7.257), the monk begins, and wishes the merchant a safe journey: "I prey yow, cosyn, wisely that ye ryde" (7.260). He thrice bids the merchant goodbye with cousinly terms: "Farewel, cosyn, God shilde yow fro care!" (7.264); "And fare now wel, myn owene cosyn deere" (7.279); and "Grete wel oure dame, myn owene nece sweete, / And fare wel, deere cosyn, til we meete!" (7.363-64). The merchant's wife proclaims her desire not to speak ill of her husband to the monk in deference to the fact that "be he youre cosyn" (7.147), but the monk immediately denies this bond that he otherwise upheld: "He is na moore cosyn unto me / Than is this leef that hangeth on the tree!" (7.149-50). And finally, the merchant calls the monk his cousin, such as when he agrees to his request for a thousand franks

("O cosyn myn, daun John, / Now sikerly [surely] this is a smal requeste" [7.282-83]) and when he confronts his wife about the missing thousand franks: "By God, as that I gesse / That ye han maad a manere straungenesse / Bitwixen me and my cosyn daun John" (7.385-87).

Hearing these many passages including *cousin* or its variants attunes one to the satiric role of kinship in the tale. In comparison, the *Knight's Tale*, which runs roughly five times as long as the *Shipman's Tale*, uses the word *cousin* only nine times in referring to Palamon and Arcite, men who are cousins by blood ("of sustren two yborn" [1.1019]), in contrast to the more ambiguous relationship between the merchant and the monk. In the *Friar's Tale* Chaucer achieves a similar satiric, if not punning, effect with *brother* and its variants: by employing the word disproportionately, he effectively characterizes the pseudo-friendship of the summoner and devil as one based on pecuniary rather than familial desires.

Further underscoring the centrality of cousinhood as a theme of the *Shipman's Tale*, the word *cosynage* appears only three times throughout Chaucer's corpus, with all occurrences in this work. More than the simple use of *cosyn* as a familial affiliation or a title of direct address, *cosynage* introduces a more abstract sense of kinship, one connected to the tale's themes of economics and exchange. Upon introducing the monk who will defraud the merchant of his money and sleep with his wife, the narrator states of their relationship; "The monk hym claymeth as for cosynage" (7.36). As envisioned in the tale, *cosynage* allows men to petition mutual support from one another and for those petitions to be respected. When planning her adulterous liaison with the monk, the merchant's wife promises her fidelity to their duplicitous plan: "Ne shal I nevere, for to goon to helle, / Biwreye [betray] a word of thyng that ye me telle, / Nat for no cosynage ne alliance, / But verraily for love and affiance" (7.137-40). Here *cosynage* represents a relationship that can be deprioritized in favor of their illicit union, yet it nonetheless stands as a fungible and assayable, if nonetheless abstract, familial resource. In its final usage, the merchant's wife alludes to *cosynage* when defending herself against her husband's question of why she did not inform him that the monk had repaid his debt:

For, God it woot [knows], I wende [supposed], withouten doute,
That he hadde yeve [given] it me bycause of yow
To doon therwith myn honour and my prow [benefit],
For cosynage, and eek for beele cheere
That he hath had ful ofte tymes heere. (7.406-10)

Here *cosynage* is restored to its prior signification as a relationship intended to uphold the honor of kinship ties. In its shifting connotations, *cosynage* attunes readers to the vagaries of familial alliances throughout the tale, as well as to the connection between shifting allegiances and shifty dealings.

The repeated use of a word does not in itself constitute punning, and so it requires an investigation into the meanings of *cosyn* to determine if any punning humor could be in play. According to the *Middle English Dictionary*, the word's meaning as "a blood relation, a kinsman or kinswoman; any relative by blood or by marriage," stands as its primary and most obvious meaning,[14] but Fisher proposes that Chaucer employs multiple senses of its meaning: "It would seem reasonable and possible then that Chaucer was playing upon the word in all three of its meanings: the familiar and affectionate meaning of 'friend' (which is ironic in any event); that of 'dupe' or 'cuckold' or 'cheated husband'; and that of 'mistress or prostitute.'"[15] While the *Middle English Dictionary* includes a denotation of *cosyn* as "an intimate, a mistress," this usage is dated after Chaucer's death; Fisher counterargues this point by tracing the word to its contextual milieu of the French fabliau. Noting additional secondary meanings of *cosyn*, David Abraham argues that Chaucer is punning on the related word *cozen*, which means "to cheat" and which interlaces with the economic themes of the *Shipman's Tale*: "*Cosyn* and *cosynage* functioning at once to describe the activities, and simultaneously, as puns, to alter and expand one's perception of the activities, define both meaning *and structure* of the tale."[16] Once again, however, the *Middle English Dictionary* does not confirm the likelihood of such a meaning and dates the signification of *cozen* as "to cheat" to 1453. But how far should one trust the *Middle English Dictionary* or even the *Oxford English Dictionary*, particularly on the secondary and slang meanings of a word, which are notoriously hard to date? For example, the *Oxford English Dictionary* misses the mark widely on the slang meaning of *trim*, dating its meaning as "sexual intercourse with a woman" to 1955 and ascribing its usage to the United States.[17] Yet William Shakespeare uses the word with this meaning in *Titus Andronicus* when Aaron recounts Lavinia's rape: "Why, she was wash'd, and cut, and trimm'd, and 'twas / Trim sport for them which had the doing of it."[18] Other early dramas document this usage, including Willfull Wanton in *The Tide Tarrieth No Man*, who desires a husband who "would trimly bebrave" her.[19] Sin in *All for Money* says of Mother Croote, who desires a young husband, "Oh, she will be a trim bride, that day she is wed!"[20]

Given this example, readers of medieval literature must be sensitive to the ways in which words in earlier historical contexts resist efforts to pinpoint their definitions, and Joseph Gerhard, contextualizing the likely pun on *cosynage* within the economic themes of the *Shipman's Tale*, proposes that "Chaucer has himself coined, has 'fallen' into that sense of the word in the process of narration: just as the tale's circulation of money has created sexual commerce among the wife, monk, and merchant . . . , so the free and easy use of a word, 'cosynage,' has produced a linguistic increment, the production of a new signification."[21] Yet thus is the paradox of Gerhard's argument: if Chaucer creates a new signification of *cosynage* by overusing it, would any of his original audience have been capable of hearing his pun? The quest to decode *cosyn* and *cosynage* results in a semantic enigma, the puzzling quandary of how to define a medieval word's slang meanings when these meanings may not have been clear even to its original audience.

Whereas the punning on *cosyn* generates some controversy, Chaucer's wordplay on *taille* and *taillynge* toward the conclusion of the *Shipman's Tale* exemplifies the deft use of an erotic pun but also its limitations. When the merchant's wife defends herself for spending the money initially borrowed by the monk, she explains how she plans to repay this debt: "For I wol paye yow wel and redily / Fro day to day, and if so be I faille, / I am youre wyf; score it upon my taille" (7.414-16). Less than twenty lines later, the Shipman concludes his story and plays on the verbal echo of his previous pun: "Thus endeth my tale, and God us sende / Taillynge ynough unto oure lyves ende" (7.433-34). Claude Jones documents the pun on *taille* and *taillynge*, with their primary denotations referring to a tally and tallying and their secondary denotations referring to the wife's vagina and sexual intercourse.[22] These punning meanings are generally accepted by Chaucerians, particularly because the sexual connotations of *tayl* appear elsewhere in the *Canterbury Tales*, such as when the Wife of Bath declares, "For al so siker [as surely] as cold engendreth hayl [hail], / A likerous [lascivious] mouth moste han a likerous tayl" (3.465-66). Male characters also refer to *tayls* when discussing sexual desire and the nether regions of their bodies, such as when the Reeve laments the unsated desires of elderly men: "For in oure wyl ther stiketh evere a nayl, / To have an hoor [white] heed and a grene tayl, / As hath a leek; for thogh oure myght be goon, / Oure wyl desireth folie evere in oon" (1.3877-80). The Reeve's Miller, Symkyn, farts in his sleep, necessitating a reference to his rear end: "This millere hath so wisely bibbed [imbibed] ale / That as an hors he fnorteth in his sleep, / Ne of his tayl bihynde he took no keep" (1.4162-64). Some critics have quibbled over whether such wordplay on *taille* and *taillynge* constitutes a pun instead of, in the words of Robert Caldwell, "a subtleness of innuendo that is artistically superior" to a mere pun,[23] but it is nonetheless clear that Chaucer ends the *Shipman's Tale* by stressing the double meaning inherent in these words, thus precisely uniting the tale's fabliau economic themes with its verbal humor—and then repeating it, lest anyone missed the joke the first time around.

With puns employed as a prevailing comic motif throughout the *Shipman's Tale*, their literary utility and limitations come into sharper focus. Rather than the subtle and sly humor of wordplay incorporated as grace notes to this story's focus on the economic and erotic business of marriage, the repetitions of *cosyn* and *cosynage* and *taille* and *taillynge* increasingly demand the reader's attention, as if the narrator stressed these words with an accompanying "wink, wink, nudge, nudge." Chaucer employs but does not quite trust the humor of his puns in the *Shipman's Tale*, undercutting his comedy through repetitions that demand more attention than warranted. And beyond the immediate realm of the *Shipman's Tale*, the issue of Chaucer's puns continues to attract defenders and detractors, those who argue that they are consonant with his literary genius and those who seek to burnish his image by downplaying his interest in them. On this issue Marsha L. Dutton advocates a moderating view: "Respect for great Chaucerians as well as common sense and self-protectiveness urges not only discretion in the recognition of puns, but also scholarly humility and an effort to avoid solecism. But to deny Chaucer his puns—to fail to be alert to them and to appreciate them when they appear—is to deny him his gift for one of the favorite games of classical and medieval rhetoricians: wordplay."[24] Chaucer did not shy away from a range of humorous styles and genres, from the fabliau shenanigans of the *Miller's Tale* to the parodic romance of the *Tale of Sir Thopas*, from the learned philosophical satire of the *Nun's Priest's Tale* to the farcical sex scene of *Troilus and Criseyde*. To envision an author so invested in humor yet averse to puns would seem an anomaly, and so the challenge of Chaucer's punning humor is not merely in locating them between the lexical shifts from Middle to Modern English, but in appreciating the paradox that the same artist created both the good and the bad, the gems and the groaners.

CHAPTER 16

The Forgiving Readers and Mitigated Antisemitism of the *Prioress's Tale*

A glaring example of Chaucer's outmoded perspectives, the *Prioress's Tale* can be deemed bad based on the simple moral tautology that virulently antisemitic works are bad, that any aesthetic effects that might be achieved are negated by the dehumanizing stereotypes that are simultaneously upheld. No one can overlook the antisemitism at the heart of the *Prioress's Tale*, yet some readers deny any imputation of prejudice to its author, Geoffrey Chaucer, and thus the *Prioress's Tale* serves as a striking example of a bad tale finding its defenders among otherwise eloquent and perceptive readers. As Heather Blurton and Hannah Johnson document, a number of critics have attempted to simultaneously praise Chaucer for the tale's literary merits while excusing him for the antisemitism at the heart of the *Prioress's Tale*, as they also note the limitations of such a recuperative project: "But we would suggest that asserting that the *Prioress's Tale* is the best example of its genre functions as a partial excuse of Chaucer's antisemitism without having to engage with it, and it functions as well to excuse the critic's embarrassment with the subject matter of the tale."[1] In this tale of murderous Jews executing a seven-year-old child for singing a hymn, the Prioress contrasts a grotesquely vicious stereotype of Jewish vice with an exaggeratedly innocent paragon of Christian virtue, uniting these bifurcated threads under the guise of an exemplary narrative that seeks to inspire devotion from the Christian faithful. Chaucer constructs a variety of narrative scaffolds to distance himself from the bigotry so central to his tale's meaning, and some readers avail themselves of these opportunities to excuse the author for his character's antisemitism. These forgiving readers illustrate the challenges of discussing any troubling elements of Chaucer's fictional works and biography, for the ironic frames of the *Canterbury Tales* create an interpretive loophole allowing the author to escape censure even when exculpatory evidence remains scanty. Excusing antisemitism as an incidental feature of an otherwise engrossing work, or by otherwise marginalizing its meaning and impact, some readers demonstrate the slippery-slope effect of extracting Chaucer from his fictions. By devising ingenious readings that mitigate the antisemitism of the *Prioress's Tale*, they reject the surface of the text for a preferred subtext that ironically highlights the need to focus even more intently on the antisemitic surface.

As with all bigotries and stereotypes, the antisemitism depicted in the *Prioress's Tale* can be contextualized without an accompanying attempt to excuse, mitigate, or minimize it. Five key dates succinctly summarize the history of Jews in medieval England.[2] In 1066, William I conquered England, with Jewish members of his court accompanying him. Thomas of Monmouth's *The Life and Passion of William of Norwich*, which depicts Jews conspiring to kill an innocent child, recounts obscure events of 1144 and is considered the first blood-libel story, a narrative tradition from which the *Prioress's Tale* descends.[3] On March 16, 1190, a minimum of 150 Jews died during the York massacre, and in 1290, Edward I expelled the Jews from England. In Jeffrey Jerome Cohen's words, this date marks the moment when "medieval Englishness became a national identity built around Jewish exclusion."[4] In 1659, Jews began returning to England in larger numbers following Menasseh ben Israel's political appeals to Oliver Cromwell.[5] Chaucer lived from roughly 150 years after the expulsion of Jews to roughly 260 years before they were allowed to return. This is not to suggest that Chaucer would never have encountered Jewish people, particularly during his European travels, which, as Marion Turner discusses, offered him the opportunity to "experience life . . . where different religions coexisted, often amicably, where accommodations were made to take into account different sets of cultural norms."[6] On the other hand, exposure to a diversity of peoples and cultures does not in itself erase stereotypes and biases, and so any argument that Chaucer would have been more enlightened than the average Englishman based on his potential encounters with Jews is perhaps more optimistic than reasoned.

Chaucer's richly satirical vision of a pampered, indolent, and flirty Prioress in the *General Prologue* stands as one of his most notable literary accomplishments, as he pays her lavish compliments that simultaneously reveal her stunted spirituality and corrupt values, as well as his utter naivete in his role as the narrative's autofictional avatar. All of her many flaws on display—coy smiling, mild swearing, nasal singing, food grabbing, and hound cosseting, among others—Chaucer phrases as virtues and thereby alerts discerning readers to her shallow understanding of her Christian faith. As much as the *General Prologue* revels in the ironies of a religious woman wholly uninterested in devotions of the spirit yet very much interested in pleasures of the flesh, the prologue of the *Prioress's Tale* invites readers to hear the voice of a woman who now sincerely pronounces her faith. "O Lord, oure Lord, thy name how merveillous" (7.453), she begins, as she then announces her key theme of the spiritual purity of children: "But by the mouth of children thy bountee / Parfourned is, for on the brest soukynge / Somtyme shewen they thyn heriynge [praise]" (7.457-59). The Prioress includes sentiments of Marian theology as well, praising Jesus's mother in a direct address—"O mooder Mayde, O mayde Mooder free!" (7.467)—that segues into a celebration of her generosity and virtue: "Lady, thy bountee, thy magnificence, / Thy vertu and thy grete humylitee / Ther may no tonge expresse in no science" (7.474-76). In this prologue's final stanza, the Prioress unites her theme of children's spiritual purity with her desire to tell an appropriate story, if Mary should grant this prayer: "But as a child of twelf month oold, or lesse, / That kan unnethes [hardly] any word expresse, / Right so fare I, and therfore I yow preye, / Gydeth my song that I shal of yow seye" (7.484-87). The Prioress's presentation of herself as a child contrasts sharply with her portrait in the *General Prologue*, particularly owing to its emphasis on her large stature ("For, hardily, she was nat undergrowe" [1.156]), yet on the whole, her prologue bears little trace of the satirical energies that previously defined her. Whereas most of the pilgrim's personalities depicted in the *General Prologue* match those depicted in their tales' prologues, the glaring discrepancies between these portraits of the Prioress emerge as particularly puzzling aspects of her character and her relationship to her tale, suggesting as well Chaucer's inattention to maintaining a consistent personality for her.

As the Prioress begins her story, it becomes clear that its minimal plot serves little purpose other than to contrast Christian virtue with Jewish vice. A widow's seven-year-old son devotedly learns the *O Alma redemptoris* (O Dear [Mother] of Our Savior), a hymn praising Mary, and sings it frequently. The Jews of the tale treat this song as an unforgivable affront and hire an assassin, who dispatches the boy and disposes of his body in a privy. The boy's mother worries over his absence, and in a miraculous turn of events, the dead child sings his hymn again, thus signaling to the Christian community the whereabouts of his body. By emphasizing the mother's concern for her missing child and her anguish over his dead body, the Prioress draws a tableau reminiscent of Mary's mourning over Jesus, as Nancy Bradley Warren proposes: "The suffering mother / martyred son dyad refigures Christ and Mary at the crucifixion, with the added parallel that each son's murder is effected by vilified Jews."[7] The Christians carry the murdered boy's body to an abbey, and the magistrate of the city orders the execution of the Jewish residents:

> With torment and with shameful deeth echon,
> This provost dooth thise Jewes for to sterve [die]
> That of this mordre wiste [knew], and that anon.
> He nolde [would not] no swich cursednesse observe.
> "Yvele shal have that yvele wol deserve";
> Therfore with wilde hors he dide hem drawe,
> And after that he heng hem by the lawe. (7.628-34)

The Prioress's Tale does not specify how many Jews are slaughtered to avenge this young boy's death, but it implies that this punishment is suffered by many, if not all of them. As Merrall Llewelyn Price notes, the tale shifts its attention "within a single thought" from "this cursed Jew" (7.570) to "thise Jewes" (7.573), which "suggest[s] that, as in the death of Christ, all Jews bear collective responsibility for the act."[8] Following this savage punishment, the tale returns to the young dead child, whose miraculous speech allows him to continue praising Mary until a curious grain—most likely a symbol of the Eucharist—is taken from his tongue.[9] After the abbot removes this grain, the child dies, and they bury this young martyr's body.

This ostensible tale of Christian virtue ends with a prayer to "yonge Hugh of Lyncoln," beseeching him: "Preye eek for us, we synful folk unstable, / That of his mercy God so merciable / On us his grete mercy multiplie, / For reverence of his mooder Marie. Amen" (7.684, 687-90). Hugh of Lincoln and William of Norwich served as archetypes of the pious Christian child purportedly murdered by Jews during clandestine anti-Christian rituals, and so the Prioress connects her tale to a wider narrative tradition of vilifying Jews. Accounts of ritual murder, in which Jews sacrifice a young child to mock Jesus's crucifixion or for other arcane purposes, differ slightly in their plot from the vengeful murder of a singing Christian child depicted in the Prioress's Tale, but the overarching themes—the evil and nefariousness of Jews—unite them.

Beyond this antisemitic plot, the Prioress's characterizations of Jews construe them as one-dimensional villains. Her opening lines establish her tale's setting in a Jewish ghetto of Asia, which as Sylvia Tomasch posits, signifies "a polluted Asia—polluted through Jewish presence and actions," with this setting "implicitly contrasted with a purified England, whose sanitized state is founded on the displacement of the Jews."[10] The Prioress disparages Jews for "foule usure and lucre of vileynye" (7.491), and it should be noted that this reference to usury represents Chaucer's innovation to antisemitic narrative traditions. As Kathy Lavezzo argues, "Chaucer's stress on usury becomes all the more striking when we consider that none of the forty miracle tales identified by scholars as analogues mentions moneylending, let alone foregrounds it."[11] The Prioress condemns Jews as "Hateful to Crist and to his compaignye" (7.492); she asserts that "the serpent Sathanas / . . . hath in Jues herte his waspes nest" (7.558-59); and she repeatedly denigrates Jews as "cursed" (7.570, 574, 599, 685). More so, Jews are depicted as lying to the widow when they falsely deny knowledge of her son's location. The stock antagonists of this antisemitic tale, Jews personify a vicious, child-murdering Other who must be eradicated to preserve the sanctity of this city's Christian citizens. In a powerful reading of the tale's construction of its Jewish characters as the Others to Christianity, Geraldine Heng espies the formulation of a racialized discourse distinguishing Jews and Christians: "Christians are bound by their inheritance of Christian blood; Jews are bound by shedding that Christian blood. The two populations—one a blood-race, the other an infernal race—are *embodied* races."[12]

Following the prayerful "Amen" that concludes the *Prioress's Tale*, the Canterbury pilgrims react reverently, and their solemnity undercuts efforts to divorce the tale's antisemitism from Chaucer's authorial presentation of it. In his joint roles as the narrator of and a character in the *Canterbury Tales*, Chaucer stresses their silent introspection over its spiritual meaning rather than their horror at its bigoted sentiment: "Whan seyd was al this miracle, every man / As sobre was that wonder was to se" (7.691-92). Florence Ridley, documenting the numerous analogues of Chaucer's tale and the accompanying legends of Hugh of Lincoln and William of Norwich, proposes the relative banality of the tale's prejudicial views in fourteenth-century England: "The average Englishman would not have looked askance at [the Prioress's] views, much less have attacked them; in all probability, he would have shared them completely."[13] Chaucer includes himself among this company—"every man"—and so it is unclear why readers would ignore his complicity in antisemitic discourse. Some readers posit that the pilgrims' muted response suggests their discomfort with the Prioress's antisemitic tale, yet most of the connotations and denotations of *sobre* in the *Middle English Dictionary* reflect its meaning as "moderate in one's desires or actions, temperate, restrained; also of spiritual love: characterized by moderation," with ancillary meanings as "prudent, reasonable, sober-minded" and "appropriately solemn, serious, . . . of demeanor, speaking, words, etc.: grave, earnest."[14] Within this context, it is unclear why *sobre* would denote the pilgrims' unease with the Prioress's sentiments rather than their prayerful meditation over them, particularly as Chaucer characterizes their joint response as a "wonder," which would suggest the miracle depicted in her tale has inspired a nearly miraculous response. With Chaucer stripping the *Prioress's Prologue* of the satiric energies of her *General Prologue* portrait, building a tale from antisemitic narrative foundations, vilifying Jews throughout the tale as "cursed," foregrounding Jewish usury in the tale's opening lines in contrast to its sources, and depicting the reverent reaction of the Canterbury pilgrims following its conclusion (rather than, for instance, allowing pilgrims to interact with the Prioress and thus to escalate the comic conflicts seen in so many prologues of the *Canterbury Tales*), little evidence suggests that the Prioress's antisemitism registers as wholly separate from the author's own. To make these points requires the necessary acknowledgment that they must be construed as textual interpretations and could never be construed as proof, yet it concomitantly raises the issue of why some readers would work so diligently to disprove imputations of Chaucer's antisemitism despite the sentiments of this tale.

The reception history of the *Prioress's Tale* documents the ways in which a number of critics have attempted to separate the author from his Prioress's antisemitism, as a brief overview of responses demonstrates. Lawrence Besserman distinguishes between "hard" and "soft" readings of the tale and its author's intentions:

Indeed, most essays on the Prioress and her tale can roughly be classified according to their handling of the *Tale*'s treatment of the Jews, as either "hard" or "soft." In "hard" readings, the idea that Chaucer intended any satire on the antisemitism of the tale is rejected because, it is argued, antisemitism was accepted as a given of the culture in which Chaucer lived, and it was therefore something which Chaucer as a man of his culture would have accepted without question. In "soft" readings, on the other hand, critics argue that Chaucer intended to satirize the bloody-minded antisemitism of the tale (and often they also argue that Chaucer thereby intended to satirize the Prioress who tells it).[15]

"Hard" readings of the *Canterbury Tales* confront the troubling ethical implications inherent in a literary genius expressing antisemitic sentiments and tackle the oversights of "soft" readings. For example, although some "soft" readers focus their interpretations on the tale's miraculous depiction of Mary's intervention rather than on its execution of the Jews, Louise Fradenburg forcefully rejects this perspective: "To say, then, that the 'real center' of the *Prioress's Tale* is the miracle of the Virgin and not the destruction of the Jews is scarcely effective in convincing me that the *Prioress's Tale* is not a text of torture."[16]

Many "soft" interpretations either highlight the culpability of the Prioress rather than Chaucer for the tale's antisemitic themes or downplay the text's representation of Jews. For example, E. T. Donaldson displaces the tale's antisemitism entirely onto the Prioress: "Chaucer . . . made the *Prioress's Tale* in some ways as pretty as her own brooch, but it is the failure of her character, not his, which makes the poem so imperfect an expression of the motto *Amor Vincit Omnia*."[17] Unfortunately, intelligent men and great poets are not immune to prejudice, as any number of intelligent men and great poets evince. Sherman Hawkins views the tale's Jews as stock villains, arguing that "the Jews, then, are not the only 'enemy,' but they are typical of all whose wisdom is without faith, who in the name of truth attack the truth they cannot comprehend."[18] Hardy Long Frank chides readers for focusing on the tale's dark subject matter, urging them instead to focus on the Christian mother's love for her lost son: "The *Prioress's Tale*, then, should be notable, not for its incidental anti-Semitism, but for the warm maternity of its heroine and of its teller."[19] To this claim it must be rebutted that antisemitism, and virtually all such bigotries and prejudices, can rarely be excused as "incidental" to those who endure their pernicious consequences. Sounding a similar note, John Archer discerns the tale's greater interest in its Marian themes than its antisemitic ones: "The legend of the little clergeoun stresses the glorification of the Virgin Mary at the expense of the sensational anti-Semitism of many of its sources and analogues."[20] Lee Patterson views Chaucer virtually as undertaking a scientific experiment with the tale. "What the *Prioress's Tale* represents is one of Chaucer's characteristically disinterested explorations of the unpredictable interaction of history and psychology," he avers, although one can only presume this medieval author's disinterested stance on such matters, in contrast to his heartfelt zeal.[21] Michael Calabrese, arguing that "poetry cannot be reduced to social history," claims that "Chaucer says nothing about the Jews in the *Prioress's Tale*. Unlike a chronicle, papal bull, sermon, or scholastic dialogue, the tale contains no information."[22] Chaucer's Jews are fictional creations, of course, but Calabrese's position would deny the impact of rhetoric and fiction in their entirety, which all too often bear real-life consequences. Many such "soft" readings of the *Prioress's Tale* explore with nuance and care its complex staging of Marian devotion and Christian faith, but virtually by necessity such an approach requires mitigating the centrality of its Jewish antagonists and the ugly caricature of their "cursed" nature.

But for Chaucer's "soft" defenders who attempt to dismiss or diminish his culpability for the antisemitism of the *Prioress's Tale*, it is not so easy to overwrite the antisemitism of the Parson. Described in glowing terms (and with little indication of typical Chaucerian irony) in the *General Prologue* as "A bettre preest I trowe that nowher noon ys" (1.524), the Parson stands as a moral paragon among the dissolute members of the pilgrimage, yet his antisemitic discourse echoes the Prioress's when he condemns swearing sinners: "For certes, it semeth that ye thynke that the cursede Jewes ne dismembred nat ynough the preciouse persone of Crist, but ye dismembre hym moore . . . Thanne semeth it that men that sweren so horribly by his blessed name, that they despise it moore booldely than dide the cursede Jewes or elles the devel, that trembleth whan he heereth his name" (10.591, 599). Furthermore, the Parson blames Jesus's crucifixion on the Jews (10.662, 888). The *Pardoner's Tale* condemns the rioters' cursing as painful to Jesus, proposing that these young men "thoughte that Jewes rente hym noght ynough" (6.475), and the *Monk's Tale* includes the story of King Antiochus, who is characterized by his antisemitism: "Unto the Jewes swich an hate hadde he" (7.2593). Whether espoused by the venal Prioress, the holy Parson, the corrupt Pardoner, or the secularly minded Monk, Chaucer's characters unite in their steady, often vehement, denouncement of Jews—and thus reveal their shared antisemitism. Many of the "soft" readers of the *Prioress's Tale* overlook the relevance of the *Parson's Tale* and other antisemitic references in the *Canterbury Tales* to their argument or simply minimize them. For instance, Stephen Spector states that "the Parson's references to Jews are merely incidental,"[23] yet members of minority and marginalized communities would seldom agree that such "incidental" dehumanizing references lessen the sting of stereotyping.

Chaucer was a man of his time and place, and his time and place were antisemitic ones, and we have not yet progressed to a state where antisemitism is simply a memory of the bad old days. Looking squarely at the antisemitism of the *Prioress's Tale* illustrates the ways in which some readers often wish to ignore that which the text states boldly on its surface. As Albert Friedman succinctly observes, "In my opinion the whole critical enterprise directed toward explaining away Chaucer's bigotry is misconceived and unnecessary."[24] We need not throw Chaucer out as a relic of a barbaric and unenlightened past, nor should we turn a blind eye to the ways in which his works contribute to antisemitic discourses of yesteryear that refuse to die the death they so richly deserve. Peering through the frames of author, narrator, tale-teller, and story allows readers to disengage Chaucer from the antisemitism at the heart of the *Prioress's Tale*, but this can result in a myopic view, one that excuses readers from the hard work of looking at the contradiction of a literary genius endorsing horrific sentiments in a tale from whose badness one cannot look away. More so, the *Prioress's Tale* lures some readers into ill-framed and exculpatory interpretations, thus demonstrating the necessity of directly looking at the badness of great authors in order not to allow their prejudices to metastasize in the present. Chaucer lived in the 1300s, and to a degree his personal regressive views can be cordoned off to this era, but not if today's readers continue to seek ingenious ways to exonerate him from his prejudices and thus to mitigate the horrors of his antisemitism and other outmoded perspectives.

CHAPTER 17

The Singsong Meter and Aural Agonies of the *Tale of Sir Thopas*

Chaucer's *Tale of Sir Thopas* stands as one of the greatest parodies of the English literary tradition—a virtually paradoxical accomplishment, for parodies are only rarely recognized as masterpieces owing to the greater respect paid to their source texts.[1] In this sharply funny, quickly paced, and dead-eyed satire, the doughty Sir Thopas quests for adventure and the love of an elf-queen, only to flee when threatened by the giant Olifaunt. After proving himself a coward, the indefatigable Thopas prepares to ride out again, with his story coming to a premature conclusion before readers learn whether he redeems himself in subsequent battle. Like Chaucer's *Squire's Tale* before it, the *Tale of Sir Thopas* parodies the romance tradition, as their narrators, whose rhetorical skills cannot match their aspirations, debase its elevated and courtly elements. Also like the *Squire's Tale*, the *Tale of Sir Thopas* is simply so bad that it becomes good, so erring in its deployment of romance conventions that it becomes unerringly amusing. "The tale is funny because it is so ineffably, exquisitely bad," comments Derek Pearsall. "It would be worth reading all the popular Middle English romances for no other reason than to savour the more its delicious absurdity."[2] Despite the many similarities between these tales, a key distinction emerges in their poetic meter: the Squire tells his tale in metrically precise heroic couplets, whereas Chaucer tells *Sir Thopas* in the verse form of tail-rhyme. With this finely drawn parody both upheld and undone by its meter, Chaucer tests the limits of bad writing in *Tale of Sir Thopas* and locates them in the singsong, jingle-jangle rhythms of a tale engrossing to read but vocally torturous to hear. That it is to say, reading the *Tale of Sir Thopas* silently allows one to enjoy the humorous pleasures of a purposefully bad story, but reading it aloud confronts one with the insufferable affront of poetry designed to aurally agonize.

By definition, parodies represent derivative art forms, in that they lampoon the styles and structures of particular cultural artifacts with the purpose of rendering masterpieces into absurdity. As J. A. Cuddon defines the term, parodies require the "imitative use of the words, style, attitude, tone and ideas of an author in such a way as to make them ridiculous. This is usually achieved by exaggerating certain traits, using more or less the same technique as the cartoon caricaturist."[3] While parodies are often denigrated as inherently inferior to the works on which they are based, Dwight McDonald regards such reformulations as an intellectually astute practice and virtually a critical art, characterizing them as "an intuitive kind of literary criticism, shorthand for what 'serious' critics must write out at length. It is Method acting, since a successful parodist must live himself, imaginatively, into his parodee. It is jujitsu, using the impetus of the opponent to defeat him, although 'opponent' and 'defeat' are hardly the words." Some authors of parodies might indeed express their disdain by ridiculing what they find ridiculous, but McDonald counters this view-point, proposing instead that "most parodies are written out of admiration rather than contempt. It is hard to make the mimetic effort unless one has enough sympathy to 'identify' with the parodee."[4] Scholars argue over the foundations of parody, yet regardless of whether Chaucer's early readers dubbed the tale as such, it is clear that they enjoyed its humor. The early scribes of the *Tale of Sir Thopas*, including those of the Ellesmere and Hengwrt manuscripts, appreciated its vibrant comedy and attempted to capture its playful form in their layouts, as Jessica Brantley observes: "The physical form of *Sir Thopas*—like so many other things about the poem—is a joke. . . . Breaking from the more familiar couplets or stanzas in single columns of text, the new layout calls attention to the literary structures of tail-rhyme through an unusual spacing of verses and an elaborate system of brackets."[5]

We need not definitively pinpoint Chaucer's attitude toward romance either as admiration or as contempt to assess the brilliance of his humor: in comically debasing the tropes of chivalric romance, he creates his own literary masterpiece. It is nonetheless worth noting Chaucer's apparent distaste for romance as documented throughout his corpus and as particularly evident in his allusions to Lancelot. In the *Squire's Tale* the narrator asks a rhetorical question about the court's festivities and posits dismissively of the only man who could answer, "No man but Launcelot, and he is deed" (5.287). The narrator of the *Nun's Priest's Tale* ironically comments on his story's veracity by referring to Lancelot with similar irony: "This storie is also trewe, I undertake, / As is the book of Launcelot de Lake, /

That wommen holde in ful greet reverence" (7.3211-13). Beyond his dis-
missive references to Lancelot, in the *Tale of Sir Thopas* Chaucer as author
and as narrator catalogs additional heroes of romances, establishing them
as a knightly standard to which Thopas is compared:

> Men speken of romances of prys [value, excellence],
> Of Horn child and of Ypotys,
>   Of Beves and sir Gy,
> Of sir Lybeux and Pleyndamour—
> But sir Thopas, he bereth the flour
>   Of roial chivalry! (7.897-902)

Unfortunately for Bevis of Hampton, Guy of Warwick, Lybaeaus Desco-
nus, and the others, this comparison to Sir Thopas undercuts rather
than enhances their chivalric reputations. The subsequent reference to
Percival—"Hymself drank water of the well, / As dide the knyght sire Per-
cyvell" (7.915-16)—likewise does little to enhance the portrait of Thopas's
puissance, for drinking water from a well hardly indicates one's knightly
fortitude. In his other narratives indebted to the romance tradition, includ-
ing the *Knight's Tale*, the *Man of Law's Tale*, and *Troilus and Criseyde*, Chau-
cer interweaves a panoply of other narrative traditions to elevate what he
apparently perceived as a somewhat debased genre.

Chaucer notably synthesizes a surface parody of romance plotlines
with an aural parody of poetic recital. On its surface level of parody, the
Tale of Sir Thopas begins, as did the *Squire's Tale*, with an apology, as Chau-
cer declares himself ill-equipped to participate in the tale-telling contest:
"For oother tale certes kan [know] I noon [not one], / But of a rym I lerned
longe agoon" (7.708-9). After displacing blame to his unnamed source,
Chaucer commences the parodic pleasures of the *Tale of Sir Thopas* with
the opening depiction of its eponymous protagonist. The poem's third
stanza describes the hero in a mock blazon, cataloging his attractiveness
with flourishes more associated with the female beloveds of romance than
with their suitors:

> Sire Thopas wax a doghty swayn;
> Whit was his face as payndemayn [white bread]
>   His lippes rede as rose;
> His rode [complexion] is lyk scarlet in grayn,
> And I yow telle in good certayn
>   He hadde a semely nose. (7.724-29)

Lauding his fair skin, red lips, and pleasing nose, this description simultaneously lionizes and effeminizes Thopas. The many women who might desire this specimen of effete masculinity face disappointment, for the narrator also records his erotic abstemiousness: "But he was chaast and no lechour" (7.745). When Thopas commences his adventuring, the narrator announces with great reverence the awaiting dangers—"He priketh thurgh a fair forest, / Therinne is many a wilde best [beast], / Ye, bothe bukke and hare" (7.754-56)—despite the unlikeliness of a deer or bunny proving itself a formidable foe. After pledging his love to a fair elf-queen and grandiosely declaring all mortal women beneath him ("For in this world no womman is / Worthy to be my make [mate]" [7.791-92]), Thopas encounters the fearful giant Olifaunt, but he promptly flees when his enemy fires at him with his slingshot: "Sire Thopas drow abak ful faste; / This geant at hym stones caste / Out of a fel [wicked, terrible] staf-slynge [slingshot]. / But faire escapeth child Thopas" (7.827-30).

The parody continues its humorously debasing depiction of Thopas and his misadventures. Apparently oblivious to the shame he should feel for bolting from his foe, Thopas opens the poem's second fit by ordering his minstrels "to tellen tales / . . . / Of romances that been roiales" (7.846-48), although it is difficult to imagine these minstrels composing melodies that resolve the tension between his self-perception and his actions. The following stanzas detail Thopas's opulent clothes and armor, stressing their luxury rather than their utility. He wears fine linen—"cloth of lake [linen] fyn and cleere" (7.858)—and his armor appears unscratched by former battles, with the narrator describing his coat of arms as "whit as is a lilye flour" (7.867), which contrasts sharply with the depiction of the Knight's battle-hardened armor in the *General Prologue*: "Of fustian [wool cloth] he wered a gypon [tunic] / Al bismotered [bespattered, soiled] with his habergeon" (1.75-76). Subsequent lines detail Thopas's golden and begemmed shield, his leather greaves, his ivory sheath and saddle, and his cypress spear. The narrator ends the second fit by speaking directly to his audience: "Loo, lordes myne, heere is a fit! / If ye wol any moore of it, / To telle it wol I fonde [attempt]" (7.888-90). But these words are nonsensical, as they first state the obvious fact that that the narrator has completed this part of his tale, and so the narrator cannot now offer "moore of it," for it has ended.

As previously mentioned, the poem's third fit compares this mock hero to other great knights of medieval romance, and as J. A. Burrow notes, the fits of the *Tale of Sir Thopas* shorten in length, from eighteen stanzas in the first to nine in the second, and then to a mere four-and-a-half in the third. Burrow praises this canny structure as a notable aspect of Chaucer's "superior joke" in the tale.[6] The *Tale of Sir Thopas* ends abruptly in this foreshortened third fit in another key similarity to the *Squire's Tale*: as the Franklin interrupted and ended the Squire's story, Harry Bailly interrupts and ends Chaucer's first contribution to the tale-telling game. Rudely expressing his exasperation, the Host cries, "Namoore of this, for Goddes dignitee" (7.919), explaining further his distaste for Chaucer's rhymes: "Now swich a rym the devel I biteche [commit]! / This may wel be rym doggerel" (7.924-25). In an apt assessment of what precisely he means by "rym doggerel," Harry assesses Chaucer's efforts in his tale: "Thy drasty rymyng is nat worth a toord!" (7.930). Harry's words make evident Chaucer's interest not merely in the content of the *Tale of Sir Thopas* but in its verbal performance as well, as Seth Lerer theorizes: "Chaucer's *Tale of Sir Thopas* is the supreme moment in the *Canterbury Tales* that actively engages the phenomenon of voice. More than any other tale it is about its speaker, not just in that its performance augments our appreciation of the Chaucerian persona, but in that its performance is the subject of its telling."[7] The stunning awfulness of this vocal performance elevates Chaucer's parody beyond the humor of its absurd plot to the parodies of poetic form as well.

With Harry Bailly denouncing the *Tale of Sir Thopas* as "rym doggerel," it is clear that Chaucer's fellow pilgrims do not appreciate his contribution to the tale-telling contest, yet it remains somewhat unclear what Harry intends by this term. The *Oxford English Dictionary* defines doggerel as "of verse: comic, burlesque, and usually composed in irregular rhythm. Also: (of verse or writing) badly composed or expressed; trivial."[8] Because these lines of Chaucer's *Canterbury Tales* stand as the initial source cited for this definition, ambiguity arises over which aspect of the *Tale of Sir Thopas* Harry finds most offensive: does he see it as a "badly composed" and "trivial" tale, or does he find its "irregular rhythm" annoying, or does he refer to these various points simultaneously? It seems likely that Harry Bailly denounces the poem on multiple levels, for he attacks its trivial and trifling take on the romance tradition (its "verray lewednesse" [7.921]); also, although the metrical structure of *Tale of Sir Thopas*, a tail-rhyme romance, is mostly uniform, he claims that his "eres aken of thy drasty speche" (7.923) and prohibits Chaucer from further rhyming: "Sire, at o word, thou shalt no lenger ryme" (7.932).

Tail-rhyme romances, while comprising a variety of forms, typically consist of six-line stanzas with a rhyming pattern of *aabaab* or *aabccb*, and the *Tale of Sir Thopas* employs both of these schemas. The *b* lines of a tail-rhyme romance often run shorter than the *a* and *c* lines, with *Sir Thopas's* *b* lines in hexameter and its *a* and *c* lines in octometer. As Judith Tschann explains, "Tail-rhyme stanzas ironically suit very well the incompetent author of this tale, since this is the verse form of many incompetent conventional romances (though of course what we get is not a conventional romance but a delightful parody)."[9] Indeed, Chaucer establishes a sharp contrast between his *Prologue to Sir Thopas* and his *Tale of Sir Thopas* by composing the former in rhyme-royal stanzas and the latter in tail-rhyme stanzas. Rhyme-royal stanzas consist of seven lines featuring a rhyme pattern of *ababbcc*, and this verse form, as its name implies, has traditionally been associated with royalty. As Marianne Børch states of this switch in poetic form: "The greater is the surprise when his own representative 'Chaucer the Pilgrim' responds to the call for a tale by offering up an oral romance, and in this case not just one of those written-stories-told which constitute the rest of the *Canterbury Tales*, but one which avails itself of a rhetoric indisputably intended for oral composition and whose form is that of the above-mentioned English tail rhyme oral-style romances preserved in manuscript."[10] Building on such observations, Martin Stevens notes the "blasphemous" humor of Chaucer as author employing rhyme-royal verse, often reserved for addressing sovereigns, for his fictional creation Harry Bailly to address his fictional version of himself.[11] The auditory discrepancy between rhyme-royal and tail-rhyme sharpens the parodic thrust of the *Tale of Sir Thopas*, with the devolution in rhyme scheme signaling the poetic travesties being unleashed.

When deftly employed, meter encourages certain readings and discourages others, and inelegantly composed tale-rhymes can result in a particularly grating and clip-clopping rhythm. In his interpretation of the poem's opening stanzas, Alan Gaylord asks readers to hear Chaucer's words and ponder their singsong effect:

> Listeth, lordes, in good entent,
> And I wol telle verrayment [truth]
> Of myrthe and of solas,
> Al of a knyght was fair and gent
> In bataille and in tourneyment;
> His name was sire Thopas. (7.712–17)

As Gaylord perceptively posits, "The overriding impression one gains from this first stanza is of a Maker who has suddenly regressed into nursery rhyme; the *underriding* effect, so to speak, is a comic monotony of metrical pace."[12] Indeed, one can almost hear the narrator's breathlessness, as he rushes headlong into a tale over which he apparently wields little control. Summarizing his viewpoint with words particularly apt for this volume, Gaylord concludes: "No bad poet could achieve this kind of bad poetry."[13] It is a striking irony that it requires nearly the same technical skill and imaginary artistry to create a parody as its source, and so Chaucer's brilliance as an author is surprisingly apparent in this poetry rendered nigh unreadable by its meter—or at least, unreadable aloud. Moreover, if reading this single stanza even broaches the possibility that auditors might find its vocal performance grating, extending this disharmony for over thirty more stanzas multiplies its discordancy.

Whereas most of *Thopas*'s stanzas feature its *b* lines in hexameter, this pattern is occasionally broken, leading to more metrical mishaps. In the stanza in which Thopas pledges his love to an elf-queen and rudely dismisses all mortal women from consideration, Chaucer virtually forces readers to trip over his meter:

> An elf-queene wol I love, ywis,
> For in this world no womman is
>   Worthy to be my make [mate]
>   In towne;
> Alle othere wommen I forsake,
> And to an elf-queene I me take
>   By dale and eek by downe! (7.790–96)

The rhythm proceeds as expected until the unexpectedly clunky "In towne" upends the poem's metrical patterns. This seven-line stanza expands the rhyme scheme into *aabcbbc*, which thus extends the space between the *c* rhymes. Great poets often create stunning effects by varying their meter, but for purposes of mellifluousness and flow, not cacophony and disjunction. In the remainder of the poem some stanzas adhere to the standard forms of tail-rhyme, while others diverge from it with similar off-rhythm results, but with little discernible purpose other than to jog readers off their verbal paths. John Matthews Manly notes these abrupt shifts in stanzaic form and concludes: "It can hardly have been Chaucer's object merely to exhibit his versatility in stanza-forms; for, in that case he has been singularly unskillful. In the first place, the variety is, after all, not very great; in the second place, the variations are not introduced climatically, but rather without any discernible principle of arrangement."[14]

Beyond its singsong rhythm and other metrical infelicities, the *Tale of Sir Thopas* is also plagued by infelicitous rhymes. Medieval English poets often struggled with the comparatively limited rhymes available in their native tongue, for in comparison to an inflected Romance language like French, English offers notably fewer of them. As Marie Boroff notes, such circumstances resulted in overused rhymes that deadened the originality of a poetic work: "In Middle English verse, the traditional words, when used again and again in the same way and for the same purpose, seem dragged in 'for the sake of the rhyme'; repetition becomes tiresome, and simplicity seems merely flatfooted."[15] Certainly, this unwelcome effect is apparent in the *Tale of Sir Thopas*, such as in the clichéd rhyme of *mynstrales* and *tales*, a pairing that features a fortuitous semantic link between performers and their performances that Chaucer overemployed. The *Tale of Sir Thopas* features the couplet in this manner—"'Do come,' he seyde, 'my mynstrales, / And gestiours for to tellen tales'" (7.845-46)—in a formulation virtually identical to a couplet in *House of Fame*: "Of alle maner of mynstralles / And gestiours that tellen tales" (1197-98). Homophonic pairs similarly result in fatigued rhymes that auditors would likely have heard before, such as when the narrator tells of Thopas's homeland—"Yborn he was in fer contree, / In Flaundres, al biyonde the see" (7.718-19)—as compared to a similar rhyme in the *Knight's Tale*: "For everemo, as out of that contree, / Ne nevere mo ne shal his lady see" (1.1345-46). Whether used as the noun *sea* or the verb *to see*, such repetitive rhymes threaten to undercut the pleasure that oral performances otherwise provide. Chaucer also rhymes on homophones when Thopas confronts Olifaunt—"The child seyde, 'Also moote I thee [as I may prosper], / Tomorwe wol I meete with thee" (7.817-18)—which prompts the ontological question of whether the same sound repeated constitutes an actual rhyme.

While one can hardly fault Chaucer for the purposefully "drasty speche" (6.923) of the *Tale of Sir Thopas*, it is to be regretted that such horrible meter prematurely cuts short this delightfully funny tale. With Harry Bailing prematurely ending the tale for quite justifiable reasons, he proves himself an apt critic of poetic rhythm if an unnecessarily surly curtailer of parodic play. For despite these issues, the *Tale of Sir Thopas* stands as a parodic treasure. In Richard Hurd's famed formulation, it is "all *Don Quixote* in little," with these two masterpieces differing only in scope, "as

a sketch in miniature from a finished and full-sized picture."[16] C. David
Benson lauds this tale as "art at its nimblest,"[17] and Lindsey Jones praises
it as "the most beautifully constructed example of *diminution* in the Chau-
cer canon."[18] Reading Chaucer's *Tale of Sir Thopas* silently to oneself is one
of the greatest literary pleasures imaginable, but reading its interminable
singsong meter aloud results in one of the greatest auditory agonies imag-
inable, with Chaucer's talents for parody balanced precariously between
the two.

CHAPTER 18

The Immoral Allegory and Boring
Maxims of the *Tale of Melibee*

It might as well be candidly admitted: many, if not most, readers of Chau-
cer's *Tale of Melibee* find it mind-numbingly boring. For the most part, its
critical reception has not been kind. C. David Benson labels it "a sound, if
somewhat dull work of moral instruction, sincere if somewhat outdated,"[1]
and in his masterful overview of this topic, in an essay tauntingly titled
"Has Anyone Here Read Melibee?," Edward Foster memorably compares
it to "a lump in [one's] oatmeal."[2] In this allegory, the house and fam-
ily of Chaucer's eponymous character are assaulted by his enemies, and
while his initial impulse is to seek vengeance, his patient wife, Prudence,
urges mercy over further violence. After over nine hundred long lines of
her patient explication, Melibee realizes the wisdom of Prudence's advice
and forgives them. Beyond the tediousness of Melibee's moral lesson, this
story of reconciliation trips over an allegorical fault line: Why should
Melibee reunite with enemies representing the evils of the world, thus
crippling one of the story's key themes of reconciliation? More so, Chau-
cer builds his discourse by stringing together an astonishing number of
axioms, aphorisms, maxims, and quotations, in an impressive display of
learning that results in an underwhelming tale. (One could scaffold a plot
around *Bartlett's Familiar Quotations* if one chose, but it would not likely
result in a coherent and unified narrative.) Tendentious and seemingly
interminable, moralizing and meandering, the *Tale of Melibee* plods to a
predestined conclusion, losing readers, allegorical coherency, and thematic
consistency along the way. Chaucer variously refers to his *Tale of Melibee*
as a "a litel thyng in prose" (7.937), "a moral tale vertuous" (7.940), and a
"murye tale" (7.964); on the contrary, it is long, not little; its moral themes
are more dubious than virtuous; and its merriment is nowhere to be found.

As commonly understood, allegories operate simultaneously on their
surface and subtextual levels: the text remains the same, but astute readers

understand that the story's surface signification carries deeper meanings than initially apparent. Perusing such famous medieval allegories as Guillaume de Lorris and Jean de Meun's *Roman de la Rose*, Dante's *Divine Comedy*, William Langland's *Piers Plowman*, and Christine de Pizan's *Book of the City of Ladies*, readers understand that the narrative journey represents a spiritual journey, that the characters frequently function more symbolically than realistically. Medieval Christians were attuned to the practice of decoding allegories, particularly owing to the interpretive practice of typology, which posits the necessity of viewing the people and events of the Christian Old Testament as precursors of those depicted in the New Testament. With the foundations of their faith built in typology, medieval Christians would recognize the likelihood of a narrative structure encouraging dual readings. Despite the prevalence of such interpretations, readers of allegories must perpetually ask whether they are interpreting the text's multiple levels correctly. As Jeremy Tambling muses, "Choosing to read something allegorically begs the question of the legitimacy of that interpretation. What governs it and gives it weight, stops it from going into free fall, from becoming interpretation that corresponds simply to the whim of the interpreter?"[3] In leaving the text's surface signification in favor of its subtextual meanings, readers must strive to build interpretations that respect textual multiplicity while not devolving into simple speculation.

Allegorical literature enjoyed widespread popularity throughout the later Middle Ages, and the social context of the *Tale of Melibee* suggests a wide range of audiences for its didactic message of patience, forgiveness, and reconciliation. One likely audience member stands out in particular: King Richard II. Richard Firth Green posits that "it is entirely credible that Chaucer should have undertaken to translate *Melibee* for the youthful Richard II," in which the author positioned himself as "adviser to kings" who advocates patience and mercy to his ruler.[4] Lynn Staley similarly notes the tale's potential courtly audience, in that it could invite the king to consider his relationship to his subjects and others: "Chaucer . . . analyze[s] a situation that only a king could remedy by creating and maintaining a hierarchical yet harmonious relationships with his subjects. As the tale implies, Richard can only accomplish such a task if he is willing to see himself as bound by and to others—hence the importance of counsel—and as needing to maintain himself as a rational, objective leader of the whole body politic."[5] Carolynn Collette places the *Tale of Melibee* within the context of contemporary works "intended to instruct women of the nobility and the aristocracy in how to govern themselves, their households, and their husbands."[6] In these and other such nuanced readings of the tale and its cultural context, a tacit assumption emerges: that the story will be interpreted correctly, or at least sympathetically, rather than dismissed for its allegorical inconsistencies and mixed thematic messages.

The *Tale of Melibee* begins, as most allegories do, on the surface level of its signification. In its opening lines, readers are introduced to Melibee's family: "A yong man called Melibeus, myghty and riche, bigat upon his wyf, that called was Prudence, a doghter which that called was Sophie" (7.967). Featuring a wife named Prudence and a daughter named Sophie (who thus represents Wisdom), the story's allegorical cast is clearly communicated to readers. As Benson notes, "The opening lines seem deliberately designed to establish its undramatic, flatly allegorical approach."[7] One of the great pleasures of allegories arises in the challenge offered to readers in decoding the shifts between the surface and subtextual levels of meaning, with the *Tale of Melibee* both offering yet constraining this practice. At several points the allegorical subtext is clearly outlined to readers, such as when Prudence divulges to Melibee the allegorical nature of his name: "Thy name is Melibee; this is to seyn, 'a man that drynketh hony.' / Thou hast ydronke so muchel hony of sweete temporeel richesses, and delices and honours of this world, / that thou art dronken and hast forgeten Jhesu Crist thy creatour" (7.1409-11). An allegory that includes its own answer key, the *Tale of Melibee* at times refuses to challenge readers with the pleasures of interpretation, instead explaining thematic connections between text and subtext that readers would likely enjoy discovering by themselves.

The tale's plot advances to an early crisis when Melibee's enemies assault Prudence and Sophie:

> Upon a day bifel that he for his desport [recreation] is went into the feeldes hym to pleye. / His wyf and eek his doghter hath he left inwith his hous, of which the dores weren faste yshette. / Thre of his olde foes han it espyed, and setten laddres to the walles of his hous, and by wyndowes been entred, / and betten his wyf, and wounded his doghter with fyve mortal woundes in fyve sondry places,— / this is to seyn, in hir feet, in hire handes, in hir erys, in hir nose, and in hire mouth—and leften hire for deed, and wenten awey. (7.968-72)

Paul Strohm elaborates on this scene's allegorical level as encapsulating "a drama of the psyche," in which "Melibee's house is his body, . . . its windows are the five senses which have succumbed to external temptations, . . . his daughter . . . is his soul, [and] Prudence is his own best judgment."[8] In this view, Melibee's family represents Melibee himself, and so the dialogue that readers hear between husband and wife represents on a secondary level the inner dialogue that Melibee should be engaging in with himself. In the ensuing lines of dialogue that comprise the bulk of the tale, Prudence lays forth her moral vision of mercy that Melibee eventually accepts, but only after he repeatedly rebuts her claims and then listens to her counterarguments. By extension, this moral lesson is projected onto the readers, who learn to interpret this allegory correctly by following along Melibee's misreadings until he reaches true comprehension—or, a bit more accurately, the thematic interpretation that his wife has determined to be the true one.

Within this allegorical framework, Prudence reframes arguments to bolster her position, despite their surface meanings. In these moments, the tale's foundations in allegory begin to crack, for the interpretations put forth by Prudence and Melibee's male advisers conflict in the relationships built between text and subtext. For example, the physicians advise Melibee that "right as maladies been cured by hir contraries, right so shul men warisshe [cure] werre by vengeaunce" (7.1017). Melibee interprets their words to mean "that right as [the attackers] han doon me a contrarie, right so sholde I doon hem another" (7.1279), and it is quite clear that this is the meaning intended by the physicians. Prudence, however, interprets their words in a strikingly different manner: "For certes, wikkednesse is nat contrarie to wikkednesse, ne vengeance to vengeaunce, ne wrong to wrong, but they been semblable" (7.1285). In this passage Prudence appears to purposefully misinterpret these men's advice by playing on the variant meanings of *contrarie*, which denotes both "one of a pair of opposed or contrasting qualities, conditions, actions, conclusions, etc.; the opposite, antithesis, or reverse" and "an adverse condition or difficulty; a hostile act, a violation."[9] The physicians employ the second meaning of *contrarie*, whereas Melibee's wife focuses on its first. As Stephen Yeager explains of these passages, "Even though Melibee's interpretation of the advice is more straightforward and even appears to reflect the advisers' intent, Prudence is the personification of practical wisdom in the text, and so we can infer that her freer interpretation of the physicians' advice is the more applicable to the circumstances in which she offers it."[10] Indeed, it is the more applicable interpretation to the argument that she is building, yet it is simultaneously a misreading of the physicians' clearly intended meaning. As this example based on the word *contrarie* aptly illustrates, the slippage between a word's multiple levels of meaning can open up radically different interpretations, no matter the intentionality of a text's speakers—with this insight applying to the potential conflicts of interpretation responding to the intentionality of a text's author as well.

As much as Prudence builds a rational and compelling moral lesson, the tale's pacing suffers, with each advance in her argument first rejected by Melibee until she overrides his objections yet again, and then he allows the dialogue to proceed incrementally. Following one series of exchanges, Melibee praises his wife and then redirects the conversation: "Dame . . . as yet into this tyme ye han wel and covenably [appropriately] taught me as in general how I shal governe me in the chesynge [choosing] and in the withholdynge of my conseillours. / But now wolde I fayn that ye wolde condescende in especial / and telle me how liketh yow, or what semeth yow, by oure conseillours that we han chosen in oure present nede" (7.1233-35). In a similar passage, Melibee again realizes the wisdom of Prudence's words, and the conversation shifts again: "I see wel, dame Prudence, that by youre faire wordes and by youre resouns that ye han shewed me, that the werre liketh yow no thyng; / but I have nat yet herd youre conseil, how I shal do in this nede" (7.1673). Through this well-worn pattern, the characters' allegorical qualities undermine their simultaneous construction as human characters. Humanity (as represented by Melibee) continually questions Prudence (as represented by Melibee's wife), thus demonstrating Humanity's incapability of development. Their patterns of argumentation also descend into repetition, with *certes* signaling transitions in the argument with a wearying regularity. To be sure, by the time Melibee cedes his will to Prudence—"Dame . . . dooth youre wil and youre likynge; / for I putte me hoolly in youre disposicioun and ordinaunce" (7.1724-25)—many readers wish he had capitulated much earlier, and there are still over 150 lines to go.

Whereas Melibee initially sees himself as the victim of his enemies' attack, Prudence patiently encourages him to view his own culpability in these events. As she explains, he willingly allowed sin to enter his heart:

Thou hast doon synne agayn oure Lord Crist, / for certes, the three enemys of mankynde—that is to seyn, the flessh, the feend, and the world— / thou hast suffred hem entre in to thyn herte wilfully by the wyndowes of thy body, / and has nat defended thyself suffisantly agayns hire [their] assautes and hire temptaciouns, so that they han wounded thy soule in fyve places; / this is to seyn, the deedly synnes that been entred into thyn herte by thy fyve wittes. / And in the same manere oure Lord Crist hath woold [willed] and suffred that thy three enemys been entred into thyn house by the wyndowes / and han ywounded thy doghter in the forseyde manere. (7.1419-25)

Again, the allegorical meaning of this scene is clear, as Prudence encourages Melibee to see that his house represents his body and that the sins of the flesh, the devil, and the world have defiled him. He is to blame for insufficiently guarding himself against their temptations, and owing to these lapses, his daughter suffers on his account. As Jamie Taylor details, "Prudence insists that Melibee understand the crime that begins the tale in allegorical terms, and specifically that Sophie's brutalized body can represent the violent trespass of sins into his soul. She is careful to claim that sin enters through the 'five wittes,' making a parallel between these wounds and Sophie's five discrete injuries."[11] Throughout the *Tale of Melibee* Prudence explains and explicates, leading Melibee to a deeper understanding of his transgressions on his path to reconciliation with his enemies.

But here the allegorical and thematic levels of the *Tale of Melibee* founder, for why should Melibee reconcile with the flesh, the devil, and the world? As Ruth Waterhouse and Gwen Griffiths demonstrate, "If the allegorical parallels [Prudence] has set up in the middle of the discourse are carried through to the end, this means that Melibee is reconciled with the world, the flesh, and the devil. Such an alliance totally contravenes church teaching; indeed, a battle to the end with these three foes is demanded of true followers of Christ."[12] Moreover, Melibee himself would become complicit in the attack on his family, which thus fractures the complementarity necessary for its allegorical themes to cohere. Yet at the tale's conclusion, Melibee does indeed forgive these enemies: "Wherfore I receyve yow to my grace / and foryeve yow outrely alle the offenses, injuries, and wronges that ye have doon agayn me and myne" (7.1880-81). The tale's allegorical registers collapse at this moment: on the text's surface level, a man may reconcile with his enemies, but on the tale's subtextual level, should a Man representative of humanity reconcile with Enemies representative of the Flesh, the Devil, and the World? Melibee then shifts the tale's allegorical themes one last time, as he, who holds the power to offer earthly forgiveness, now positions himself before God, who "wole at the tyme of oure diynge foryeven us oure giltes that we han trespassed to hym in this wrecched world. / For doutelees, if we be sory and repentant of the synnes and giltes which we han trespassed in the sighte of oure Lord God, / he is so free and so merciable / that he wole foryeven us oure giltes" (7.1884–87). David Aers outlines the ways in which Melibee's words are strangely divorced from their religious context: "Repentance and forgiveness certainly are at the core of the closing lines. But . . . they are presented without any mention of the Church in which the Catholic Christian was taught to fulfill the sacrament of penance and to seek union with others and with Christ."[13] More so, Melibee aggrandizes himself through the allegorical connection between God and himself, thus assigning himself a divine-like authority that undercuts Prudence's moral lessons, for who would presume to teach God his catechism?

Beyond the *Tale of Melibee*'s confused allegory and themes, its overreliance on maxims slows the narrative's forward movement such that, all too frequently, it metaphorically spins its wheels in well-worn ruts. Along with its debts to allegorical literature, the *Tale of Melibee* appears inspired by the genre of *florilegium*, which consists of notable excerpts from esteemed authors, with Chaucer erecting a narrative structure to link them together. Certainly, Prudence is a well-read woman who cites numerous classical, Christian, and contemporary authorities, but her quotations serve more to bolster her spiritual authority than to advance the story's plot. For example, she quotes Ovid ("He is a fool that destourbeth the mooder to wepen in the deeth of hire child" [7.977]); Paul ("Man shal rejoyse with hem that maken joye and wepen with swich folk as wepen" [7.989]); and Petrus Alphonsus ("Whoso that dooth to thee oother good or harm, haste thee nat to quiten [repay] it, for in this wise [way] thy freend wole abyde and thyn enemy shal the lenger lyve in drede" [7.1053]), among many, many more. Chad Crosson notes the exhausting effect of these maxims: "Prudence reproduces aphorisms, but those aphorisms effect not change in Melibeus but simply more aphorisms. The repetition of *sentence* stalls the narrative progression, even seeming to suppress the tale's movement to the next topic and series of proverbs."[14] That is to say, this colloquy's didacticism dulls its narrative tension, with readers encountering a range of vibrant authors whose words are stripped from their context in service of a separate argument.

Furthermore, as much as Prudence cites authorities, so too do Melibee's other advisers offer a range of advice, often predicated on the sayings of others. Within a few exchanges of dialogue, a surgeon cites the Hippocratic oath ("we do to every wight the beste that we kan, where as we been withholde, and to our pacientz that we do no damage" [7.1012]); a lawyer cites the common proverb "He that soone deemeth, soone shal repente" (7.1030); and the young men advise "right so as whil that iren is hoot men sholden smyte" (7.1035). Maxims, aphorisms, and morals play an important role in much literature, whether explicitly didactic or not, but in the case of the *Tale of Melibee*, they impede the narrative flow, offering Prudence the opportunity to share her wide-ranging wisdom but not enhancing the story. In a real sense, the *Tale of Melibee* simply pits warring axioms against one another, in a narrative that devolves into an extended analysis of their rhetorical strengths and weaknesses. But of course, virtually every maxim is contradicted by its opposite—for example, if one person posits, "Many hands make light work," another can quickly rebuff this viewpoint with "Too many cooks spoil the broth"—thus demonstrating the inherently flimsiness of axioms in rhetorical discussions and as literary themes. Strikingly, Prudence pits her own axioms against one another. At one point she cites Solomon and affirms that "right as the herte of a man deliteth in savour that is soote [sweet], right so the conseil of trewe freendes yeveth swetnesse to the soule" (7.1157); soon after she cites Cato and cautions, "Avyse thee wel, and eschue the wordes of swetnesse and of plesaunce" (7.1180). Chaucer appears to realize in his introductory matter that the *Tale of Melibee* packs in too many proverbs, alerting the Canterbury pilgrims that he will "telle somwhat moore / Of proverbes than ye han herd bifoore / Comprehended in this litel tretys here" (7.955-57). Somewhat more, indeed.

As with all discussions of Chaucer's badness, opposing views about the *Tale of Melibee* should be taken into account. Archival evidence points to its popularity in the Middle Ages, as it exists in five manuscripts independent of the *Canterbury Tales*. Several readers have passionately defended it, such as William Witherle Lawrence's regretful assessment that it stands as "the neglected stepchild" of the *Canterbury Tales*; he praises it as "primarily a humanitarian document."[15] Diane Bornstein commends Chaucer's prose style, declaring that he "set an example for fifteenth-century writers in prose as well as in verse."[16] Respectfully responding to these countervailing opinions, Foster muses over the efforts of Chaucer's defenders to defend the aesthetically and narratively indefensible: "I suspect that such an enterprise is the last infirmity of the noble critical mind—the impulse to find hidden genius where none is apparent."[17] With a particularly clever interpretation that both defends Chaucer's genius and justifies the tediousness of the *Tale of Melibee*, John Gardner acknowledges its dullness but believes it to be a practical joke that Chaucer played on his auditors: "Here, obviously, Chaucer is creating intentionally bad art, originally no doubt a prank on the courtly audience that had assembled to hear him, expecting, as always, something vivid and delightful."[18] If so, the *Tale of Melibee* devolves into an excruciatingly long buildup for a punch line that never arrives. But if this example of intentionally bad art with a mishmashed theme simply appears to be bad art to most readers, the joke might just have been on Chaucer himself.

CHAPTER 19

The Hundred Endless Threats and Tragic Genres of the *Monk's Tale*

As signaled by the pilgrims' interruptions that abruptly end narratives threatening to proceed well past their welcome, the *Monk's Tale*, along with the *Squire's Tale* and the *Tale of Sir Thopas*, represents one of Chaucer's evident exercises in the genres of bad storytelling. As the Franklin gently interrupts the *Squire's Tale*, as Harry Bailly rudely suspends Chaucer's *Tale of Sir Thopas*, the Knight exasperatedly curtails the *Monk's Tale*. Following the seventeen brief tragedies that constitute this tale, the Knight apparently recalls that the Monk knows one hundred such stories, as the latter declared, "first, tragedies wol I telle, / Of whiche I have an hundred in my celle [storeroom]" (7.1971-72); one can hardly blame the Knight for expressing exhaustion at the prospect of eighty-three more. While the annals of Western literature herald tragedies as a highly esteemed literary and theatrical tradition, the Monk's tragedies reveal the contested nature of the form in the Middle Ages, in that Chaucer both receives inspiration and innovates from the classical past and his contemporaries. The resulting specimens of tragedy, at least according to the Knight, devolve into tendentiousness and tedium in their repetitive structures and conflicting themes, and thus further exemplify Chaucer's genre troubles.

Like the satirized Prioress in the *General Prologue* who is transformed into a woman of devout spirituality in her prologue, the Monk of the *General Prologue* appears notably different when his prologue commences. M. C. Seymour believes that the tale was composed independently of the *Canterbury Tales*—"The likelihood is strong that the *Monk's Tale* is a virtually unrevised early poem"—and thus advocates that it "deserves a separate existence" and should be read "removed from its final context" as voiced by the Monk.[1] Seymour's points bear much merit, for in his former depiction, the Monk appears uninterested in his spiritual vocation, preferring hunting over prayer: "He yaf [gave] nat of that text a pulled hen, / That seith that hunters ben nat hooly men" (1.177-78). Rather than simple clothing reflective of his concern for the poor, the Monk is well dressed, with the enigmatic accessory of his pin and love knot suggestive of carnal pursuits: "He hadde of gold ywroght a ful curious pyn; / A love-knotte in the gretter ende ther was" (1.196-97). In contrast to these images, the prologue of the *Monk's Tale* depicts Harry Bailly engaging with the Monk as he was described in the *General Prologue* yet with the Monk responding as if he were a wholly reimagined character. Harry Bailly encourages the Monk to "be myrie of cheere" (7.1924) and to "brek nat oure game" (7.1927). He then comments on this man's unsuitability for a religious lifestyle: "I pray to God, yeve hym confusioun / That first thee broghte unto religioun!" (7.1943-44). Harry Bailly also opines on the Monk's sexual virility: "Haddestow as greet a leeve as thou hast myght / To parfourne al thy lust in engendrure [engendering, intercourse], / Thou haddest bigeten ful many a creature" (7.1946-48). As evident from his joking words, Harry Bailly astutely assesses the Monk's character as he was portrayed in the *General Prologue*, and perceptive readers would likely expect the Monk to reply jokingly in kind, yet this character now appears rather dour and humorless. The narrator reports that he accepts Harry's words with forbearance ("This worthy Monk took al in pacience" [7.1965]), with the Monk's dialogue employing an unlikely lexicon for a man who prefers hunting over religion. He speaks of his "diligence" and "honestee" (7.1966-67) and promises later to tell the Canterbury pilgrims "the lyf of Seint Edward" (7.1970). St. Edward the Confessor lived circa 1003 until 1066, over three hundred years prior to Chaucer's creation of the *Canterbury Tales*, and so the Monk's knowledge of this historical figure, sufficient to tell a promised tale about him, partially contradicts the vision of him as choosing hunting in the field over studying in the cloister—a contradiction also evident in the seventeen tragedies he succeeds in telling before the Knight ends this litany of despair.

Instead of a biography of St. Edward, the Monk shares with the pilgrims a bounteous supply of tragedies. As the term is understood today, *tragedy* refers to a serious drama in which the (usually male) protagonist struggles against situations seemingly beyond his control, and even beyond his ken. Tragedies end calamitously: death and despair flourish, with the protagonist and often an array of friends, family, and foes left dead or devastated by the cataclysmic flow of events. Among classical authors Seneca (4-65 CE) most directly influenced medieval conceptions of tragedy, with his works filtering into the ideas and themes of his descendants.[2] Aristotle believed that tragic heroes should represent morally complex characters, those neither wholly good nor wholly evil but recognizably human in their struggle to navigate between these two moral poles. Within this classical conception of the genre, tragic heroes evince a notable flaw, typically an error of judgment unleashing an unstoppable chain of events, known as hamartia. Hubris, or excessive pride, is commonly featured as this flaw. Aristotle also discussed the appeal of tragedies for their audiences, positing that they incite feelings of pity and fear, and that viewers experience a catharsis, or purging, of these emotions. Some of these aspects of classical tragedy echo in the *Monk's Tale*, particularly the frequent depiction of pride as a motivating factor in the protagonist's downfall, evident in the accounts of the "proude kyng" Nebuchadnezzar (7.2159, cf. 7.2167), "proud" Belshazzar (7.2186, cf. 7.2212, 7.2223), Nero ("Moore proud was nevere emperour than he" [7.2472]), Antiochus (and his "proude wordes" [7.2580]), and the "proude kyng" Croesus (7.2759, cf. 7.2741). Given Shakespeare's reverence for Chaucer, the Monk's tragedy of Julius Caesar surely influenced the Bard's version of this tale, although his version clearly adheres to the Aristotelian theories of the genre.

Notwithstanding these echoes of Senecan drama and Aristotelian theory, Chaucer's view of tragedy was more directly influenced by conceptions of it as a reversal of fortune, as recorded in Boethius's *The Consolation of Philosophy*. In this account of his unjust imprisonment, Boethius debates Fortune over the meaning of injustice and human suffering, and in his translation of this work, Chaucer repeats Boethius's definition of tragedy: "What other thynge bywaylen the cryinges of tragedyes but oonly the dedes of Fortune, that with an unwar [unexpected] strook overturneth the realmes of greet nobleye [nobility]? (*Glose. Tragedye is to seyn a dite* [verse, narrative] *of a prosperite for a tyme, that endeth in wrecchidnesse*)" (book 2, poem 1, prose 2). This perspective, largely distinct from Aristotelian theories, discerns tragedy in stories in which Fortune's metaphoric wheel turns, and those who were formerly at the world's heights fall into suffering and despair. Fortune gives with one hand and takes away with the other, and humanity's cries of protest do little to move her.

Although many readers, like the Knight, find the *Monk's Tale* rather dull, it nonetheless highlights Chaucer's innovative literary style, particularly in his formulation of tragedy as an amalgam of traditions. Certainly, it displays his vast knowledge of classical and contemporary literature, including Lucan's *Pharsalia*, Valerius Maximus's *Facta et dicta memorabilia*, and Dante's *Inferno*. Among these many sources Boccaccio's *De casi-*

bus virorum illustrium (On the Falls of Famous Men) stands as particularly important, for as Henry Ansgar Kelly proposes, Chaucer was inspired by this text to link a Boethian sense of tragedy to Boccaccio's tales of famous men who fell from their lofty heights:

> If there was no tradition of *"De casibus* tragedy" for Chaucer to be influenced by, he must have arrived on his own at the conclusion that Boccaccio's series was a collection of tragedies; and Boccaccio's unintended example undoubtedly inspired him to create his own series of tragedies, to which he gave the same title, *De casibus virorum illustrium,* a rubric found in both major families of manuscripts of the *Monk's Tale.* In other words, Chaucer did not get the idea of writing tragedies from Boccaccio, but he got the idea of writing a *series* of tragedies from him. Chaucer, then, not only resurrected tragedy but also invented *De casibus* tragedy.[3]

It is furthermore evident that Chaucer grappled with the multiple meanings of tragedy and his vision of it, for in a rather remarkable strand of literary theory expressed in metadiscourse, he defines the genre three times in the *Monk's Prologue* and *Tale.* In the first instance, the Monk succinctly summarizes a Boethian view of tragedy:

> Tragedie is to seyn a certeyn storie,
> As olde bookes maken us memorie,
> Of hym that stood in greet prosperitee,
> And is yfallen out of heigh degree
> Into myserie, and endeth wrecchedly. (7.1973-77)

This passage ironically paints the Monk as a scholar who has memorized the "olde books" that were dismissed in his *General Prologue* portrait. The Monk also explains the metrical expectations of tragedy: "And they ben versified communely / Of six feet, which men clepen *exametron.* / In prose eek been endited [composed] many oon, / And eek in meetre in many a sondry wyse" (7.1978-81). Hexameters, lines of poetry with six feet, served as the default meter of much Greek and Latin epic poetry, including Homer's and Virgil's epics, as well as such influential works as Ovid's *Metamorphoses.* Ironically, the *Monk's Tale* is composed neither in hexameters nor in prose, providing a startling discontinuity between the Monk's theory of tragedy and his specimens of the form, and as Jonathan Hsy observes, "Generations of editors and scholars have grappled with the many imperfections of the Monk's metadiscourse on form."[4] Nonetheless, with this concise yet precise definition, the Monk would apparently be ready to begin his tale.

Yet when the Monk commences his story a few lines later, he oddly begins by redefining the term that he has just defined:

> I wol biwaille in manere of tragedie
> The harm of hem that stoode in heigh degree,
> And fillen so that ther nas no remedie
> To brynge hem out of hir adversitee.
> For certein, whan that Fortune list to flee,
> Ther may no man the cours of hire withholde.
> Lat no man truste on blynd prosperitee;
> Be war by thise ensamples trewe and olde. (7.1991-98)

Little distinguishes "greet prosperitee" from "heigh degree," and little is added to this definition from the previous one other than the direct mention of Fortune. Lest any reader or Canterbury pilgrim miss these repeated definitions, the *Monk's Tale* concludes with another restatement of the genre's parameters:

> Tragediës noon oother maner thyng
> Ne kan in syngyng crie ne biwaille
> But that Fortune alwey wole assaille [assail, attack]
> With unwar strook the regnes [reigns, kingdoms] that been proude;
> For whan men trusteth hire, thanne wol she faille,
> And covere hire brighte face with a clowde. (7.2761-66)

Whereas a single definition of a key term may be helpful in introducing a narrative, this thrice-told accounting of tragedy more bespeaks the Monk's exhausting rhetorical style than the necessity of its repetition. That is to say, not only does the learned narrator of the *Monk's Tale* appear remarkably different from the hunter of the *General Prologue* portrait, he now appears annoyingly pedantic. More so, noting the subtle shifts in these definitions of tragedy, Eleanor Johnson proposes that the Monk wavers in his understanding of this key term: "In his negative phrasing, 'Tragediës noon oother maner thyng / Ne kan in syngyng crie ne biwaille,' [the Monk] reveals a shift from how tragedy works to how it *fails* to work. The Monk, that is, shifts from talking about tragedy as lamentation to lamenting the limitations of tragedy itself. At the end of his performance, the Monk has thus troubled the working definition or definitions of tragedy he set out in the beginning."[5] Without a clear sense of his own vision of tragedy, the Monk's examples of the genre begin to appear oddly disconnected from one another.

Certainly, the Monk does not always adhere to his repeated definitions of tragedy, particularly as Fortune herself plays a muted, if not absent, role in his first several narratives. In his opening sequence depicting Lucifer's expulsion from heaven, the Monk admits the irrelevance of this example because "Fortune may noon angel dere [harm]" (7.2001). Without Fortune as the motivating agent of this tragedy, it loses its moorings in Boethian thought and becomes an example of one who "From heigh degree yet fel he for his synne" (7.2002). Surely, though, Lucifer was justly punished for his rebellion against God, and so his appearance in the Monk's first tragedy undercuts the term as he recently defined it. Fortune fails to appear in the Monk's accounts of Adam and Samson as well. His portrayal of Adam depicts the heights of Adam's status ("Hadde nevere worldly man so heigh degree" [7.2011]) and then his punishment to endure "labour," "helle," and "meschaunce" (7.2014). The tragedy of Samson similarly depicts his fall into suffering (7.2075-78) but then shifts into an exemplum, advising men not to trust their wives: "Beth war by this ensample oold and playn / That no men telle hir conseil til hir wyves" (7.2091-92). It is only in the fourth of the Monk's minitragedies, with Hercules as its protagonist, that the narrative aligns with his definition of tragedy. Hercules stands as the world's "sovereyn conquerour" (7.2095) until his lover Dianira gives him a shirt poisoned by the centaur Nessus; the shirt dissolves his flesh and leaves him in such agonizing pain that he burns his remaining skin with hot coals. "Lo, who may truste on Fortune any throwe?" (7.2136), the narrator asks, as he then concludes the tale: "Beth war, for whan that Fortune list to glose [deceive], / Thanne wayteth she her man to overthrowe / By swich a wey as he wolde leest suppose" (7.2140-42). With Hercules's gruesome demise, the Monk depicts the grim consequences of Fortune's caprices, as the celebrated hero falls to his adversary's machinations.

As strongly hinted in the account of Adam, God sometimes replaces Fortune as the architect of these tragic protagonists' falls. Nebuchadnezzar thinks of himself as more powerful than God and is immediately punished—"But sodeynly he loste his dignytee" (7.2170)—until God grants him mercy: "Til God relessed hym a certeyn yeres, / And yaf [gave] hym wit, and thanne with many a teere / He thanked God" (7.2177-79).

Rather than simply falling to the bottom of Fortune's wheel, Nebuchad-nezzar apparently spins right back to the top, with this ending further eroding the coherency of the Monk's definition of tragedy. In the follow-ing account of Nebuchadnezzar's son Belshazzar, Fortune and God are virtually conflated, with Fortune first receiving credit for his punishment ("Fortune caste hym doun, and ther he lay" [7.2189]) and then God ("And therfore God greet wreche [retribution] upon hym sente" [7.2213]). The story of Belshazzar, as told in Jewish scriptures, foregrounds Daniel's her-oism rather than Belshazzar's tribulations, but the Monk's retelling of the story shifts its focus from the protagonist to its antagonist. The follow-ing tragedy of Zenobia adheres well, if perhaps too rigidly, to the Monk's skeletal outline of tragedy. Her courage and blamelessness contrast with the transgressions of others, for she lives bravely and virtuously until Aurelianus defeats her in battle. Whereas the Monk aligned the rebel-liousness of Lucifer and Adam with their falls, thus tacitly contesting the presumption that Fortune always acts capriciously, Zenobia, in contrast, proves the arbitrariness of Fortune's interventions.

The Monk shifts the pacing of his tale with the three very short trag-edies of Pedro of Castile (two stanzas), Pierre de Lusignan (one stanza), and Bernabò Visconti (one stanza). Pedro is killed by his brother, Pierre by his lieges, and Bernabò by his nephew, and the quick pacing of these tales attests to the threadbare story lines of some of the Monk's tragedies. The next tales paint lurid pictures of death and despair. Imprisoned with his children, Ugolino of Pisa rails against Fortune, as his children beseech him to cannibalize them ("Fader, do nat so, allas! / But rather ete the flessh upon us two" [7.2449-50]). Nero's many depravities—burning Rome, murdering senators, fratricide, matricide, and incest—are recounted, until Fortune punishes him, and in this decision, she breaks character as a disinterested intercessor in human affairs: "By God! I am to nyce / To sette a man that is fulfild of vice / In heigh degree, and emperour hym calle" (7.2522-24).

In the next two tragedies—of Holofernes and Antiochus—the Monk chooses antagonists of Jewish scriptures—Holofernes from Judith, Antio-chus from Maccabees—as his protagonists, thus reversing the perspec-tive from which these tales are typically told. The Monk incorporates a sly inversion of Holofernes's ostensible tragedy. In the scriptural account, Judith executes Holofernes, who has been seduced by her beauty; in the Monk's version of the tale, Fortune seduces him instead: "Fortune ay kiste [Holofernes] / So likerously [lasciviously], and ladde hym up and doun / Til that his heed was of, er that he wiste [knew]" (7.2556-58). Fortune and

God are portrayed as collaborating on Antiochus's downfall: the former "hadde enhaunced [Antiochus] so in pride" (7.2583), and the latter punishes him with an "invisible wounde" (7.2600) such that "thurgh his body wikked wormes crepte, / And therwithal he stank so horribly" (7.2616-17). By recalibrating these tales from their original perspectives, the Monk creates protagonists from antagonists and tacitly asks us to "biwaille" their downfalls, despite the evident providence of their demises in scriptural traditions.

For his final three tragedies, the Monk selects protagonists from the histories and legends of the classical past: Alexander the Great, Julius Caesar, and Croesus. The narrator weeps over Alexander's fate—poisoned by his own people—and ironically, in this tale so focused on the excesses of pride, Alexander is praised for acting virtually as an agent of Fortune himself, as he strips the prideful of their pretensions: "The pride of man and beest he leyde adoun, / Wherso he cam, unto the worldes ende" (7.2637-38). The account of Julius Caesar accords well with the Monk's formulation of tragedy, beginning with Caesar's rise "from humble bed to roial magestee" (7.2672) and concluding with his assassination, thus illustrating the theme that "Fortune was first freend, and sitthe [afterward] foo" (7.2723). Croesus, defeated by Cyrus the Great, escapes death by fire when Fortune sends a rainstorm; believing himself divinely favored, he begins a new war, but soon finds himself hanged on the gallows. The *Monk's Tale* ends with a summary of Croesus's fate—"Anhanged was Cresus, the proude kyng; / His roial trone myghte hym nat availle" (7.2759-60)—and then by defining *tragedy* for the third time, as cited previously.

After this long, seemingly interminable, litany of tragedies, the pilgrims revolt, as the Knight, who in his authoritative position on this journey would seem more likely to model forbearance than impatience, interrupts: "Hoo! . . . Good sire, namoore of this! / That ye han seyd is right ynough, ywis, / And muchel moore; for litel hevynesse / Is right ynough to muche folk, I gesse" (7.2767-70). As Kemp Malone explains of the dramatic effect of this interruption: "Chaucer makes the knight do the stinting partly for variety's sake and partly because he thereby heightens the dramatic effect. To have so gentle a person as the knight do so rude a thing makes the stinting far more dramatic than it could possibly be if put in the hands of the host, from whom politeness was not be expected."[6] Soon Harry Bailly joins the fray: "Youre tale anoyeth al this compaignye. / Swich talkyng is nat worth a boterflye, / For therinne is ther no desport ne game" (7.2789-91). Certainly, the terms that Harry established for the competition—that tales should evince "sentence" and "solaas" (1.798)—appear ignored in the Monk's litany of tragedies, for there is little meaning in them beyond the obvious moral that Fortune's wheel turns, and there is little pleasure in them in their repeated images of death and desolation.

Despite the tale's apparently abrupt ending, scholars debate whether the Knight's interjection prematurely concludes the *Monk's Tale* or simply coincides with the Monk's plan for his narrative. For instance, Robert Boenig notes the bookending effect of the Monk's definitions of tragedies and proposes that the tale should be read as completed.[7] Moreover, the interaction between the Knight and Monk continues Chaucer's earlier linking of the men, when Harry Bailly invited the Monk to respond to the *Knight's Tale*: "Now telleth ye, sir Monk, if that ye konne, / Somwhat to quite with the Knyghtes tale" (1.3118-19). R. E. Kaske observes that the Knight and the Monk "are depicted in the *General Prologue* with obvious reference to the two great Christian ideals of chivalry and monasticism, the Knight the unlikely fulfillment of his ideal as the Monk is the too-likely negation of his; of all the pilgrims, in fact, it would be difficult to find two whose portrayal depends more directly on this relationship between the ideal and its fulfillment or lack of fulfillment in the individual."[8] The *Knight's Tale* depicts "hevynesse" in Arcite's death, as well as in the weeping women mourning their husbands slain by Creon, yet its darker themes are counterbalanced by its depiction of romance and Palamon's marriage to Emelye. In an intriguing defense of the *Monk's Tale*, Shawn Normandin places it within the context of monastic reading practices and metamorphoses the literary vice of boredom into a virtue by detailing the ways in which it "is an experience integral to monastic writing and reading. Monks knew how boring the repetitiveness of their lives could be."[9] Yet most of the *Monk's Tale*'s readers are not monks, and do not read like monks, and thus concur: the *Monk's Tale* is rather boring. "Hoo," indeed.

CHAPTER 20

The Cock's Words and Chaucerian Triple-Talk of the *Nun's Priest's Tale*

One might not expect fornicating chickens and herb laxatives to appear in one of the masterpieces of the literary canon, but the *Nun's Priest's Tale* accomplishes this improbable feat through an irrepressible display of erudition, wit, and humor. At its core, it is a beast fable, telling the simple tale of the rooster Chauntecleer, his marriage with his wife Pertelote, and his hair-raising escape from a hungry fox. Chaucer enwraps and interlaces this basic structure with a striking number of literary traditions, including elements of romance, epic, dream vision, and philosophical disquisition, and readers have responded rapturously to his accomplishments, with many lauding it as the finest of the *Canterbury Tales.* After summarizing some of the ebullient praise heaped upon it, Peter Travis concludes, "Urbane, playful, humanistic, learned, and quintessentially Chaucerian, the *Nun's Priest's Tale* has rarely suffered from underappreciation,"[1] including in his litany Morton Bloomfield's position that "an inability to enjoy [the *Nun's Priest's Tale*] should disqualify anyone from the study of literature."[2] With chickens conversing and copulating, a fox conniving but ultimately confounded, and a narrator simultaneously unleashing and directing its joyful humor, the *Nun's Priest's Tale* triumphantly navigates a complex network of discourses and discursive strategies, with Harry Bailly's delighted gratitude to the Nun's Priest—"faire falle yow for youre tale!" (7.3460)—indicative of the widespread response of readers over the centuries.

Yet the ebullient humor of the *Nun's Priest's Tale* is undercut by its narrator's repeated misogynistic attacks, which he recognizes as potentially offensive to the women members of his audience. At the same time, the Nun's Priest deflects any criticism by attributing these viewpoints solely to Chauntecleer, despite that he ventriloquizes himself through the rooster's voice. Chaucer as author benefits from an additional level of narrative distance through his rooster's misogyny; in effect, he creates a structure not merely of double-talk but of triple-talk, as Chauntecleer speaks, the Nun's Priest comments, and Chaucer, as ventriloquist of both speakers and their commentaries, remains above the fray while controlling it. This structure is additionally complicated, but not undermined, by critical readings that propose that Chaucer encodes himself in the text either as the Nun's Priest or as Chauntecleer or even as both. Such interpretations should lessen the distance between the characters' words and the author's voice, but the power of ventriloquized triple-talk is such that Chaucer can withstand efforts to link him to his words. This rhetorical structure of doubled and tripled voices stands in place throughout the *Nun's Priest's Tale*, and it is strikingly apparent when the discussion turns to misogyny, when apologies are both proffered and recanted in virtually the same breath. Thus, as an example of Chaucer's outmoded perspectives, the *Nun's Priest's Tale* expresses misogynistic viewpoints recognized as such in the Middle Ages yet preserves the author from responsibility for them.

As the Nun's Priest begins his tale, the very setting of his story can be viewed as a form of double-talk (or at least of doubled description) that reflects negatively on women, in that he juxtaposes the poverty of the poor widow's farm and its women inhabitants against the royal splendor of Chauntecleer's court. The story begins by mentioning "A povre wydwe, somdeel stape in age [advanced in years], / Was whilom dwellyng in a narwe [humble] cotage" (7.2821-22), in which she led "a ful symple lyf, / For litel was hir catel [property] and hir rente" (7.2826-27). It is striking that, in this initial description, the inhabitants of the farm are human women and female animals. In addition to the widow, residents include "doghtren two," "thre large sowes," "three keen [cows]," and a "eek a sheep that highte [is named] Malle" (7.2829-31). The Nun's Priest contrasts the modesty of this poor widow's farmyard with the grandiosity of its grandiloquent protagonist, Chauntecleer the rooster, who is praised in superlative terms—"In al the land, of crowyng nas his peer" (7.2850)—and who rules the roost of all that he surveys with Pertelote and his six other wives at his side. The narrator's physical description of Chauntecleer details this bird's exquisite beauty, with Pertelote's comeliness noted as well.

Following the gendered divergence evident in the tale's setting, Chauntecleer and Pertelote argue, with their viewpoints increasingly linked to their genders. Chauntecleer suffers from a restless night featuring an ominous nightmare and foresees a beast's murderous attack against him, but Pertelote shames him for his cowardice and advises him to take a laxative. They argue about the premonitory power of dreams, and Chauntecleer marshals a range of examples and authorities to argue that dreams foretell the future. At the climax of the *Nun's Priest's Tale*, the rooster is proved correct when a fox captures him, only then to escape by appealing to the fox's pride and eagerness to taunt his foes. Thus, the *Nun's Priest's Tale* builds to a confrontation pitting male protagonist against male antagonist, as female characters rush in to Chauntecleer's defense when he is threatened. Accentuating the gendered contours of this narrative trajectory, Chaucer avails himself of triple-talk discourse to express misogynistic ideas on several occasions.

The antifeminist sentiment of the *Nun's Priest's Tale*, while within the norms of gendered discourse in the Middle Ages, should not therefore be overlooked. Chauntecleer speaks out of both sides of his mouth, a tactic cunningly evident through the linguistic subterfuge of mistranslation. Concluding his disquisition concerning the significance of dreams, Chauntecleer segues into seducing Pertelote, with his words signifying through both their literal and their misinterpreted meanings: "For al so siker [certain] as *In principio*, / *Mulier est hominis confusio*," he states, as he then mistranslates the meaning of this phrase: "Madame, the sentence of this Latyn is, / 'Womman is mannes joye and al his blis'" (7.3163-66). Chauntecleer's Latin more accurately translates as "In the beginning, woman is the ruin of man," with the phrase *In principio*, which Chauntecleer does not bother to translate, meaning "In the beginning" and alluding to the first words of Genesis and the Gospel of John in the Vulgate. Notably, these two narratives that begin "In the beginning" allow Chauntecleer to assert men's preeminence over women. Genesis includes the account of Adam and Eve's expulsion from Eden, which numerous medieval theologians attributed to Eve's actions rather than to Adam's. The Gospel of John does not include the story of Jesus's birth, thus downplaying Mary's role in her son's salvific mission. Instead, this gospel commences, "In the beginning was the Word, and the Word was with God, and the Word was God" (John 1.1). With Eve blamed and Mary marginalized, Chauntecleer's *In principio* establishes biblical precedent for men's words to assess and then dismiss women's worth, and it is surely not coincidental that, following Pertelote's initial speech, his voice silences hers. The mistranslation of *Mulier est hominis confusion* as "Womman is mannes joye and al his blis" raises many questions—does Chauntecleer mistranslate these words ignorantly or purposefully? Is his objective to rewrite or to reinscribe scriptural interpretations blaming women for humanity's fall?—yet the utility of this passage for misogynistic discourse is that either interpretation can be readily claimed, depending on the reaction of the men and women in the audience. Such is the power of double-talk.

As the Nun's Priest alludes to biblical phrases and employs mistranslation to establish Chauntecleer's dominion over his wives, he likewise refers to the legends of King Arthur and his knights to affirm masculine prerogatives while lampooning women's ability to interpret narratives. In a jesting tone, he asks his auditors to evaluate the veracity of his tale: "Now every wys man, lat him herkne me; / This storie is also trewe, I undertake, / As is the book of Launcelot de Lake, / That wommen holde in ful greet reverence" (7.3210-13). Tellingly, the Nun's Priest addresses "every wys man" with these words, inviting them to laugh at his ironic assessment of his story as true, while also inviting them to deride the women who ostensibly would not realize its fictionality because they revere the legends of Lancelot. Here the Nun's Priest construes men as learned and women as gullible, which is further evident in Chauntecleer's subtle insinuation that Pertelote is less educated than he is. Pertelote cites Cato to buttress her argument ("Lo Catoun, which that was so wys a man, / Seyde he nat thus, 'Ne do no fors of dremes'?" [7.2940-41]) and appears well versed in medicinal practices, but after citing the legend of St. Kenelm, Chauntecleer implies that she lacks his extensive knowledge: "By God! I hadde levere [rather] than my sherte / That ye hadde rad his legende, as have I" (7.3120-21). Within this formulation, men's learning trumps women's ignorance, even when it is unclear why the woman in question should be viewed as ignorant in the first place.

Ironically, a similar misogynistic volley follows the Nun's Priest's admission of his own ignorance concerning the issue of free will and predestination. Medieval theologians struggled with the question of humanity's volition versus God's foreknowledge of one's actions, and the narrator confesses that these debates have flummoxed him:

> Wheither that Goddes worthy forwityng [foreknowledge]
> Streyneth [constrains] me nedely for to doon a thyng—
> . . . .
> Or elles, if free choys be graunted me
> To do that same thyng, or do it noght,
> Though God forwoot it er that I was wroght,
> . . . .
> I wol nat han to do of swich mateere. (7.3243-44, 3246-48, 3251)

The Nun's Priest admits the limits of man's knowledge—in this case, his own—and segues back to Chauntecleer: "My tale is of a cok, as ye may heere" (7.3252). By returning to his story's narrative action, he returns as well to its theme that men's knowledge outpaces women's, for Chauntecleer's belief in the prophetic nature of dreams is soon validated, and thus Pertelote's conviction that they lack prophetic force is disproved. The narrator then adds that Chauntecleer "tok his conseil of his wyf, with sorwe, / To walken in the yerde upon that morwe" (7.3253-54). But this statement is nonsense: Pertelote, while disbelieving the prophetic force of dreams, never advises Chauntecleer to walk in the yard; on the contrary, she asserts her willingness to venture out "in oure yeerd" (7.2951) to find the herbs necessary for the laxative she promises to prepare for him. Moreover, Chauntecleer, regardless of the question of free will versus divine predestination, surely enjoys sufficient agency to determine for himself whether to proceed into the yard, whether or not his wife encourages him to do so.

Echoing Chauntecleer's earlier invocation of the biblical phrase *In principio*, the narrator returns his audience's attention to the Genesis account of Adam and Eve's expulsion from Eden and denigrates women's advice to their husbands: "Wommennes conseils been ful ofte colde; / Wommannes conseil broghte us first to wo / And made Adam fro Paradys to go" (7.3256-58). Such interpretations of this biblical scene circulated throughout the Middle Ages, yet they are based on rather flimsy evidence, for the scene in question is remarkably succinct: "And the woman saw that the tree was good to eat, and fair to the eyes, and delightful to behold: and she took of the fruit thereof, and did eat, and gave to her husband who did eat" (Genesis 3.6). From this passage that includes no mention of Eve's motivations or of Adam's response to her sharing of the fruit arose long-standing traditions blaming Eve for humanity's fall; the Nun's Priest endorses such viewpoints through his debasement of women's counsel. Yet the Nun's Priest then denies that these words reflect his beliefs: "But for I noot [do not know] to whom it myght displese, / If I conseil of wommen wolde blame, / Passe over, for I seyde it in my game" (7.3260-62). The Nun's Priest claims to be joking, but, as is well known, jokes often contain a kernel of truth, in that they allow people to express ideas, particularly unpopular and hostile ideas, that they hold but know not to speak aloud. Sigmund Freud, in his analysis of humor and the unconscious, proposes that aggressive wit is often triangulated: "Besides the one who makes the wit there is a second person who is taken as the object of the hostile or sexual aggression, and a third person in whom the purpose of the wit to produce pleasure is fulfilled."[3] Such a triangulated structure of humor is in effect in this scene, with women as the object of the statement's humor, men as the narrator's ideal audience, and the tripled construction of Chauntecleer / Nun's Priest / Chaucer behind this triple-talk statement.

The Nun's Priest then directs his audience to the textual authorities and exegetes who would endorse the viewpoint he claims to repeat only "in my game": "Rede auctours, where they trete of swich mateere, / And what they seyn of wommen ye may heere" (7.3263-64). Piero Boitani unpacks the contradictions and triple-talk of the Nun's Priest's words: "Exactly! The only problem is that 'authors,' beginning with Genesis, say pretty contrasting things about women. Thus, Pilate-like, the Priest washes his hands of the whole business, and with a triple somersault attributes what he has just said to the subtle interpreter of Scripture, Chauntecleer."[4] In the final words of this passage that seesaws between condemning women and positioning the speaker as one who would never condemn women, the Nun's Priest assigns his words to Chauntecleer: "Thise been the cokkes wordes, and nat myne; / I kan noon harm of no womman divyne" (7.3265-66). The very nature of irony encourages opposed readings of the same words, and the Nun's Priest avails himself of this rhetorical subterfuge to state before the women members of his audience what they would presumably prefer not to hear.

Continuing the narrative's sideways appeals to misogyny, Pertelote plays hardly any role in the tale's climax but is partially blamed for Chauntecleer's dire fate, despite the narrative's focus on his succumbing to the fox's flattery. The fox promises that "the cause of my comynge / Was oonly for to herkne how that ye synge. / For trewely, ye have as myrie a stevene [voice] / As any aungel hath that is in hevene" (7.3289-92); Chauntecleer, "ravysshed with his flaterie" (7.3324), begins his song but is so distracted that he fails to guard himself against his foe's attack. As these baleful events unfold, the narrator blames destiny, Chauntecleer, and Pertelote: "O destinee, that mayst nat been eschewed! / Allas, that Chauntecleer fleigh fro the bemes! / Allas, his wyf ne roghte nat of dremes!" (7.3338-40). The first of these lines refers to the Nun's Priest's earlier discussion of predestination versus free will, the second line regretfully assesses Chauntecleer's decision to fly into the farmyard, and the third line blames Pertelote for not believing in the prophetic force of dreams. Oddly, the fox escapes the Nun's Priest's censure altogether—but then again, this is how misogyny works, in finding a way to fault women for men's actions.

In his final act of triple-talk, the narrator hopes that readers who might dismiss his tale as frivolous discern its spiritual value:

> But ye that holden this tale a folye,
> As of a fox, or of a cok and hen,
> Taketh the moralite, goode men.
> For Seint Paul seith that al that writen is,
> To oure doctrine it is ywrite, ywis;
> Taketh the fruyt, and lat the chaf be stille. (7.3438-43)

The genre of beast fable asks readers to discern the deeper meaning of its surface stories, and in most instances the interpretation is readily inferable from the actions depicted. A thorny challenge presented by the *Nun's Priest's Tale* is that it suffers from a surfeit of morals. One could reasonably argue that it demonstrates that one should avoid flattery and flatterers ("Lo, swich it is for us to be recchelees / And necligent, and truste on flaterye" [7.3436-37]); or that one should recognize the ephemerality of life's pleasures and enjoy them while able ("For evere the latter ende of joye is wo. / God woot that worldly joye is soone ago" [7.3205-6]); or that one must remain vigilant against one's foes ("For he that wynketh, whan he sholde see, / Al wilfully, God lat him nevere thee [prosper]!" [7.3431-32]), or other such possibilities. With readers encouraged to choose among the plethora of morals, the Nun's Priest evades assigning a meaning to his tale, much as he evades responsibility for his cock's words.

The Nun's Priest stands virtually as a blank slate, with little to individualize him, and the emptiness of his characterization enhances the obfuscating strategies of Chaucer's triple-talk scaffolding. The *General Prologue* introduces him simply as a member of the Prioress's entourage—"Another NONNE with hire hadde she, / That was hir chapeleyne, and preestes thre" (1.163-64). Jumbled in with two other priests, an insurmountable conundrum of the *Canterbury Tales* arises in the simple question of which of these three is the Nun's Priest who tells the *Nun's Priest's Tale*. The prologue of the *Nun's Priest's Tale* depicts him in threadbare terms, for he simply acquiesces to Harry Bailly's request for a story: "'Yis, sir,' quod he, 'yis, Hoost, so moot I go, / But I be myrie, ywis I wol be blamed'" (7.2816-17). The barest hint of a personality emerges in these lines, as the Nun's Priest's realizes that his merry tale might offend some of the pilgrims, and Chaucer as narrator concludes this prologue with an assessment of this man's character: "This sweete preest, this goodly man sir John" (7.2820). Such a skeletal portrait offers little, and as John Finlayson theorizes: "In so far as we can identify the Nun's Priest, he is created by his Tale rather than presenting a story through his personality."[5]

Notably, several critics have identified the Nun's Priest as Chaucer's autofictional representation of himself, in effect replacing a literary character, albeit an underdeveloped one, with the author who created him.[6] Authors have long been identified with their characters, and, in many instances, rightfully so. To deny David Copperfield as an autofictional representation of Charles Dickens misunderstands the author and his intentions with this novel, as well as the numerous parallel points between author and protagonist: their impoverished childhoods, misadventures in love, and writing careers. Yet not only the Nun's Priest but his rooster emerges as a potential link between Chaucer and this tale. Dolores Warwick Frese, examining medieval poets' onomastic wordplay, suggests that "by supplying 'Ge' for 'Geffrey'—the poet's own spelling of his name—the name CHAUnteCleER engenders the epithet '(ge)ntele Chaucer.'" Frese posits further that Chaucer's Pertelote "contains within the characters of her new name the initial 'P' and the surname 'Roet,' possibly furnishing us with the name of Chaucer's own wife, P[hillipa] Roet." Frese offers these interpretations "with a certain amount of reservation," concerned that she should not be remembered "like Pinte, the literary ancestress of Pertelote, who is epithetically referred to in Le Roman de Renart as 'the one who laid the big eggs.'"[7] The overlap between the paired names of Chaucer and Chauntecleer and Phillipa Roet and Pertelote is nonetheless striking, and it is amusing, if unprovable, to consider that Chaucer depicted his own marital life through the fictional facade of a doughty rooster bickering with his devoted wife. And while there is no great harm in identifying the Nun's Priest as Chaucer and/or as Chauntecleer, there is no real benefit to it, either, and critics do not evince a similar tendency to identify Chaucer with many of his other pilgrims who tell the best tales. Few readers assume that Chaucer aligns himself so thoroughly with his Miller, his Franklin, or his Wife of Bath, or most other of the Canterbury pilgrims. On a rhetorical level, however, these frames perform important work by distancing the author from controversial viewpoints, allowing him to plausibly deny that any such opinions are his own.

Through the multiple frames of narration throughout the Canterbury Tales, through the voices of characters and narrators that sometimes do and sometimes do not align, through the construction of rhetorical double-talk and triple-talk (and surely one could further theorize qua-druple- and quintuple-talk, if not even more such levels), Chaucer can indulge in misogynistic humor while deflecting attention from himself as its author. In the *Legend of Good Women* the God of Love chastises Chaucer for his misogynistic writings while Alceste pardons him, which depicts the author's recognition of his responsibility for his words and his rhe-torical strategies for excusing them. Throughout the *Canterbury Tales*, Chaucer speaks in one voice and comments in another, adopting a wily strategy that allows him to evade being pinned down while also recogniz-ing that he should be held accountable for his words. In the God of Love's court, Chaucer is both guilty of and allowed to exculpate himself from the charge of misogyny, an accomplishment achieved throughout much of the *Canterbury Tales* on a range of additional subjects that he pronounces on yet distances himself from any repercussions. Through his triple-talking apologies, Chaucer can insult women while ingratiating himself to them as well, which is hardly a feat worth crowing about, whether in the Middle Ages or today.

CHAPTER 21

The Invisible Nun and Chaste Orgasms of the *Second Nun's Tale*

Chaucer's Second Nun tells a torrid tale of chastity, one in which her surface focus on virginity masks a vivid meditation on the carnality of divine love. This hagiographical account of St. Cecilia's marriage and martyrdom celebrates her virginity as a preeminent ideal while concomitantly infusing elements of eroticism that trouble its facade of virtuous chastity. As told by the unknowable Second Nun, a character of whom Chaucer withholds any description, the tale thus cannot enhance our understanding of her character in any meaningful way. Is she a devout woman whose hagiographic narrative reflects deeply held beliefs, or is she, like the Prioress of the *General Prologue*, only reluctantly ensconced in a religious vocation, with her tale thus exposing fleshly desires that must be repressed (and thus latently expressed) within her ecclesiastical milieu? The fascinating duality of the *Second Nun's Tale*—chaste on its surface, orgasmic in its subtext—provides Chaucer with a unique and compelling opportunity to deepen the portrait of this mostly invisible nun, of whom we see only the barest of outlines. Without any understanding of her character or motivations, readers can never perceive the purposes behind this conflicted narrative, beyond the obvious connection between its woman tale-teller and her women-centered tale. As Karen Arthur rightly affirms, "The presence of women on the Canterbury pilgrimage as well as ambiguities in the *Prologue* should alert us to the possibility that Chaucer's version of the legend of St. Cecilia is unique in allowing for the distinct interests of a female teller."[1] While representing distinctly feminine interests, the *Second Nun's Tale* also obfuscates our understanding of the woman who tells this strangely bifurcated story, in which chastity cloaks the blissfully eroticized pleasures to be enjoyed by both Cecilia and her readers. From this perspective, Chaucer's Second Nun, virtually invisible to readers, stands as one of the most striking and disappointing absences in his fiction.

Like the Nun's Priest, who tells the brilliant *Nun's Priest's Tale*, the Second Nun remains a cipher. Following the *General Prologue*'s lengthy portrait of the Prioress, Chaucer simply records, "Another NONNE with hire hadde she, / That was hir chapeleyne" (1.163-64). Because she is never described through Chaucer's ironic frames, readers can do little more than visualize a hazy, generic image of a fourteenth-century English nun. Carolyn Collette states that "the tale lacks a clearly defined 'personality' as its teller" and describes the Second Nun as a "shadowy figure" whose absence undermines efforts to interpret her tale.[2] Moreover, the segue between the *Nun's Priest's Tale* and the *Second Nun's Tale* is notably disjointed, for nothing in the former's conclusion suggests that the Second Nun is envisioned as the next speaker. On the contrary, the epilogue to the *Nun's Priest's Tale* simply states, "And after that [Harry Bailly], with ful merie chere, / Seide unto another, as ye shuln heere" (7.3461-62). The "another" is never specified in this passage, and so such boilerplate language could have been appended following virtually any tale. The prologue of the *Second Nun's Tale* then disproves what was just spoken, for in it Harry Bailly does not speak; rather, the Second Nun, without acknowledging the Host or the other pilgrims, immediately commences her prologue. Indeed, this prologue offers little indication that the Second Nun is speaking within the context of the Canterbury pilgrimage, and it is likely that Chaucer wrote this hagiography earlier and then incorporated it into the *Canterbury Tales*. The *Legend of Good Women* catalogs several of Chaucer's earlier works, including the *House of Fame*, the *Parliament of Fowls*, and his translation of Boethius's *Consolation of Philosophy*, as well as two tales later reconceived for the Canterbury pilgrimage: "the love of Palamon and Arcite / Of Thebes" (F420-21), which became the *Knight's Tale*, and "the lyf also of Seynt Cecile" (F 426), which became the *Second Nun's Tale*.

The conflicted spiritual and sexual themes of the *Second Nun's Tale* are foreshadowed in its prologue, in which the Second Nun connects herself to the subject of her hagiography.[3] The opening stanza condemns Idleness as the "norice [nurse] unto vices" (8.1) and the "porter of the gate is of delices [delights, pleasures]" (8.3). Contrasting idleness with activity, she praises the virtue of "leveful [pleasing] bisynesse" (8.5) and aligns herself with it, declaring that in her tale she has "heer doon my feithful bisynesse" (8.24). By busily telling her tale, the Second Nun aligns herself with her protagonist Cecilia, whose energetic "busyness" in winning new converts to Christianity provides a key theme of her story. Cecilia's body serves as a conflicted site of denial and desire in her tale, and the Second

Nun embodies such a contested identity when she calls herself an "unworthy sone of Eve" (8.62). Seeing herself as a male woman, the Second Nun corrupts strict categories of gender and sex, with this decoupling of the body and gender latently connected to eroticism and its denial. Original sin—a sin of sexuality, in many exegetical interpretations—clashes with the human desire for heavenly bliss, and when invoking Mary, the Second Nun prays that she will be cleansed of sin: "And of thy light my soule in prison lighte, / That troubled is by the contagioun / Of my body, and also by the wighte [weight] / Of erthely lust and fals affeccioun" (8.71-74). With this close attention to her body, which is contaminated by earthly lust and false affection, the Second Nun focuses her audience's attention on human sinfulness and its close ties to corporeality. Within theological terms, the Second Nun fears that her *sensualitee* might overrule her reason and thus that her bodily desires will endanger her soul; as Chaucer's Parson avows of the rightful order of human dominion: "God sholde have lordshipe over resoun, and resoun over sensualitee, and sensualitee over the body of man" (10.261). The Second Nun seeks to purge her body and spirit of lust by following the chaste example set by Cecilia, yet the fraught suggestion of God's erotic interest in Cecilia undercuts the achievability, even the desirability, of this goal. The "contagioun" of the Second Nun's body threatens her vision of transcendent unity with God, but the future destruction of this body, a carnal prison, in death allows her to envision a spirit finally freed. To develop this theme, the final stanza of her prologue describes heaven as "swift and round and eek brennynge [burning]" (8.114) and Cecilia as "brennynge evere in charite ful brighte" (8.118). These passages link Cecilia to the heavenly award awaiting her, while also adumbrating her death by fire at the narrative's end.

In the first stanza of the *Second Nun's Tale*, readers learn Cecilia's heartfelt prayer—"to kepe hir maydenhede" (8.126)—and in the second stanza they learn that she faces the imminent abnegation of this desire because the "day was comen of hir marriage" (8.130). This quick introduction establishes the conflict between Cecilia's spiritual desires and the prevailing cultural expectation that she will marry her suitor Valerian and reproduce, yet readers versed in hagiographical literature have little reason to expect that she will lose her virginity. In the Middle Ages, virginity and chastity were prized in a variety of circumstances, even within the context of marriage. Spiritual marriages, in which husbands and wives married but pledged chastity, were widely known in the English Middle Ages. For example, Margery Kempe's autobiographical *Book* includes a famed passage in which she negotiates the cessation of sex with her husband, on the condition that she pay his debts: "Grawntyth me that ye schal not komyn in my bed, & I grawnt yow to qwyte [pay] yowr dettys [debts] er I go to Ierusalem. & makyth my body fre to God so that ye neuyr [never] make no chalengyng in me to askyn no dett of matrimony [marital debt, sex] aftyr this day whyl ye leuyn [live]."⁴ As Dyan Elliot explains of spiritual and sexless marriages of the Middle Ages, the legend of St. Cecilia "possesses three irreducible elements that are common to most hagiographical depictions of virginal marriage: reluctance to marry, conversion of the spouse on the wedding night, and a secret resolve to preserve virginity."⁵ More so, Mary Beth Long notices the specificity of Cecilia's wishes—"In hind sight, Cecilia's marital status seems inevitable: the text opens with her desire to remain chaste, not to remain unmarried"⁶—with this slight but telling distinction between desiring chastity and desiring to remain unmarried key to the erotic tensions surrounding the tale's celebration of chastity.

Because Cecilia does not alert Valerian to her preference for a spiritual, not sexual, marriage, readers can likely sympathize with his surprise on their wedding night. The stanza begins by discreetly suggesting the two are preparing for intercourse: "The nyght cam, and to bedde moste she gon / With hire housbonde, as ofte is the manere" (8.141-42). The customary acts of a wedding night, however, will not be enacted in this tale. Cecilia greets Valerian warmly—"O sweete and wel biloved spouse deere" (8.144)—but then warns him of his impending doom should their marriage be consummated. An angel is watching over her, she states, and he will execute Valerian if he deflowers his bride: "And if that he may feelen, out of drede, / That ye me touche, or love in vileynye, / He right anon wol sle yow with the dede, / And in youre yowthe thus ye shullen dye" (8.155-58). The stark disparity in choices offered to Valerian—sexual intercourse resulting in his imminent execution, sexual abstention resulting in divine favor—establish a clear binary between eroticism and abstinence. Although Cecilia's words establish marital chastity as a preeminent virtue, Elizabeth Robertson points out the occluded erotics of the scene: "Cecilia warns Valerian that if the Angel should 'feelen' his touch, he will kill Valerian. Not only has the intimate encounter of two newlyweds become triangulated by the unexpected presence of a third being in the bedroom, but, uncannily, another being seems to inhabit Cecilia's body: if Valerian reaches out to touch Cecilia, the angel rather than Cecilia will feel his touch."⁷ By touching Cecilia, Valerian would touch this angel, with the latter responding violently both to the heteroerotic desire directed toward Cecilia and to the latently homoerotic desire directed toward him. Moreover, the consummation of a marriage tacitly alludes to the couple's potential procreation, yet rather than bearing Valerian's children and consequently adhering to the biblical injunction to "increase you and multiply, and go upon the earth, and fill it" (Genesis 7.9), Cecilia aspires to "multiply" the followers of her Christian faith through "clene love," which she requests from Valerian and which Valerian, upon agreeing to her desire for a chaste marriage, will win from her angel. Truly, as Lynn Staley Johnson concludes of the unexpected erotics of Cecilia and Valerian's wedding night, "The 'fruit' of Cecilia's wedding night is the re-birth of her husband as a Christian."[8]

Following the confused erotics of Cecilia's wedding, the remainder of the *Second Nun's Tale* repeatedly employs imagery that destabilizes the binary between chastity and sexuality, thereby ironically painting images of God's highly eroticized pursuit of Cecilia. Initially suspecting that Cecilia has taken another man as her lover, Valerian demands proof of the divine revelation granted to her. Deprived of the erotic pleasure of penetrating Cecilia, he envisions a violent penetration of her and her suspected paramour: "And if thou love another man, for sothe / Right with this swerd thanne wol I sle yow bothe" (8.167-68). As much as the *Second Nun's Tale* concentrates on the eroticized relationship between Cecilia and God, Valerian too learns that forgoing earthly eroticism prepares him to enjoy eternal bliss. When Valerian visits Pope Urban to confirm the truth of Cecilia's message, Urban responds with words laden in images of chastity that he subverts in the same breath:

> "Almyghty Lord, O Jhesu Crist," quod he,
> "Sower of chaast conseil, hierde [shepherd] of us alle,
> The fruyt of thilke seed of chastitee
> That thou has sowe [sown] in Cecile, taak to thee!
> Lo, lyk a bisy bee, withouten gile,
> Thee serveth ay thyn owene thral [servant] Cecile." (8.191-96)

Employing the mixed metaphor of a planter sowing seeds who also works as a shepherd, Urban envisions Jesus as propagating chastity among his believers. Yet the inherent contradiction of this imagery arises in the simple fact that humans cannot reproduce asexually, and so the reference to the "fruyt of thilke seed of chastitee" exposes the carnality obscured but impossible to overlook in this metaphor. The fact that Jesus sowed this "seed of chastitee" in Cecilia cannot help but bear traces of human eroticism, particularly because it stands in contrast to Valerian's semen, which is indicative of human procreation but was forbidden to multiply in her womb. Both erotic and antierotic, Jesus's "seed of chastitee" will allow Cecilia to increase and multiply the number of Christian believers. The subsequent description of Jesus serving Cecilia "lyk a bisy bee" deepens the antierotic tenor of the passage because bees symbolized chastity in the Middle Ages.[9] In a final oxymoronic image that complements the tale's interest in eroticized chastity, Jesus, Cecilia's heavenly lord, serves her, his servant.

Adhering to its key theme of Cecilia's energetic proselytizing mission, alluded to in the prologue's description of her as "swift and bisy evere in good werkynge" (8.116), the plot of the *Second Nun's Tale* advances quickly. Following his conversion, Valerian is advised to live with "body clene and with unwemmed [unblemished] thoght" (8.225) and to "be chaast and hate vileynye" (8.231); his newfound chastity coincides with his newfound ability to win converts to Christianity. His brother Tiburce soon joins the fledgling faith, and as news of this religion spreads, the prefect Almachius sends Maximus to execute those who will not sacrifice to Jupiter. Upon witnessing Valerian's and Tiburce's execution, in which they display their "humble herte and sad devocioun" (8.397), Maximus is converted, and, like Cecilia, he succeeds in winning numerous new followers to Christianity—"And with his word converted many a wight" (8.404)—that results in his execution as well. Summoned before Almachius, who orders her either to offer a sacrifice to Jupiter or to recant her faith, Cecilia eloquently responds: "O juge, confus in thy nycetee [foolishness], / Woltow that I reneye [abjure] innocence, / To make me a wikked wight?" (8.463-65). Rather than renouncing her innocence, which denotes a range of virtues including her faith, her devotion, and her chastity, Cecilia further challenges Almachius, pointing out to him the limitations of his authority as a secular ruler.

By the necessity of Chaucer's plot and themes, Almachius cannot be converted to Cecilia's viewpoint. This courtroom scene, in Roger Ellis's words, is designed "to produce not a convert but a martyr. . . . [T]hough both sides go through the motions of attempting to change one another's positions, they are locked into a situation whose possibilities diminish as the argument proceeds, until at the end only martyrdom remains."[10] Frustrated and angry, Almachius orders her execution:

... "In hire hous," quod he,
"Brenne [burn] hire right in a bath of flambes rede."
And as he bad, right so was doon the dede;
For in a bath they gonne hire faste shetten,
And nyght and day greet fyr they under betten. (8.514-18)

According to V. A. Kolve, the traditional iconography of this scene hums with erotic tension, with the virgin's placement in a bath titillatingly suggesting her naked body surrounded by flames symbolizing sexual lust.[11] Chaucer does not specify Cecilia's nudity in this account of her martyrdom, yet it is clear that, rather than a rising heat with hints of eroticism, she remains coolly detached: "She sat al cool and feelede no wo. / It made hire nat a drope for to sweete [sweat]" (8.521-22). This scene inverts Paul's famed admonition that one should marry rather than indulge in sinful sexuality: "But I say to the unmarried, and to the widows: It is good for them if they so continue, even as I do. But if they do not contain themselves, let them marry. For it is better to marry than to be burnt" (1 Corinthians 7.8-9). Paul admonishes Christians to marry rather than to face the metaphorical fires of lust and the spiritual fires of damnation; Cecilia, in contrast, patiently abides the fires of her martyrdom to prove her commitment to her chastity and her faith.

Frustrated by Cecilia's supernatural survival, Almachius sends his servant to behead the martyr. Despite this executioner striking her three times, she survives, as the narrator reports:

He myghte noght smyte al her nekke atwo [in two];
And for ther was that tyme an ordinaunce
That no man sholde doon man swich penaunce
The ferthe [fourth] strook to smyten, softe or soore,
This tormentour ne dorste do namoore. (8.528-32)

This odd law prohibits the executioner from striking Cecilia's neck a fourth time, with the story thus curiously emphasizing three strokes. With three a number of symbolic significance in Christian traditions, it would appear that the three strokes numerologically align Cecilia with the Trinity in this scene laden with erotic imagery. The gashes on her neck crudely acknowledge that the executioner's sword has penetrated her body, and Cecilia's blood thus adumbrates not merely a physical wound but a spiritual deflowering. The rupturing of her hymen, a liminal event delayed from her wedding night, now metaphorically transpires as she ascends to her rightful place as God's eternal lover. Certainly, Cecilia's blood dominates the iconography of this scene: "But half deed, with hir nekke ycorven there, / He lefte hir lye, and on his wey he went. / The Cristen folk, which that aboute hire were, / With sheetes han the blood ful faire yhent [caught]" (8.533-36). As Paul Strohm trenchantly points out, "Bloody beds are rife in late medieval literature," and he cites the appearance of these over-determined tropes of intercourse in the *Wife of Bath's Prologue*, Julian of Norwich's *Showings*, Beroul's *Tristan*, and Chrétien de Troyes' *Lancelot*.[12] These examples of bloody sheets testify to the persistence and prevalence of this sexual symbolism in various highly charged erotic scenes. Most obviously, bloody sheets indicate the penetration of a bride's hymen, with the red stains providing visual evidence of her prior virginity. The scene of marital consummation that was promised on Cecilia's wedding night to Valerian now transpires, albeit metaphorically, as Cecilia assumes her new position as a martyred spouse of Christ.

Moreover, although Cecilia refused intercourse with Valerian and thus refused to procreate with him, her symbolic marriage to Christ allows her to multiply the faithful even more than previously. During the three days she lives in torment, she "nevere cessed [ceased] hem the feith to teche / That she hadde fostred; hem she gan to preche" (8.538-39). As a married couple typically establishes a new household together, Cecilia accomplishes this feat in her dying moments, donating her personal possessions to Pope Urban and endowing her home as a church: "Hir hous the chirche of Seint Cecilie highte [is called]; / Seint Urban halwed [blessed] it, as he wel myghte; / In which, into this day, in noble wyse, / Men doon to Crist and to his seint servyse" (8.550-53). Rejecting the earthly roles of wife and mother, Cecilia assumes these positions in their spiritual forms. Within this medieval economy of sex and its repression, a woman cannot become a mother without losing her virginity, yet Cecilia eludes this biological necessity and metamorphoses into a virgin mother, one modeled on Mary herself. Somewhat ironically, in her prologue, the Second Nun prays to Mary and praises Jesus's assumption of a human body: "That no desdeyn [disdain] the Makere hadde of kynde [mankind, humanity] / His Sone in blood and flessh to clothe and wynde" (8.41-42). The human body offers a fitting cloak for divinity but a debasing shell for humans, and transcending its desires requires steadfast action to build the church that will guide believers to their heavenly rewards. Ever busy in life and even in dying, Cecilia dedicates herself to multiplying the faithful through acts metaphorically suggestive of marriage and intercourse that nonetheless stress her devoted chastity.

From the mouth of this invisible nun comes a tale of sexual abstemiousness that abounds with eroticized imagery, undoing the imagery of women's virginity so central to its meaning. While speaking of a text's subconscious bears the risk of anthropomorphism, it nonetheless aptly captures the self-contradictions of the *Second Nun's Tale*, in which this unknowable nun speaks of chastity while subverting her messages through divine carnality. With Cecilia as a martyr rejecting all human advances but penetrated, naked, and burning in her desire for God, and with God apparently returning her ardor, the cool chastity of martyrdom proves merely a facade for desires that refuse to be denied. With this stunning divergence between the Second Nun's intentions and her tale's conflicting significations, Chaucer creates a character of impenetrable objectives, for her invisibility cloaks any interpretation we might devise to account for them. In what could be considered as much a fault of etiquette as of narrative construction, Chaucer did not introduce this character to his readers, and so we are left with a one-sided conversation in which this Second Nun stands mutely alongside her verbose tale. By assigning this tale to a placeholder character, Chaucer lost the opportunity to heighten the satire, or the piety, or the humor, or the devotion of the *Canterbury Tales* as a whole, thus diminishing what could have been an even loftier achievement in favor of a blank slate simultaneously overwritten with sex.

CHAPTER 22

The Textbook Rhetoric and Pedantic Poetics of the *Canon's Yeoman's Tale*

Nineteenth-century showman P. T. Barnum famously proclaimed, "There's a sucker born every minute," and as long as suckers have fallen for get-rich-quick schemes, scammers, hucksters, and grifters have preyed on the gullible. In his Canon's Yeoman's prologue and tale, Chaucer seeks to expose to his readers the sleights of hand behind the pseudoscience of alchemy, warning them of its meretricious allure and phantom payoffs. In assigning this lesson to the Canon's Yeoman, however, Chaucer creates a narrative voice unsure of his authority yet steeped in alchemical knowledge. Such tensions between a depth of experience but a lack of expertise enhance the characterization of the Canon's Yeoman, yet they simultaneously handicap his exposé of alchemy's false promises, as the influence and rhetorical style of alchemical textbooks undercut the presentation of his lesson. The Canon's Yeoman envisions alchemists as scholars poring over books—"Though he sitte at his book bothe day and nyght / In lernyng of this elvysshe nyce loore" (8.841-42)—but such books frequently cramp his tale-telling efforts, thus highlighting the poetic perils of pedantry. The genre of a textbook, perhaps not too surprisingly, does not translate into a particularly effective narrative form, thus resulting in another example of Chaucer's genre troubles.

Whereas many of the prologues of the *Canterbury Tales* begin with an exchange of words, often quite pointed, the Canon's Yeoman's prologue begins with a striking scene of dramatic action. Following the conclusion of the *Second Nun's Tale*, a man in black clothes, accompanied by his yeoman, chases down the pilgrims in a mad dash on sweating horses (8.558-60). This Canon hopes to "riden in this myrie compaignye" (8.586), and his Yeoman soon makes an amazing claim of alchemical wonder: that the Canon "koude al clene turnen up-so-doun, / And pave [the road to Canterbury] al of silver and of gold" (8.625-26). Harry Bailly, suspicious of these claims, rudely asks the Yeoman, "Why artow so discoloured of thy face?" (8.664). This blunt query sparks a change of heart in the Yeoman, who then admits that alchemists can only "doon illusioun" (8.673) of transmuting base metals into gold, and the Canon, realizing that his accomplice has unveiled their scam, "fledde awey for verray sorwe and shame" (8.702). Segueing from prologue to tale, the Canon's Yeoman promises to divulge the secrets and scams of alchemy to the pilgrims: "Now wolde God my wit myghte suffise / To tellen al that longeth [belongs] to that art!" (8.715-16). Many of the strengths and weaknesses of the Canon's Yeoman's ensuing tale derive from his incorporation of alchemical lore into an otherwise engrossing narrative of con men always on the make for a mark. In alternating between his autobiographical account of the misfortunes that alchemy spawns and his pedagogical account of its lore, the Canon's Yeoman wavers in the delivery of his lesson that one must be wary of pseudoscientific grifters, mixing genres to ill effect.

Congruent with the pedagogical focus of the *Canon's Yeoman's Tale*, one of its dominant themes treats the perils of ignorance. Knowledge is a virtue, but alchemical knowledge has brought the Canon's Yeoman only misery, and so his perspective on education is necessarily colored—or discolored, as is his face—by his experiences in the field. Indeed, Chaucer employs the word *lewed*, meaning "uneducated," "ignorant," and "unlettered," more in the Canon's Yeoman's prologue and tale than in any other of his works, which alerts readers to the centrality of this theme.[1] After Harry Bailly's suspicious questions about alchemy, the Canon's Yeoman proposes that overconfidence in wisdom is folly: "Wherfore in that I holde hym lewed and nyce. / For whan a man hath over-greet a wit, / Ful oft hym happeth to mysusen it" (8.647-49). Despite his extensive experience with alchemy, he says simply of himself, "I am a lewed man" (8.787), and he dismisses the possibility of teaching this pursuit to another: "Al is in veyn, and parde, muchel moore. / To lerne a lewed man this subtiltee— / Fy! Spek nat therof, for it wol nat bee" (8.843-45). When a group of alchemists are discussing an experiment gone explosively awry, one blames another: "Straw! . . . ye been lewed and nyce. / It was nat tempred as it oghte be" (8.925-26). The Canon's Yeoman also cites Arnaldus of Villanova: "Lan no man bisye hym this art for to seche, / . . . / And if he do, he is a lewed man" (8.1442, 1445). Collectively, these references to "lewedness" establish alchemy as a paradoxical site of learning: ignorant men are handicapped because they do not know its secrets, but its practitioners are likewise revealed to be "lewed" because they seek answers that can never be found.

Alchemy, in a real sense, is a lesson both unlearnable and unteachable, as these contrasting uses of "lewed" demonstrate.

The Canon's Yeoman's prologue foreshadows the tale's interest in pedagogical rhetoric in its allusion to Cato, whose *Distichs* was widely used as a textbook throughout the Western Middle Ages. As Paul Clogan documents, "Composed in the third century . . . the *Distichs of Cato* offered easy and practical wisdom in a collection of philosophical maxims put in distichs or couplets."[2] Chaucer as narrator employs his knowledge of the *Distichs* in depicting the Canon's realization of his Yeoman's confession:

> Whil this Yeman was thus in his talkyng,
> This Chanoun drough hym neer and herde al thyng
> Which this Yeman spak, for suspecioun
> Of mennes speche evere hadde this Chanoun.
> For Catoun seith that he that gilty is
> Demeth alle thyng be spoke of hym, ywis. (8.684–89)

Chaucer's translation captures the essence of Cato's words: "Ne cures, si quis tacito sermone loquatur: / Conscius ipse sibi de se putat omnia dici."[3] The allusion to Cato's lesson establishes the prologue's and tale's interest in pedagogical themes, as it also models their effective deployment, with Chaucer as pilgrim imputing motives to the Canon based on his own understanding of school lessons learned long ago.

Winding down his prologue, the Canon's Yeoman vows to teach the pilgrims the full extent of his alchemical knowledge. "Al that I kan anon now wol I telle" (8.704), he states, and soon adds, "Now wolde God my wit myghte suffise / To tellen al that longeth to that art!" (8.715–16). The final line of the prologue affirms his aspiration to share the full range of his alchemical experiences: "Swich thyng as that I knowe, I wol declare" (8.719). Preparing to deliver this extensive lecture on alchemy, the Canon's Yeoman strengthens the tale's thematic consideration of "lewedness" by first admitting his ignorance of the subject: "With this Chanoun I dwelt have seven yeer, / And of his science am I never the neer [nearer]" (8.720–21). While his words most likely indicate his continued ignorance of this complex topic, one could also interpret them as signifying that, despite these seven years of study, there is no science of alchemy for the Yeoman to have learned, and so that he is stressing the emptiness of the subject rather than the limits of his learning. In either case, his ambition is to reveal alchemy as a fraudulent pursuit, as he explains further: "Whan we been there as we shul exercise / Oure elvysshe craft, we semen wonder wise, / Oure termes been so clergial and so queynte" (8.750-52). The Yeoman's reference to an "elvysshe craft" refers primarily to alchemy while also capturing the wider rhetorical skills necessary for understanding and teaching its "clergial" and "queynte" lexicon. In an intriguing parallel, *craft* also refers to rhetorical manipulation, as noted by the author of the handbook *Rhetorica ad Herennium*: "Craft is exercised by means of money, promises, dissimulation, accelerated speed, deception, and the other means."[4] The thematic overlaps between alchemy as an "elvysshe craft" and as deceitful rhetoric are striking, in that both focus on financial gain, overbroad assertions, trickery, quick talking, and other such falsehoods. In exposing the "elvysshe craft" of alchemy, the Canon's Yeoman also exposes the rhetorical craftiness necessary to advance it.

Continuing his speech, the Canon's Yeoman stresses that he lacks the necessary knowledge of alchemy to impart a meaningful lesson:

> Ther is also ful many another thyng
> That is unto oure craft apertenyng.
> Though I by ordre hem [them] nat reherce kan,
> . . . .
> Yet wol I telle hem as they come to mynde,
> Thogh I ne kan nat sette hem in hir kynde. (8.784-86, 788-89)

The Canon's Yeoman positions himself as an ineffective teacher, one who knows his subject matter but lacks a proper framework for imparting it to others. In the following twenty-eight lines, he catalogs alchemical ingredients and equipment with little purpose other than to say the words aloud, with occasional interjections testifying to his ability to add even more terms. This list begins:

> As boole armonyak, verdegrees, boras,
> And sondry vessels maad of erthe and glas,
> Oure urynales and oure descensories,
> Violes, crosletz, and sublymatories,
> Cucurbites and alambikes eek,
> And othere swiche, deere ynough a leek. (8.790-95)

It is quite likely that many medieval readers, and most modern readers as well, could not identify the more esoteric of these terms. For example, the

Middle English Dictionary cites only one example of *descensorie* (from the *Canon's Yeoman's Tale*, of course), only two examples of *sublymatorie*, and only eight examples of *cucurbite*, all of which appear in rather technical passages.[5] In a real sense, many of these actual words could be substituted with nonsense words, and the rhetorical effect would be similar. This passage is key to assessing the Canon's Yeoman's expertise and thus his character as well. Edgar Duncan observes that "the yeoman pours forth a helter-skelter list of materials, apparatus, and processes which he cannot give in order because he is a 'lewed' man."[6] Robert Cook rebuts Duncan's reading, arguing that the passage "does not reveal a confused and ignorant mind but is rather a deliberate attempt to portray the great and hopeless complexity of the practice of alchemy."[7] In a third view, Jackson Campbell asserts that, in the Yeoman's long list of alchemical terms, Chaucer aspires to humor: "Chaucer the poet doubtless meant to achieve comic effects with this excessive detail. . . . As [the] monologue proceeds, it appears that this extensive list has very little function and leads nowhere, but it clearly shows that even in his reformed state the Yeoman retains his fascination for the craft."[8] Despite the differences in these viewpoints, they converge on the challenges of imparting alchemical knowledge, for alchemy muddies interpretive clarity owing to the very fact of its arcane lore, deceptive practices, and imaginary results.

A particularly frustrating feature of the Canon's Yeoman's rhetorical style emerges in his apparent realization of this humdrum litany yet his decision to continue regardless. Following his dismissive assessment of alchemical equipment and ingredients as "deere ynough a leek"—in other words, worthless—he states, "Nat nedeth it for to reherce hem alle" (8.796). Despite his apparent realization that only rarely does a list in itself pique the interest of one's students, he immediately returns to the list. "Watres rubifying, and boles galle, / Arsenyk, sal armonyak, and brymstoon" (8.797-99), he begins, and again it matters little whether his medieval or modern audiences understand the alchemical signification of reddening water, bull's gall, arsenic, sal ammoniac, and brimstone (sulfur). He then turns to another category of ingredients: "And herbes koude I telle eek many oon, / As egremoyne, valerian, and lunarie, / And othere swiche, if that me liste tarie" (8.799-801). Any hope the Canterbury pilgrims likely hold that the Canon's Yeoman will indeed prefer not to tarry and instead proceed with his tale are quickly dashed, for he continues with his slap-dash rehearsal of alchemical terms for seventeen more lines.

Ironically, although the Canon's Yeoman proclaimed that he could "by ordre . . . nat reherce" the various ingredients and equipment of alchemy, his next lessons are structured according to the lessons through which he learned this material. "I wol yow telle, as was me taught also, / The foure spirites and the bodies sevene" (8.819-20), he states, and the following lines impart this information. The "foure spirites," or volatile substances, refer to quicksilver (mercury), orpiment (arsenic trisulfide), sal ammoniac, and brimstone (8.822-24), and the "bodies sevene" refer to celestial bod-ies: the sun, the moon, Mars, Mercury, Saturn, Jupiter, and Venus. This orderly lesson, however, is delivered through pedantic poetics structured on a singsong rhythm:

> The bodyes sevene eek, lo, hem heere anoon:
> Sol gold is, and Luna silver we threpe [assert],
> Mars iren [iron], Mercurie quyksilver we clepe [call, identify],
> Saturnus leed [lead], and Juppiter is tyn,
> And Venus coper, by my fader kyn! (8.825-29)

As Helen Cooper proposes, the Canon's Yeoman's lessons "read like nursery-rhyme mnemonics, like 'Thirty days hath September,' which as poetry leaves . . . much to be desired."[9] Mnemonic verses were used in a variety of pedagogical settings throughout the Middle Ages, for both lower-level and advanced students. Indeed, eleventh-century educator Egbert of Liège, in his *Fecunda ratis* (The Well-Laden Ship), endorses the pedagogical function of such verse, first by denigrating scurrilous rhymes but then detailing the utility of mnemonic verse.[10] Unsophisticated poetry can serve gainful purposes, Egbert acknowledges, yet such doggerel need not then be conscripted into literary works.

As much as the textbook rhetoric of the Canon's Yeoman detracts from the narrative arc of his story, his wide-ranging knowledge of alchemical practices enhances it in numerous other instances. When the Canon's Yeo-man refrains from teaching alchemy yet uses knowledge of its practices to enrich his autobiographical account of its dangers, he paints detailed images for his auditors, such as when describing his shame over his for-mer duplicities:

> Evere whan that I speke of this falshede,
> For shame of hym my chekes wexen rede.
> Algates they bigynnen for to glowe,
> For reednesse have I noon, right wel I knowe,
> In my visage. (8.1094-98)

The Canon's Yeoman's cheeks once glowed with redness before he undertook alchemical pursuits, lost their radiance owing to the "fumes diverse / Of metals" (8.1098-99), and now blaze again in shame, much like a flickering fire heating an alembic in which various ores are alchemically transmuting. As Joseph Grennen states of such imagery and its effects, "The point is that in the aggregate the details of physical description of the Canon and the Yeoman relate themselves more satisfactorily to a pattern built upon a comic inversion of alchemical theory than they do to a pattern based upon humanly realistic appearances."[11] Grennen also points to the following passage, in which the Yeoman describes the protean mutability of the Canon: "On his falshede fayn wolde I me wreke [avenge myself], / If I wiste [knew] how, but he is heere and there; / He is so variaunt, he abit [abides, remains] nowhere" (8.1173-75). "This looks very much like a Chaucerian version of an alchemical description of mercury," Grennen states,[12] and thus the Canon's Yeoman captures the mercurial qualities of his former ally by metaphorically depicting him as the element.

Moving from alchemical theory to flimflam artistry, the Yeoman explains in detail the Canon's scam for deceiving their dupes. The plan, as John Reidy summarizes, is both simple and precise:

> The crucible containing one ounce of quicksilver (8.1120-21) is put on the fire, and the canon throws in the purported "powder of projection." The canon has the priest build up the charcoal (1157), but, pretending to correct him, sets a special piece above the crucible (1189-91). This contains silver filings in a hole stopped with wax (1160-64); when the wax melts the silver drops into the crucible. The trick depends on the fact that the quicksilver boils and vaporizes at about 357° C, leaving only the silver, which melts at 962° C (1196-1200). The canon pours the molten silver into an ingot or mold, which he has cut to measure out of chalk (1222-23, 1232-33), and drops it into cold water. The result is a one-ounce bar of silver, to all appearance, transmuted from quicksilver.[13]

The Canon's Yeoman interjects, "What, devel of helle, sholde it elles be? / Shaving of silver silver is, pardee!" (8.1238-39), as he then recounts how the Canon further convinces his dupes of his alchemical abilities, employing a hollow stick in which he packs an ounce of silver filings (8.1264-82) and a sleight-of-hand trick in which he replaces copper with silver (8.1296-1340). Thrilled by the appearance of these alchemical transformations, the victim pays the Canon forty pounds to learn his secrets, and the Canon's Yeoman concludes his lesson by warning the Canterbury pilgrims to avoid alchemical pursuits: "Medleth namoore with that art, I mene, / For if ye doon, youre thrift is goon ful clene" (8.1424-25).

By the end of his tale, the Canon's Yeoman speaks ambiguously on the topic of alchemy, thus further undermining the efficacy of his lesson. He cites Arnaldus of Villanova, the author of the treatise *Rosarie*, to conclude, "Lat no man bisye hym this art for to seche, / But if that he th'entencioun and speche / Of philosophres understonde kan" (8.1442-44). Arnaldus leaves open the possibility that scholars of sufficient wisdom might indeed discover the secrets of alchemy, and the Yeoman also cites an encounter between Plato and a student, in which they discuss the mysteries of the philosopher's stone. Plato admonishes, "The philosophres sworn were everychoon / That they sholden discovere it unto noon [no one], / Ne in no book it write in no manere" (8.1464-66), yet similarly alludes to alchemy's potential benefits to inspire humanity. The Canon's Yeoman advises, "Thanne conclude I thus, sith [since] that God of hevene / Ne wil nat that the philosophres nevene [name] / How that a man shal come unto this stoon, / I rede [advise], as for the beste, lete it goon" (8.1472-75). George Keiser traces the ways in which readers have responded to these concluding passage in sharply divergent ways, as either an endorsement or a rejection of alchemy: "It is both interesting and ironic to observe how, in the history of these readings, past and present readers have found assurances in these lines for the views of alchemy that have prevailed in their own worlds."[14]

The Canon's Yeoman's ambiguous ending echoes the sentiments of contemporary alchemists such as Geber, who shroud the mysteries of alchemy in secrets that simultaneously foster belief and disbelief: "If they say that philosophers and leading men of this world have desired this science and have not found it, we answer that they lie. For we read that certain leaders (though few) and especially the ancient, and wise men of our time have by their own industry found out . . . this science, but would not either by word or by writings discover it to such men because they are unworthy of it."[15] Also, as much as the quest for alchemical transformations strikes modern readers as hopelessly misguided, the Canon's Yeoman repeatedly links it to the quest for God's inspiration: "[God] had ymaad us spenden muchel good, / For sorwe of which almoost we wexen wood, / But that good hope crepeth in oure herte" (8.868-70). Ann Astell notes the ambiguity arising from the Canon's Yeoman's contrasting views of alchemy: "Sometimes the Yeoman represents his contract with his lord as a pact with the devil; at other times, he virtually identifies God with the 'philosophres stoon.'"[16] Alchemists thrive on elusive hope, both their own and of others, with even their failures potentially reimagined as a quest for greater understanding of God's creation.

By employing the pedagogical strategies of textbooks, the Canon's Yeoman illuminates his themes but undermines his rhetorical eloquence. For the most part, however, he achieves his goal of alerting his auditors to the physical and spiritual degradation accompanying alchemy. Certainly, most textbooks of the Middle Ages were written for the ultimate glory of God, as evident in Theophilus's words, in his twelfth-century manual *On Divers Arts*: "When you have read this again and again and entrusted it to your memory, you will repay your instructor for his pains if every time you have made good use of my work, you pray for me that I may receive the mercy of Almighty God who knows that . . . I have given aid to many men in their need and have had concern for their advancement to the increase of the honor and glory of His name."[17] In his final words, the Canon's Yeoman advises his audience not to "maketh God [their] adversarie" (8.1476) and prays that "God sende every trewe man boote [reward] of his bale [suffering]!" (8.1481). With this empathetic valedictory, the Canon's Yeoman concludes his tale that demonstrates the ways in which the genre of a textbook deadens one's rhetoric, even when the lesson remains worthy of students' attention.

CHAPTER 23

The Empty Birdcage and Paradoxical Punishment of the *Manciple's Tale*

Is a bird vanquished from its cage punished or emancipated? Chaucer implicitly poses this perplexing thematic question in the *Manciple's Tale*, which features such paradoxes as a god of chaos who fosters order, a god of reason who acts unreasonably, a punishment that fails to punish, and a theme unmoored from its thematic meaning. Probing the constraints of civilization as one of its key story lines, the *Manciple's Tale* dramatizes rebellions against authority that expose the pretense of ostensibly civilized protocols; in these portrayals of disorder, however, Chaucer chooses not to endorse anarchy but to reinstate order at the tale's conclusion, resulting in a narrative that teeters between insurrection and control. In the concluding lines in which the Manciple ventriloquizes his mother urging him to heed his tale's lesson, its theme is both confirmed and ridiculed, reinstated and parodied, which calls into question the exemplary meaning that the Manciple ostensibly imparts in it.

As critics have long discussed, the *Manciple's Prologue* and *Tale* contrast two diverging perspectives on civilization: the Dionysian and the Apollonian. In Greek mythology, Zeus's son Dionysius represents wine and inebriation, chaos and disorder, unbridled desire and bodily pleasure; another son, Apollo, represents the sun and clarity, rationality and order, music and harmony. The *Manciple's Prologue* begins with the Canterbury pilgrims noticing a key indicator of the Dionysian worldview: their fellow pilgrim, the Cook, is drunk. Realizing that the Cook seems to be drowsing on horseback, Harry Bailly inquires, "Hastow had fleen [fleas] al nyght, or artow dronke?" (9.17). The Manciple tells the Cook bluntly, "thy breeth ful soure stynketh" (9.32), and then points out to the pilgrims, "See how he ganeth [yawns], lo, this dronken wight, / As though he wolde swolwe [swallow] us anonright" (9.35-36). Proving Harry Bailly's and the Manciple's assumptions correct, the Cook falls off his horse in a drunken stupor. Harry Bailly attempts to bring order to this chaotic scene by requesting the Manciple to tell a tale instead of the Cook; the Manciple agrees, and in an ironic twist, silences the Cook by giving him more wine (9.92-93). Pleased with the Manciple's solution to the Cook's misbehavior, Harry Bailly discerns the positive value of alcoholic beverages: "I se wel it is necessarie, / Where that we goon, good drynke with us carie; / For that wol turne rancour and disese / T'acord and love, and many a wrong apese [appease, mollify]" (9.95-98). One can readily envision a contrasting viewpoint to Harry's, one that decries wine's ability to foment discord and dissension and instead urges Apollonian moderation, but within this Dionysian worldview, the disorder that wine produces through drunkenness unexpectedly preserves the social order. Harry Bailly concludes the *Manciple's Prologue* with a prayer to Bacchus—"O Bacus, yblessed be thy name, / That so kanst turnen ernest into game! / Worshipe and thanke be to thy deitee!" (9.99-101)—as he then requests the Manciple to proceed with his tale. Within the worldview of the *Manciple's Prologue*, the standard dichotomy between Dionysian and Apollonian worldviews is overturned, with Dionysian disorder ultimately contained by Dionysian order. This ironic conclusion to the *Manciple's Prologue* demonstrates both that Apollonian order does not always triumph over Dionysian bacchanals and that the Dionysian can trump the Apollonian according to its own terms.

In introducing his primary character—Dionysus's brother, Phoebus Apollo—the Manciple shifts his thematic perspective from the Dionysian to the Apollonian. Chaucer invokes Apollo in his *House of Fame*, "O God of science and of lyght" (1091), and the Manciple begins his tale by sketching Phebus's personal traits, frequently with superlatives. "He was the mooste lusty bachiler / In al this world, and eek the beste archer" (9.107-8), the Manciple begins, as he also cites the god's heroic accomplishments, notably the slaying of the Python. The defeat of monstrous adversaries accords with Phebus's reputation as a preserver of the social order, and his musical performances delight all who hear them: "Pleyen he koude on every mynstralcie, / And syngen that it was a melodie / To heeren of his cleere voys the soun" (9.113-15). Atonal compositions aside, music's sonorous aesthetics arise from harmonies, which serve as an apt metaphor for the Apollonian view of culture and society. The Manciple also notes Phebus's attractiveness: "Therto he was the semelieste man / That is or was sith that the world bigan" (9.119-20). Physical attractiveness is often praised on the basis of symmetries; as music is an aural harmony, beauty is an optical one. Moreover, Phebus models the values "of gentillesse, / Of honour, and of parfit worthynesse" (9.123-24).

Yet as much as Phebus represents social order and harmony, the *Manciple's Tale* indicates that he imposes his view of civilization on his household, which, as the tale unfolds, hints that his Apollonian values seek to quell others' Dionysian instincts. In paired lines, the narrator introduces the tale's other primary characters: "Now hadde this Phebus in his hous a crowe" (9.130) and "Now hadde this Phebus in his hous a wyf" (9.139). Phebus has tamed his white crow, putting it "in a cage," fostering it for "many a day," and successfully teaching it to speak (9.132). The crow is originally depicted in much the same terms as Phebus himself. Its physical description—"Whit was this crowe as is a snow-whit swan" (9.133)—points to its beauty, and it is sufficiently civilized to speak: "And countrefete the speche of every man / He koude, whan he sholde telle a tale" (9.134-35). Nightingales are frequently praised for the beauty of their songs, but this crow surpasses their vocal stylings: "Therwith in al this world no nyghtyngale / Ne koude, by an hondred thousand deel, / Syngen so wonder myrily and weel" (9.136-38). Notably, the crow exponentially improves on the nightingales' performance, which further points to the ways in which it fractures any firm border between the natural and the civilized worlds.

Treating his wife similarly to his crow, Phebus metaphorically encages her in their home, despite the narrator's observation that faithful wives require no surveillance: "A good wyf, that is clene of werk and thoght, / Sholde nat been kept in noon awayt [under watch], certayn" (9.148-49). Strong marriages should not be based on rigorous monitoring, and so this passage points to two possibilities: either Phebus wrongfully mistrusts his wife (who will remain faithful) or he rightfully mistrusts his wife (who will cuckold him). Either option foreshadows the breakdown of the order ostensibly upheld in his household. From the Manciple's portrait of Phebus, it is clear that he demands his pet and his wife to adhere to his standards of civilized behavior and order, thus to keep life's Dionysian elements at bay.

The tale's plot is simple: Phebus's wife cuckolds him with a "man of litel reputacioun, / Nat worth to Phebus in comparisoun" (9.199-200), as the crow witnesses this betrayal. When Phebus returns home, the crow sings, "Cokkow! Cokkow! Cokkow!" (9.243), with the pun on *cuckold* upsetting the god. Before revealing what he witnessed, the crow accentuates the contrast between Phebus and his wife's lover. "For al thy beautee and thy gentilesse, / For al thy song and al thy mynstralcye" (9.250-51), he stresses, as he then dismisses Phebus's wife's lover as "oon of litel rep- utacioun, / Noght worth to thee, as in comparisoun, / The montance [value, extent] of a gnat" (9.253-55). It is intriguing to ponder which adverb would best capture the bird's intonations—"impassively"? "compassionately"? "tauntingly"?—for this exercise encourages readers to contemplate its motivation for informing Phebus of this adulterous affair. As Brian Strair documents of Chaucer's influences for this tale, "Almost all of the sources imply or explicitly state that the bird deserves punishment: the bird is either warned by another bird against jangling; . . . or the bird tells Phoebus for the selfish reason of hoping to receive a reward; or the bird is referred to as a 'fals bridd' and one who is wont to jangle."[1] In a fit of sorrow ("his sorweful herte" [9.262]) and anger ("his ire" [9.265]), Phebus murders his wife: "His bowe he bente, and sette therinne a flo [arrow], / And in his ire his wyf thanne hath he slayn" (9.264-65). He immediately repents his actions and blames the crow. "Traitour . . . with tonge of scorpioun" (9.271), he lambastes his pet, as he then eulogizes his wife. Significant to the conflicting themes of the tale, Phebus now refuses to believe the crow's revelation of her liaison, apostrophizing her as "O deere wyf" and lauding her as "so sad and eek so trewe" (9.274-75). Throughout Phebus's pursuit of murderous revenge, he loses the veneer of civilization so central to his mythic identity, now employing his iconic bow and arrow to kill his wife in an act of domestic violence rather than to destroy a monstrous adversary with the goal of preserving the social order (as he did with the Python).

In the tale's account of his final acts, Phebus apparently aspires to pun- ish the crow, thus to begin the process of restoring order to his fractured household. He excoriates the bird as a "false theef" (8.292) and promises vengeance: "I wol thee quite anon thy false tale" (9.293). For this punish- ment, Phebus deprives it of its melodious voice and white feathers: "Thou songe whilom lyk a nyghtyngale; / Now shaltow, false theef, thy song forgon, / And eek thy white fetheres everichon, / Ne nevere in al thy lif ne shaltou speke" (9.294-97). Phebus also condemns the crow's descendants—"Thou and thyn ofspryng evere shul be blake" (9.299)—with these words imbuing an etiological theme concerning the origin of crows' black feathers. Given his harsh words and actions, Phebus appears to be punishing the crow, and many scholars agree with this assessment. Britton Harwood notes that Phebus "proceeds to punish the crow, principally by rendering him speech- less,"[2] and Michaela Paasche Grudin likewise avows that the tale ends with "a punishment for truthtelling complete with the crow's banishment."[3]

Phebus's retribution nonetheless appears thematically paradoxical, for he emancipates the crow as part of this "punishment." The narrator records that Phebus "out at dore hym [the crow] slong / Unto the devel" (9.306-7), with the additional threat that it will "evere crie agayn tempest and rayn" (9.301) now that it has lost its cage in Phebus's household. Presumably the crow lived in nature before Phebus tamed it, and so its return to the natural world would simply reinstate the status quo. Moreover, as David Raybin pointedly queries of this crow's desires, "Why would a crow value human speech or even wish to possess a song better than the nightingale's? Is it unreasonable to assume that a bird momentarily possessed of Reason might choose to give up that Reason?"[4] Anthropomorphic preconceptions undergird any belief that a crow would embrace the encumbrances and protocols of human civilization—that is to say, would embrace Apollonian restraints over Dionysian freedoms. Ann Astell views the crow's obscure motivation for informing Phebus of his wife's adultery as connected to the equivocal nature of its punishment: "Indeed, the ambiguity about the crow's underlying motivation contributes to Chaucer's antisacrificial depiction of the bird as a scapegoat, a figure cursed and blessed."[5] Cursed *and* blessed or cursed *or* blessed, the crow eludes simplistic identifications as victim, villain, or possibly trickster. From a Dionysian perspective, the crow has been liberated from its former imprisonment and restored to its natural habitat, but from an Apollonian perspective, it has been justly punished for destroying the civilized protocols that Phebus sought to maintain for his home, even if they were only a facade.

These converging yet contradictory themes indicate that, although Phebus is assuredly attempting to punish the crow, the crow is unlikely to perceive freedom as a punishment. Earlier in the tale, the narrator explicitly states that birds prefer the untamed forest over gilded prisons:

> Taak any bryd, and put it in a cage,
> And so al thyn entente and thy corage
> To fostre it tendrely with mete and drynke
> Of alle deyntees that thou kanst bithynke,
> And keep it al so clenly as thou may,
> Although his cage of gold be never so gay,
> Yet hath this brid, by twenty thousand foold,
> Levere [prefer] in a forest that is rude and coold
> Goon ete wormes and swich wrecchednesse.
> For evere this brid wol doon his bisynesse

To escape out of his cage, yif he may.
His libertee this brid desireth ay. (9.163-74)

This passage, which follows the lines in which Phebus trains and encages the crow, ironically underscores the futility of his civilizing mission. Chaucer considers similar concepts in his translation of Boethius's *Consolation of Philosophy*, in which readers learn that "the janglynge brid that syngeth on the heghe braunches . . . and after is enclosed in a streyte cage, althoughe that the pleyinge bysynes of men yeveth [hym] honyed drynkes and large metes with swete studye, yit natheles yif thilke bryd skippynge out of hir streyte cage seith [sees] the agreables schadwes of the wodes, sche . . . seketh mornynge oonly the wode" (book 3, metrum 2, lines 21-30). Resisting humanity's impulse to anthropomorphize the animal kingdom, this bird rejects a cosseted life in a cage in exchange for its accustomed accommodations in nature. In an irony of particular relevance to the *Manciple's Tale*, Boethius links the nature of birds to the nature of Phebus in his role as the sun: "The sonne, Phebus, that falleth at even in the westrene wawes [western waves], retorneth ayen eftones his cart, by a pryve path, there as it is wont t'aryse" (book 3, metrum 2, line 39). Immutable in his daily regimen of rising in the east and setting in the west, Phebus fails to recognize the mutability of others when interacting with his bird and his wife. This section of the *Consolation of Philosophy* posits, "Alle thynges seken ayen to hir propre cours, and alle thynges rejoysen hem of hir retornynge ayen to hir nature" (book 3, metrum 2, line 40), with the pairing of a bird and the sun illuminating their similar pairing in the *Manciple's Tale*.

If one views the *Manciple's Tale* as thematically narrating a clash between nature and civilization, it becomes apparent that Phebus loses the markers of civilization following the murder of his wife. The Manciple states that he abandons his musical pursuits ("For sorwe of which he brak his mynstralcie, / Both harpe, and lute, and gyterne, and sautrie" [9.267-68]); he also breaks his bow and arrows (9.269). Indeed, Phebus even alludes to the possibility of the ultimate act of dissolution by suicide: "Allas! For sorwe I wol myselven slee!" (9.291). By rejecting music, hunting, and life, Phebus no longer symbolizes civilization, as Michael Kensak proposes: "Whether Phebus literally kills himself at the end of the tale is of less significance than his iconicide. Chaucer's audience knew Apollo by his bow, lyre, and crow. . . . By the time Phebus wishes that he were dead, he has already destroyed the symbols that represent him in medieval iconography."[6] Further along these lines, Phebus's moral character can no longer exemplify the *gentilesse* that served as one of his defining traits. To look at another violent man in Chaucer's corpus, the rapist knight of the *Wife of Bath's Tale* loses any claim to this virtue following his cruel act, as his wife pointedly reminds him: "Thanne am I gentil, whan that I bigynne / To lyven vertuously and weyve [avoid] synne" (3.1175-76). Gentility depends on one's actions, not simply on presumptions of one's virtue, and Phebus's murderous rage strips away one of his defining features.

In his *Manciple's Prologue* and *Tale*, Chaucer subverts any balance or definition between the Dionysian and Apollonian worldviews, with the prologue portraying the creation of Dionysian order and the tale portraying the rise of Apollonian disorder. In itself, such an ironic dismantling of these contrasting perspectives would stand as one of Chaucer's most provocative themes, in the deconstruction of their presumed opposition in favor of a deeper understanding of the ways in which the Dionysian informs the Apollonian and vice versa. This profound theme imbues the *Manciple's Prologue* and *Tale* with philosophical depth, as it exposes the limitations inherent in rigid categories of human experience, yet this meaning is belied by its surface story of an errant crow, its paradoxical punishment, and the narrator's insistence that a moral theme should be excavated from this story.

After completing his tale's narrative action, the Manciple identifies its genre as an "ensample" (9.309), which builds on his earlier citation of Plato: "The wise Plato seith, as ye may rede, / The word moot nede accorde with the dede" (9.207-8). As words must conform to the deeds they describe, so too should a tale's theme conform to the actions described therein, and the Manciple explicitly summarizes the lesson he intends to divulge: "Ne telleth nevere no man in your lyf / How that another man hath dight his wyf" (9.311-32). Contradicting the long-standing proverb that one should not shoot the messenger for delivering unwelcome tidings, the Manciple urges messengers to realize that their fate is inextricably intertwined with the news that they impart, as Helen Phillips explains: "Phoebus punishes the servant who, in fact, faithfully brings a message, and would clearly prefer not to receive it; his later remorse restores a truer moral balance. The cynical overt message that ends Chaucer's tale is that servants act best by keeping true reports away from lords."[7] Indeed, Phebus earlier states, "Ne trowe [believe] no thyng withouten strong witnesse" (9.284), which suggests both his belief that accusations should be confirmed before punishments are executed and ironically highlights the fact that, in this instance, the crow testified candidly about what he witnessed.

One might presume the tale should end at this moment when the Manciple explicitly declares the theme of his exemplary narrative, yet in a surprising twist, he then begins ventriloquizing his mother's voice. Just as it is intriguing to consider the ways in which the crow intoned his revelation of Phebus's wife's adultery, it is similarly productive to ponder how the Manciple mimics his mother in this extended passage of verbal transvestism. Does he speak in his own voice and relate her advice neutrally, or adopt an inflection suggestive of a woman's pitch, or exaggerate a feminine voice such that it becomes a caricature? Notwithstanding these multiple possibilities of vocal performance, the rhetoric attributed to the Manciple's mother registers as excessive. "My sone, thenk on the crowe, a Goddes name! / My sone, keep wel thy tonge, and keep thy freend" (9.318-19), she begins, and this maternal advice continues until the tale's conclusion, with repeated apostrophes to the narrator as "sone" and "my sone" (9.321, 322, 325, 329, 332, 335, 346, 351, and 359). The repetition of "sone" functions as virtually a rhetorical cage, foreclosing the narrator's agency as a tale-teller and textual interpreter whose mother monitors his speech, which then hints at his likely exaggeration of her words as a means of reinstating masculine prerogatives. Celeste Patton espies in this exaggerated rhetoric the subversion of women's agency: "In his positioning of final authority in a female speaker at the end of the tale [the Manciple] seems to be giving pride of place to her *sententia*. Yet the worldly expedience of her advice and the Manciple's parodying of her motherly voice undermines her as a figure of authority."[8] Few discourses are as resistant to parody as advice, for one typically offers advice sincerely, yet the Manciple corrupts the clear intentionality of his mother's words through the excess of his performance. Throughout these muddied lines, maternal advice contrasts sharply with filial rhetoric, and even though the *Manciple's Tale* concludes with her words—"Whereso thou come, amonges hye or lowe, / Kepe wel thy tonge and thenk upon the crowe" (9.361-62)—they are spoken by her son, and thus subject to the imposition of his intonation, whether sincere or parodic.

In the final analysis, the sharp disjunction between Phebus's attempted punishment of the crow and the Boethian philosophy recognizing the natural tendencies of animals to live as animals cannot be smoothly aligned, and neither can the tale's final passages of maternal advice voiced by a male character. Without a punishment, the theme of the Manciple's exemplary tale collapses, for instead of an admonition against speaking unwelcome truths to powerful authorities, its theme transforms into an endorsement of the unexpected benefits of a punishment that simply reinstates the world's natural order. The tale's closing words of maternal ventriloquism further accentuate the meaningless of its message, as this voice, worriedly fretting over her child's future, encourages him to ponder the meaning of the crow's experience without understanding its full meaning. The paradox of a punishment that rewards is never resolved, leaving the *Manciple's Tale* a purportedly exemplary narrative that exemplifies the confusion in a world where Dionysian chaos brings order and Apollonian civilization foments the murder of a woman and the meaningless punishment of a bird. After all, the crow flies freely away from the chaos he leaves behind, a perhaps apt metaphor for Chaucer's conclusion of a tale that promises meaning but leaves behind only contradictions.

CHAPTER 24

The Meek Heretic and Narrativeless Narrative of the *Parson's Tale*

Heretics rarely play by the rules. By the very fact that their spiritual beliefs conflict with the established practices of their religions, they tend more to be firebrands than blushing violets, agitators than pacifiers. With Chaucer's Parson, however, readers have long sensed hints, albeit rather softly spoken, of his antagonistic stance toward the prevailing practices of medieval Christianity. In his portrait in the *General Prologue* and as evidenced by accusations aimed against him by Harry Bailly and the Shipman, the Parson appears supportive of the sharp critiques promoted by such reformers as John Wycliffe and the Lollards, with these sympathies calling into question the orthodoxy of his beliefs. His tale adopts a more orthodox tone in its call for Christians to participate in the sacrament of penance, yet it too contains whispered references to Lollardy. Beyond the issue of his religious beliefs, the Parson reimagines the requirements of the tale-telling game by sharing a penitential treatise rather than a narrative tale. Although not quite a spoilsport, the Parson does not engage in the tale-telling game with the same recreational enthusiasm shared by many of his fellow pilgrims. By characterizing his Parson as a meek heretic, Chaucer ends his *Canterbury Tales* on a note of questionable orthodoxy and of mirthless play.

A fourteenth-century reformatory movement spearheaded by theologian John Wycliffe, Lollards railed against the abuses of the medieval church. One of their foundational documents, the treatise "Twelve Conclusions of the Lollards," outlines their tenets and condemns such matters as the connections of the English priesthood to "the grete chirche of Rome," which they denigrated as a "stepmother" to their reformed church. Lollards censured the requirement of priestly chastity, which they alleged promoted sodomy, and the "feynid miracle" of the Eucharist, which they argued "inducith alle men but a fewe to ydolatrie." Exorcisms and even some blessings were castigated, as were pilgrimages. The sacrament of penance spurred great concern because Lollards asserted that priests possessed only "a feynid power of absoliciun."[1] The Lollards' critique of penance corresponds with their endorsement of vernacular preaching, for they believed that individual Christians should not require priestly intercessions to commune with God. To this end, Wycliffe participated in efforts to translate the Christian Bible into English, which represented a radical rupture with past traditions. As Frances McCormack notes of the intersection of penance and translation, "It seemed as though, by denying the miraculous power of the clergy, Wycliffe and the Lollards were trying to usurp clerical authority and to return it to the lay person. The call for vernacularity was therefore the ultimate threat."[2] Predating by several decades Martin Luther's 1517 promulgation of his Ninety-Five Theses, also known as the *Disputation on the Power and Efficacy of Indulgences*, the Lollards laid the foundations of the Protestant Reformation, with many of the ensuing branches of Christianity enacting reforms that they advocated.

Long before the Parson tells the last of the *Canterbury Tales*, Chaucer, in his joint roles as author and narrator, glowingly characterizes the Parson with terms that nonetheless admit the possibility of his Lollardy. His portrait in the *General Prologue* begins: "A good man was ther of religioun, / And was a povre PERSOUN OF A TOUN, / But riche he was of hooly thoght and werk" (1.477-79). In his role as naive narrator, Chaucer refers to various pilgrims as good, including the Shipman (1.395), the Wife of Bath (1.445), the Plowman (1.531), and the Knight (1.850), and so readers should not accept this endorsement at face value; however, the following lines of this character sketch praise the complementarity of the Parson's material poverty with his spiritual riches, thus corroborating the appropriateness of the simple epithet "good." The Parson, along with the Knight and the Plowman, is traditionally viewed as one of the three Ideal Pilgrims of the *Canterbury Tales*, each of whom represents a key segment of society: the religious orders, the aristocracy, and the workers. As Jill Mann explains in her definitive study of Chaucer's depiction of social class: "When Chaucer describes an 'ideal' representative, he takes care to indicate also what is the 'normal'; the account of the Parson's virtues inevitably suggests the sins of the average priest, and his portrait thus becomes representative of the estate in both its good and its bad aspects."[3] Chaucer as narrator records that the Parson is "in his techyng discreet and benygne" in the hope "To drawen folk to hevene by fairnesse, / By good ensample, this was his bisynesse" (10.518-20). As this character sketch winds down, Chaucer adds simply, "A bettre preest I trowe that nowher noon ys" (1.524).

Along with such words of high praise, Chaucer includes accounts of the Parson's preaching methods, and these passages contain hints of his Lollard sympathies. Lollards endorsed learning the Christian faith directly from the Gospels rather than from church fathers and other authorities, and the portrait of the Parson in the *General Prologue* speaks to this belief by stressing the centrality of the Gospels for educating the laity. Commencing this aspect of his portrait, Chaucer writes, "He was also a lerned man, a clerk, / That Cristes gospel trewely wolde preche" (1.480-81). These words may not appear very controversial, as the Gospels play a central role in medieval preaching (as they continue to play in modern Christian preaching), but the portrait further emphasizes the ways in which the Parson models his own life and behavior on the lessons of the Gospels: "This noble ensample to his sheep he yaf, / That first he wroghte, and afterward he taughte. / Out of the gospel he tho [those] wordes caughte" (1.496-98). These words allude to Jesus's admonition, "He therefore that shall break one of these least commandments, and shall so teach men, shall be called the least in the kingdom of heaven. But he that shall do and teach, he shall be called great in the kingdom of heaven" (Matthew 5.19), and thus demonstrate that the Parson incarnates through his actions Jesus's words. In this portrait's final reference to the Gospels, Chaucer as narrator notes of the Parson: "Cristes loore and his apostles twelve / He taughte; but first he folwed it hymselve" (1.527-28). As a whole, these passages paint the Parson as a man of spiritual action, inspired by the Gospels to act on his parishioners' behalf and to lead by spotless example. In his reading of the Parson's portrait in the *General Prologue*, R. S. Loomis affirms, "It is safe to say that when Chaucer spoke of the Parson as teaching Christ's lore and that of the apostles, he left no doubt in the minds of contemporary readers that here was the ideal priest conceived according to the Lollard view."[4] While offering a more refined view of the nuances in this portrait, Katherine Little speaks to the ways in which "the accusation of Lollardy . . . seems to be confirmed by the portrait in the *General Prologue*. This Parson 'Cristes gospel trewely wolde preche' (1.481), and his single-minded adherence to interpreting and teaching the gospel . . . supports the term 'Lollere.'"[5]

Over the course of the *Canterbury Tales*, the Parson next appears in the epilogue of the *Man of Law's Tale*, and this encounter gives further credence for viewing him as a Lollard. Harry Bailly praises the Man of

Law's story and requests the Parson take the next turn in the tale-telling game: "Sir Parisshe Prest . . . for Goddes bones, / Telle us a tale" (2.1166-67), he requests, as he also associates him with other "lerned men in lore" (2.1168). The Parson, offended by Harry's sacrilegious reference to God's body, upbraids the Host: "Benedicite! / What eyleth the man, so synfully to swere?" (2.1170-71). Harry replies with an accusation of Lollardy—"O Jankin, be ye there? / I smelle a Lollere in the wynd" (2.1172-73)—and then continues: "Abydeth, for Goddes digne passioun, / For we schal han a predicacioun [sermon]; / This Lollere heer wil prechen us somwhat" (2.1175-77). The Shipman interjects himself into the dispute and denies the Parson his turn in the game: "Heer schal he nat preche; / He schal no gospel glosen [interpret] here ne teche" (2.1179-80). Notably, the Shipman's words reestablish the connection between the Parson and the Gospels earlier seen in the *General Prologue*, as it also brings up the vexing issue of the Shipman's motivation in halting the Parson's tale. One might reasonably presume that this pirate, only euphemistically granted the neutral epithet of a "shipman," would object to the Parson's sermon because he would likely find it tedious or that, as a sinful man, he would prefer not to be reminded of his sinful state. The Shipman puts forth a different reason, however, that again links the Parson to heresy: "We leven [believe] alle in the grete God . . . / He wolde sowen som difficulte, / Or springen cokkel [weeds] in our clene corn" (2.1181-83). The Latin word *lollium* translates as "weed," with this pun between *lollium* and *Lollard* casting these believers as weeds among the faithful. The reference to *cokkel* also alludes to Jesus's parable of a farmer who sowed his field with wheat but whose enemies spread cockle over it. As the parable concludes, this farmer commands his harvesters, "Suffer both to grow until the harvest, and in the time of the harvest I will say to the reapers: Gather up first the cockle, and bind it into bundles to burn, but the wheat gather ye into my barn" (Matthew 13.30). This parable advocates earthly patience in the promise of divine justice, with the Shipman thus hinting at the Parson's future judgment for disseminating heresies among the faithful. Through this strikingly paradoxical scene, the Shipman appears to be an immoral man of devout belief, and so the ideal portrait of the Parson from the *General Prologue* is now cast in doubt. Lollardy raises vexing spiritual questions of belief, counterbelief, faith, and truth, and as Andrew Cole posits, "Chaucer here is . . . figuring in rather minute detail the larger cultural context in which 'lollardy' is both an object of sympathy and scorn alike."[6]

The Parson next appears toward the close of the *Canterbury Tales*, as the day winds down, with the tale-telling competition apparently winding down as well (despite the fact that many of the pilgrims have not told a tale, and none have told the four tales allotted in Harry Bailly's plan for two on the way to Canterbury and two on the return trip). Connected to the heretical hints in the Parson's depiction in these earlier scenes, the *Parson's Prologue* highlights that priests do not agree with one another on their preferred methods of preaching to the faithful. When Harry Bailly requests, "Telle us a fable anon, for cokkes bones" (10.29), the Parson refuses— "Thou getest fable noon ytoold for me" (10.31)—and he cites Paul's epistle to Timothy as the textual authority for his decision: "For Paul, that writeth unto Thymothee, / Repreveth hem that weyven soothfastnesse / And tellen fables and such wrecchednesse" (10.32-34; cf. 1 Timothy 1.4, 4.7 and 2 Timothy 4.4). With these words the Parson is apparently snubbing the Nun's Priest, his fellow priest and pilgrim who told a beast fable and justified his tale by similarly citing Paul: "But Seint Paul seith that al that writen is, / To our doctrine it is ywrite, ywis [certainly]" (7.3441-42; cf. Romans 15.4). Indeed, the parallels between the passages extend further, as the Parson asks, "Why sholde I sowen draf [chaff] out of my fest [fist, hand], / Whan I may sowen whete, if that me lest?" (10.35-36); his words echo the Nun's Priest's advice to "Taketh the fruyt, and lat the chaf be stille" (7.3443). Chaucer does not develop this clerical disagreement further, instead allowing the disjunction in the Parson's and the Nun's Priest's perspectives to speak for themselves. The earlier accusation of Lollardy against the Parson haunts this passage, for it implicitly asks readers to consider the fact that priests do not agree on central tenets of their sacred practice.

As his prologue continues, more contradictions undercut the coherency of the Parson's character. Appropriate to his position as the final tale-teller, he agrees to "telle a myrie tale in prose / To knytte up al this feeste and make an ende" (10.46-47), and he states the spiritual purpose behind his tale is to "shewe yow the wey, in this viage [voyage], / Of thilke parfit glorious pilgrymage / That highte [is called] Jerusalem celestial" (10.49-51). Here Chaucer links the earthly pilgrimage to Canterbury to the spiritual pilgrimage to salvation, with the boisterous voices heard throughout the *Canterbury Tales* ceding to the Parson's spiritual leadership. The Parson, however, apologizes in advance for any unorthodox statements he might make in his tale:

But nathelees, this meditacioun
I putte it ay under correccioun
Of clerkes, for I am nat textueel;
I take but the sentence, trusteth weel.
Therfore I make protestacioun
That I wol stonde to correccioun. (10.55-60)

This passage would apparently rebut any efforts to paint the Parson as a heretic, for the simple reason that heretics do not allow themselves to be corrected by the authorities against whom they have already rebelled. The Parson, in effect, retracts any errors he might make before he makes them, as, following the *Parson's Tale*, Chaucer retracts any spiritual blunders he might have committed in the *Canterbury Tales* after he has (incompletely) completed them.

In contrast to the jumble of genres preceding the *Parson's Tale*, including romance, fabliau, allegory, hagiography, parody, and more, the Parson opts for a tale without a narrative, thus corrupting the prevailing sense of what constitutes a tale. Even Chaucer's *Tale of Melibee*, the one most similar to the *Parson's Tale* in its moral themes, its prose construction, and its longwinded exposition, includes a story line of Melibee's eventual forgiveness of his enemies. Richard Newhauser identifies the genre of the *Parson's Tale*, concluding that it "belongs to a specific genre among this mass of late-medieval religious prose, that of the penitential manual, a literary form which is well represented in Latin from the thirteenth-century onwards and, by the late Middle Ages, in all European vernaculars as well."[7] As Thomas Bestul explains further of its generic conventions, "The *Parson's Tale* marks a transition in the *Canterbury Tales* from the public oral, fictional mode of the tales to the private realm of the treatise." He also points out that the *Parson's Tale* is twice referred to as a "meditacioun"— first by the Parson (as cited above) and then by Harry Bailly, who requests of the Parson, "Telleth . . . youre meditacioun" (10.69). As the *Canterbury Tales* comes to its conclusion, the Parson replaces narrative action with meditative contemplation, redirecting the often frenetic energies of carnival and celebration to the reverential reflection that should accompany the sacrament of penance.

If the Parson should be considered a Lollard, it is odd that in this "meditacioun" he mulls over the protocols of penance, for Lollards harshly condemned several aspects of this sacrament. Karen Winstead summarizes their objections: "Wycliffe held that contrition alone is essential for obtaining absolution; since only God can know the heart of a sinner, only God can forgive sins."[8] In light of the Lollards' condemnation of the sacrament of penance because it requires clerical intercession, it is then difficult to see evidence of Lollardy in the *Parson's Tale*, for the Parson's "tale" is hardly one in the sense of a narrative with a plot, setting, and characters and instead is a penitential tract explaining the processes that lead to the atonement of one's sins. Also, following his disquisition on the Seven Deadly Sins, the Parson states, "Now after that I have declared yow, as I kan, the sevene deedly synnes, and somme of hire braunches and hire remedies, soothly, if I koude, I wolde telle yow the ten comandementz. / But so heigh a doctrine I lete [leave, grant] to divines" (10.956-57). By deferring to the "divines" on this matter, the Parson acknowledges the hierarchical nature of the medieval Christian church, thus further distancing him from accusations of Lollardy.

Within this penitential tract, readers can nevertheless discern murmurs of Lollard thought, such as in the ways in which the Parson marginalizes the role of priests in confession by focusing on the need for privacy: "Pryvee penauance is thilke that men doon alday for privee synnes, of which we shryve [confess] us prively and receyve privee penaunce" (10.106). In a detailed analysis of the Lollards' lexicon, Frances McCormack scrutinizes their multivalent use of the word *order*, such as in these lines from the Parson: "And al be it so that God hath creat alle thynges in right ordre, and no thyng withouten ordre, but alle thynges been ordeyned and nombred; yet, natheless, they that been dampned been nothyng in ordre, ne holden noon ordre, for the erthe ne shal bere hem no fruyt" (10.218-19). As McCormack demonstrates, "These two lines are loaded with key Lollard terms used frequently in reference to the fraternal orders. 'Order' itself is used in most Lollard sermons, and is occasionally qualified, as in 'ordre of Crist,' which is used to refer to the Lollards themselves. Such a phrase obviously sets the sect in contrast with the orders of the religious clergy, deemed, by the Lollards, to be corrupted by their failure to adhere to the rules that were supposed to define them."[9]

The prominent metaphor of priests as shepherds to their congregations as flocks appears both in the *General Prologue*'s portrait of the Parson and in the *Parson's Tale* and offers another opportunity to consider the orthodoxy of the Parson's faith. The shepherd should serve as a moral paragon for his congregation to follow, and the *General Prologue* stresses that the Parson fulfills this role: "And shame it is, if a prest take keep, / A shiten [fouled, shit-stained] shepherde and a clene sheep. / Wel oghte a preest ensample for to yive, / By his clennesse, how that his sheep sholde lyve" (1.503-6). When discussing the deadly sin of sloth, the Parson cautions: "Thanne comth lachesse [laziness]; that is he that whan he biginneth any good werk anon he shal forleten [forsake] it and stynten [cease], as doon they that han any wight to governe and ne taken of hym namoore kep anon as they fynden any contrarie or any anoy [annoyance]. / Thise been the newe sheepherdes that leten [allow] hir sheep wityngly go renne to the wolf that is in the breres [briars, prickly bushes], or do no fors of hir owene governaunce" (10.720-21). In condemning these "newe sheepherdes," the Parson upbraids men who neglect their pastoral responsibilities, yet it is intriguing to consider precisely whom he considers a "newe sheepherde." One could reasonably propose that he refers to newly ordained priests uninterested in their duties or to Lollards attempting to initiate a new model of the church.

In a final irony, if readers believe that Chaucer depicts his Parson as breaking away from Catholic orthodoxy in the hints of Lollardy in his pro-logue and tale, they must confront the fact that this heretical Parson falls into hypocrisy by joining the pilgrimage. A contemporary Lollard tracts advises that "shulden grete men and comyners in the rewme avowe rather, and to do it in dede, and trist in God in her owne just lif, and not in siche veyn pilgrymagis."[10] With the Parson vacillating between a heretical version of Catholicism and a lax adherence to the critiques of Lollardy, one must question by what standards he merits the simple affirmation as a "good man . . . of religioun" (1.478). By pointing to the limitations of both orthodoxy and heterodoxy, Chaucer leaves readers unsure of his Parson's beliefs, and thus of the ways in which Christianity inspires his righteous living. To this end Chaucer's theology may suffer from internal contradictions that call into question his characterization of the Parson and the meaning of the final entry in the *Canterbury Tales*, but through these conundrums his understanding of human nature seems even more perceptive, for many devout members of a faith do not subscribe to all of its doctrines.

As the last of the *Canterbury Tales*, the *Parson's Tale* is tasked with bringing closure to an unfinished work, a paradoxical and improbable assignment grounded more in readers' desire for finality than in the tale's own ambitions. Without a closing frame narrative, readers can never know whether Chaucer envisioned this treatise as winning the tale-telling game, although such a conclusion is readily imaginable in the move from the secular pleasures of romance and fabliau to the Parson's excursus on penance and proper living. As Charlotte Gross proposes, this concluding narrative of the *Canterbury Tales* need not be imagined as achieving or even attempting for closure, as its deeper ambition arises in its call for its audience to examine their values: "Along with its strong movements towards ending and its many intimations of closure . . . the *Parson's Tale* introduces an equally strong anti-closural movement of 'not ending.' This is the forward-looking 'goode wey' (10.77), which leads the Chaucerian audience away from the fictional world of pilgrims and tales—not towards transcendent reality, but instead towards the English here and now, towards a practical scrutiny of self guided by the Parson's careful treatment of penitence."[11] Ending yet not ending, seemingly orthodox while heretical, the *Parson's Tale* embraces the multiplicity of meaning and interpretation available throughout the *Canterbury Tales* and results in Chaucer's paradoxical characterization of a meek heretic, one who is granted the final word in the tale-telling game and perhaps, or perhaps not, Harry Bailly's prize of a free supper for its winner. We'll really never know.

Conclusion

The Better Badness of Chaucer's Retraction

Chaucer retracts his *Canterbury Tales* with a short valedictory address headlined, "Heere taketh the makere of this book his leve," in which he beseeches his readers to pray for him and to forgive him for "any thyng that displese hem." He would have done better if he could have done better, Chaucer insists, requesting any dissatisfied readers to blame his errors "to the defaute of myn unkonnynge [ignorance] and nat to my wyl, that wolde ful fayn have seyd bettre if I hadde had konnynge" (10.1082). He then explains that, even if he failed in the execution of his tales, his intentions were praiseworthy, echoing a defense spoken earlier by his Nun's Priest that cites the apostle Paul: "'Al that is writen is writen for oure doctrine,' and that is myn entente" (10.1083; cf. *Nun's Priest Tale* 7.3441-43). Here Chaucer alludes to Paul's letter to the Romans, in which he advocates: "For what things soever were written, were written for our learning: that through patience and the comfort of the scriptures, we might have hope" (15.4). Not to make too fine a point of it, but it is difficult to see how thunderous farts, copulating chickens, a rapist knight, pear-tree fornication, alchemical con games, among numerous such other topics, would contribute to one's spiritual development. Chaucer apparently acknowledges such a rebuttal by specifically apologizing for "the tales of Caunterbury, thilke [those] that sownen into [lead toward] synne" (10.1086). One might question the sincerity of such an apology, for surely if Chaucer truly recanted these works, he might have sought to destroy the manuscripts, or not to have written such morally dubious materials in the first place.

In recognizing that some readers might criticize his works as sinful—which is to say, morally bad—Chaucer's Retraction buttresses the aims and scope of this book, although the "badness" under investigation herein has not included the potential sinfulness of the tales within medieval

Christian belief but has instead focused on a wider range of lapses and blunders in the fields of genre troubles, themeless themes, mischaracterized characters, outmoded perspectives, and pleasureful and purposeful badness. While I hope that these short excurses have proved persuasive in detailing the effects of Chaucer's literary faults, I must also follow Chaucer's lead and, if not quite retract my interpretations, place them in a fuller context. Perfection looms as an unattainable goal for all artists and all artworks, and so their flaws and lapses, misjudgments and misfires, deserve not merely to be discussed and analyzed but also to be recognized as part of their very greatness. Perfection would be boring; blunders enhance the humanity of a work. As Tristanne Connolly lyrically observes, "One of the great projects of life is to learn to love real human beings (including oneself) instead of imagining, and not finding, perfection. Loving flawed poetry (including one's own) is good exercise."[1] And so is loving Chaucer's.

Notes

Introduction

1. John Ruskin, *The Stones of Venice*, 2.171.
2. Aldous Huxley, *Point Counter Point*, 162.
3. Günter Grass, *The Tin Drum*, 90.
4. Quentin Bell, *Bad Art*, 9.
5. For example, see the studies of Per Algander ("Bad Art") and John Dyck and Matt Johnson ("Appreciating Bad Art").
6. Edmund Becke, "The Bible versus Canterbury Tales, 1549," qtd. in Derek Brewer, *Chaucer*, 1.102; some spelling modernized.
7. Sir Philip Sidney, "The Defence of Poesie," in *The Prose Works of Sir Philip Sidney*, 1-46, at 37.
8. Joseph Addison, *The Poetical Works of Joseph Addison*, 27-28, lines 9-16.
9. Daniel Defoe, "Against Printing Indecent Books," qtd. in William L. Alderson and Arnold C. Henderson, *Chaucer and Augustan Scholarship*, 205.
10. Samuel Johnson, "The History of the English Language," in *A Dictionary of the English Language*, 1.1-45, at 19.
11. George Gordon, Lord Byron, qtd. in Derek Brewer, *Chaucer*, 1.249.
12. Matthew Arnold, "Introduction," *The English Poets*, xxxv.
13. Thomas Lounsbury, *Studies in Chaucer*, 3.319-20.
14. Pierre Bourdieu, *Distinction*, 5.
15. David Raybin and Susanna Fein, *Chaucer and Aesthetics*, in *Chaucer Review* 39.3 (2005): 225-340. This issue includes Warren Ginsberg, "Aesthetics *sine Nomine*," 234-40; Peggy A. Knapp, "Aesthetic Attention and the Chaucerian Text," 241-58; Deborah Horowitz, "An Aesthetic of Permeability," 259-79; John M. Hill, "The Countervailing Aesthetic of Joy in *Troilus and Criseyde*," 280-97; Karla Taylor, "Social Aesthetics and the Emergence of Civic Discourse from the *Shipman's Tale* to *Melibee*," 298-322; and Ann W. Astell, "Nietzsche, Chaucer, and the Sacrifice of Art," 323-40.
16. Peggy A. Knapp, *Chaucerian Aesthetics*, 4.
17. Robert Graves, "What Is Bad Poetry?," 355.
18. Robert Graves, "What Is Bad Poetry?," 358.
19. Sarah Baechle and Carissa M. Harris, "The Ethical Challenges of Chaucerian Scholarship," 316.
20. Nahir I. Otaño Gracia, "Borders and the Global North Atlantic," 41.

21. Cord J. Whitaker, *Black Metaphors*, 87.
22. A. S. G. Edwards, "Gladly wolde he lerne?," 8.
23. H. Marshall Leicester Jr., *The Disenchanted Self*, 5–6.
24. Helen Cooper, *Oxford Guides to Chaucer*, 132.

Chapter 1

1. Winthrop Wetherbee, "Romance and Epic," 304.
2. Over the course of Western literature, male characters have enjoyed the role of epic protagonist far more frequently than female ones. On the masculinist bias of epic, see Bernard Schweizer, *Approaches to the Anglo and American Female Epic*.
3. Derek Pearsall, *Arthurian Romance*, 21.
4. W. P. Ker, *Epic and Romance*, 4.
5. Alexandra Cook, "'O swete harm so queynte,'" 28.
6. Colin Burrow, *Epic Romance*, 3. Ironically for the purposes of this chapter, Burrow begins with Homer and Virgil, ends with Spenser and Milton, and skips Chaucer almost entirely.
7. The Knight's identification as a model pilgrim, along with the Parson and the Plowman, has been vigorously debated, most notably in Terry Jones's *Chaucer's Knight*.
8. Robert Haller, "*The Knight's Tale* and the Epic Tradition," 67.
9. John Finlayson, "The *Knight's Tale*," 139.
10. In a further gaffe, classical legends do not tell of the men's adventures in hell; Guillaume de Lorris and Jean de Meun's *Roman de la Rose* (lines 8148–51) is a more likely source for this material.
11. Edmund Spenser, *The Faerie Queene*, canto 1, stanzas 1, 4, and 8.
12. Gertrude Stein, *Everybody's Autobiography*, 289.
13. Northrop Frye, *Anatomy of Criticism*, 319.

Chapter 2

1. D. S. Brewer, "The Fabliaux," 296–97.
2. For *Heile of Beersele*, see Robert M. Correale and Mary Hamel, *Sources and Analogues*, 2.266–75. Frederick Biggs argues that the *Miller's Tale* was not based on, but likely a source of, *Heile of Beersele*, in "The *Miller's Tale* and *Heile van Beersele*."
3. For *Le chevalier a la corbeille*, see Carter Revard, "Four Fabliaux from London, British Library MS Harley 2253."
4. Giovanni Boccaccio, *The Decameron*, 257–58.
5. *MED*, s.v. "leued," 1 (a).
6. Jennifer Bryan, "'A berd! A berd!'" 27. Bryan documents that John is referred to as "sely" in lines 3404, 3423, 3509, 3601, and 3614 of the tale.
7. *MED*, s.v. "sely," 2 (a).
8. Nicholas refers both to Noah's troubles attempting to "gete his wyfe to shipe" (1.3540) and to his preference that "she hadde had a ship hirself allone" (1.3543). Such portraits of Noah's wife are not found in Genesis but in such sources as the Towneley Plays, the Chester Mystery Cycle, and other medieval dramatizations of biblical events.
9. Dawn Simmons Walts, "Tricks of Time in the *Millers' Tale*," 404.

10. Derek Pearsall, "The *Canterbury Tales* II," 110.

11. Cicero, *Cicero on Oratory and Orators*, 151 (from *On the Character of the Orator*, chapter 58).

12. Morton Bloomfield, "The Miller—an UnBoethian Interpretation," 206.

Chapter 3

1. Gale Sigal, *Erotic Dawn-Songs*, 1.

2. Pamela Barnett, "'And shortly for to seyn,'" 145.

3. Carissa M. Harris, *Obscene Pedagogies*, 29.

4. Holly Crocker, "Affective Politics," 246.

5. For *Le meunier et les .II. clers* and *Een bispel van .ij. clerken*, see Robert Correale and Mary Hamel, *Sources and Analogues*, 1.23-73.

6. Giovanni Boccaccio, *The Decameron*, 711.

7. *Auberée*, in Nathaniel Dubin, *The Fabliaux*, 276-315; line numbers cited parenthetically.

8. Nicole Nolan Sidhu, "'To late for to crie,'" 4.

9. John Plummer, "Hooly Chirches Blood," 57.

10. R. E. Kaske, "An Aube in the *Reeve's Tale*," 310.

11. Tamarah Kohanski, "In Search of Malyne," 236.

12. Donald Howard, *Chaucer*, 317.

13. Christopher Cannon, "Raptus in the Chaumpaigne Release," 92. See also his "Chaucer and Rape."

14. Rachel E. Moss, "Chaucer's Funny Rape."

15. Euan Roger and Sebastian Sobecki. "Geoffrey Chaucer, Cecily Chaumpaigne, and the Statute of the Laborers," 435.

16. Samantha Katz Seal, "Whose Chaucer?"

17. Lindy West, *Shrill*, 165.

Chapter 4

1. Barbara Herrnstein Smith, *Poetic Closure*, 36.

2. Rachel Blau Duplessis, "Endings and Contradictions," 284.

3. *MED*, s.v. "herbergage," 2 (a; b).

4. These words attributed to Solomon are found in the apocryphal book of Ecclesiasticus: "Do not invite everyone into your home, for many are the tricks of the crafty" (11.29). Misattributions to Solomon occur frequently in medieval literature.

5. For the historical inspirations of these characters, see Stephen H. Rigby, *Historians on Chaucer*, esp. Christopher Woolgar, "The Cook," 262-76, and Martha Carlin, "The Host," 460-80.

6. John Manly, *Some New Light on Chaucer*, 79. See also Thomas C. Richardson, "Harry Bailly," 325.

7. Edith Rickert, "Chaucer's 'Hodge of Ware,'" 761.

8. For this scribe's markings, see Geoffrey Chaucer, *The Canterbury Tales: A Facsimile and Transcription of the Hengwrt Manuscript*, 224.

9. M. C. Seymour, "Of This Cokes Tale," 259.

10. Jim Casey, "Unfinished Business," 188.

11. M. C. Seymour, "Of This Cokes Tale," 260.

12. David Lorenzo Boyd, "Social Texts, Bodley 686, and the Politics of the *Cook's Tale*," 97.

13. John M. Manly and Edith Rickert, *The Text of the "Canterbury Tales"*, 3.446.

14. Douglas Gray, "Explanatory Notes," in *Riverside Chaucer*, 853.

15. On these points, see E. G. Stanley, "Of This Cokes Tale," 39–43.

16. E. G. Stanley, "Of This Cokes Tale," 59.

17. V. A. Kolve, *Chaucer and the Imagery of Narrative*, 276.

18. V. J. Scattergood, "Perkyn Revelour and the *Cook's Tale*," 22.

19. John Bowers, *The Canterbury Tales: Fifteenth-Century Continuations and Additions*, 33–39, lines 91–94.

20. Daniel Pinti, "Governing the *Cook's Tale* in Bodley 686," 386.

21. Jim Casey, "Unfinished Business," 185 and 191.

Chapter 5

1. Ian McFarland, "Prosperity Gospel," 414 and 415.

2. Additional passages relevant to prosperity theology include Deuteronomy 8.18; 2 Corinthians 8.9; Galatians 3.9; and Philippians 4.19.

3. Kate Bowler, *Blessed*, 11.

4. Laura Hodges, *Chaucer and Costume*, 106.

5. *MED*, s.v. "thrifti" (1a). Secondary definitions include "1. (b) healthy, thriving; (c) skillful, adept; also, learned; (d) well made, of good quality."

6. Diane Cady, "Damaged Goods," 146.

7. Innocent III, *De miseria condicionis humane*, 114–17. Chaucer documents his knowledge of Innocent's writings in his *Legend of Good Women*: "He hath in prose translated Boece, / And Of the Wreched Engendrynge of Mankynde, / As man may in Pope Innocent yfynde" (Prologue G 413–15).

8. Innocent III, *De miseria condicionis humane*, 114 and 116.

9. William Quinn, "String Theory," 52. Quinn's work coincides with this chapter's thesis in his proposition that "the Mercers of London might buy into this anticipation of 'prosperity theology' at face value" (52).

10. Chauncey Wood, "Chaucer's Man of Law," esp. 182–90.

11. Laurel Hendrix, "'Pennance profitable,'" 165.

12. Jill Mann, *Chaucer and Medieval Estates Satire*, 89.

13. Roger Ladd, "The Mercantile (Mis)Reader," 18.

Chapter 6

1. Jennifer Martin, "The *Crossing* of the Wife of Bath," 71.

2. *MED*, s.v. "seli" (1a, 2a, and 2c).

3. Mary Carruthers, "The Wife of Bath," 216.

4. Marilynn Desmond, *Ovid's Art and the Wife of Bath*, 139.

5. Gertrude Jobes, *Dictionary of Mythology*, 1.1596. On the phallic symbolism of the tongue, see Steven Olderr, *Symbolism*, 139.

6. Chelsea Skalak, "The Unwilling Wife," 138.

7. Susan Nakley, "'Rowned she a pistel,'" 71.

8. Arthur Lindley, "'Vanysshed was this daunce,'" 9.

9. Angela Jane Weisl, *Conquering the Reign of Femeny*, 14.

Chapter 7

1. Katie Homar, "Chaucer's Novelized, Carnivalized Exemplum," 90.
2. R. T. Lenaghan, "The Irony of the *Friar's Tale*," 284.
3. Nevill Coghill, *The Poet Chaucer*, 121.
4. David Raybin, "'Goddes instrumentz,'" 99.
5. Brantley Bryant, "'By extorcions I lyve,'" 190.
6. Christopher Dyer, *Standards of Living*, 170.
7. "A Greedy Bailiff," Robert Correale and Mary Hamel, *Sources and Analogues*, 1.96-99. See John Scattergood, "*Goodfellas*," 26.
8. Arthur Brandeis, *Jacob's Well*, 8-9.
9. T. A. Stroud, "Chaucer's Friar as Narrator," 68.
10. Przemyslaw Mroczkowski, "The *Friar's Tale*," 119.
11. Joan Young Gregg, *Devils, Women, and Jews*, 14.

Chapter 8

1. Mikhail Bakhtin, *Rabelais*, 21 and 27.
2. Mikhail Bakhtin, *Rabelais*, 21.
3. Mikhail Bakhtin, *Rabelais*, 15.
4. The title character of *The Sacristan* faces an untimely end, thus serving as a counterexample to this general principle.
5. Giovanni Boccaccio, *The Genealogy of the Gentile Gods*, 423.
6. Simon Critchley, *Very Little*, 25.
7. Stephanie Bird, "Death, Being," 144.
8. Patrick O'Neill, "The Comedy of Entropy," 92.
9. Patrick O'Neill, "The Comedy of Entropy," 92.
10. J. Allan Mitchell, *Ethics and Exemplary Narrative*, 97.
11. Marc Cels, "'An irous man,'" 321.
12. Susan Crane, "Cat, Capon, and Pig," 319-20.
13. Mikhail Bakhtin, *Rabelais*, 410.
14. Alan Levitan, "The Parody of Pentecost," 243.
15. Glending Olson, "Measuring the Immeasurable," 414.
16. Patrick O'Neill, "The Comedy of Entropy," 100.
17. Agnes Heller, *Immortal Comedy*, 7.

Chapter 9

1. Chad Schrock, "Neoplatonic Theodicy," 27-28.
2. J. Ramsay McCallum, *Abelard's Christian Theology*, 45.
3. Julian of Norwich, *Showings*, 201 (fifth revelation, thirteenth chapter).
4. Charlotte Morse, "The Exemplary Griselda," 86.
5. Shawn Normandin, "'Non intellegant,'" 202.
6. Eric Carlton, *Dancing in the Dark*, 99.
7. Leah Schwebel, "Redressing Griselda," 288.
8. Lee Patterson, *Temporal Circumstances*, 62.
9. Helen Cooney, "The *Parlement of Foules*," 373.

Chapter 10

1. Robert Jordan, "The Non-dramatic Disunity," 299.
2. Holly Crocker, "Performative Passivity," 181.
3. For an interpretation concerning the Friar, see Albert Baugh, "The Original Teller"; for the Monk, see Thomas Jay Garbáty, "The Monk and the *Merchant's Tale*."
4. Donald Howard, *The Idea of the "Canterbury Tales"*, 261.
5. Donald Benson, "The Marriage 'Encomium,'" 58.
6. Jacob McDonie, "'Ye gete namoore of me,'" 327.
7. John Finlayson, "The *Merchant's Tale*," 570.
8. Christine Rose, "Women's 'Pryvete,'" 61.
9. J. A. Burrow, "Irony in the *Merchant's Tale*," 205.
10. Karla Taylor, "Chaucer's Reticent Merchant," 200.
11. Emerson Brown, "Chaucer, the Merchant, and Their Tale," 143.
12. To this point a slight caveat should be added: January's voice remains distinct and is demarcated by clear objectives and a consistent tone except during the confusion of the marriage encomium, during which some readers hear his voice but others do not.

Chapter 11

1. Paul Strohm, "Jean of Angoulême," 72.
2. This brief chapter concentrates on the camp humor flourishing in the badness of the *Squire's Tale*. For a more politically and ethically engaged reading that grapples with the tale's "deliberate, wondrous wrongness" in its propensity to "willfully misrecognize peoples, objects, and animals across racial, gender, historical, geopolitical, and species registers," see Wan-Chuan Kao, "In the Lap of Whiteness," 543.
3. Susan Sontag, *Against Interpretation*, 279.
4. Susan Sontag, *Against Interpretation*, 284.
5. Susan Sontag, *Against Interpretation*, 280.
6. Cicero, *De inventione*, 44–45.
7. Ironically, Cicero was long believed to be the author of this anonymous text. See *Rhetorica ad Herennium*, 234–35.
8. Michelle Karnes, "Wonders, Marvels, and Metaphor," 462; see also Patricia Ingham, "Little Nothings."
9. Shirley Sharon-Zisser, "The *Squire's Tale*," 392.
10. For the legend of Canacee, see Ovid, *Heroides and Amores*, chapter 11, pp. 132–41.
11. In his *Legend of Good Women*, Chaucer includes Canacee in a litany of worthy figures (F265 and G219), which complicates simplistic assessments of her character. Chaucer chooses for these legends several problematic famous women, including Medea, and so Canacee's potential inclusion in the *Legend of Good Women* would not definitively overwrite troubling aspects of her story.
12. John McCall, "The Squire in Wonderland," 107.
13. Elizabeth Scala, "Canacee," 27.
14. Robert Miller, "Chaucer's Rhetorical Rendition," 220.
15. Lindsey Jones, "Chaucer's Anxiety," 305.
16. A. C. Spearing, *Medieval to Renaissance*, 37.

Chapter 12

1. Mark Taylor, "Sergeant and Lord," 67.
2. E. Jane Burns, "Courtly Love," 28-29.
3. Leah Otis-Cour, "True Lover," 166.
4. Wan-Chuan Kao, "Conduct Shameful," 104.
5. Jacques Lacan, *The Seminar of Jacques Lacan*, 150-51.
6. Slavoj Žižek, *The Metastases*, 96.
7. Andrea Rossi-Reder, "Male Movement," 105.
8. Emily Houlik-Ritchey, "Dwelling with Humans," 127-28.
9. Bonnie Wheeler, "*Trouthe* without Consequences," 106.
10. Susan Crane, *Gender and Romance*, 111.
11. Chrétien de Troyes, *Arthurian Romances*, 323.
12. Mary Bowman, "'Half as she were mad,'" 247.
13. Alastair Bennett, "'The emprentyng of hire consolacioun,'" 172.
14. Janemarie Luecke, "Dorigen," 118.

Chapter 13

1. Samantha Katz Seal, "Reading Like a Jew," 299.
2. R. Howard Bloch, "Chaucer's Maiden's Head," 153.
3. Glenn Burger, "Doing What Comes Naturally," 125.
4. Anne Laskaya, *Chaucer's Approach to Gender*, 159.
5. Linda Lomperis, "Unruly Bodies and Ruling Practices," 30.
6. Daniel Kline, "Jephthah's Daughter and Chaucer's Virginia," 79.
7. Judson Boyce Allen and Theresa Anne Moritz, *A Distinction of Stories*, 161 and 174 n. 49.
8. Sandra Pierson Prior, "Virginity and Sacrifice," 169.
9. Anne Middleton, "The *Physician's Tale*," 13.
10. Thomas Hanson, "Chaucer's Physician," 138.
11. John Pitcher, "Chaucer's Wolf," 15.
12. Richard Hoffman, "Jephthah's Daughter," 21.
13. Sandra Pierson Prior, "Virginity and Sacrifice," 165.
14. Kate Manne, *Down Girl*, 13.

Chapter 14

1. William Frost, "A Chaucerian Crux," 555.
2. Robert Sturges, *Chaucer's Pardoner*, 40.
3. Robert Merrix, "Sermon Structure in the *Pardoner's Tale*," 247.
4. Steven F. Kruger, "Claiming the Pardoner," 131.
5. George Lyman Kittredge, *Chaucer and His Poetry*, 215.
6. Marie Padgett Hamilton, "Death and Old Age," 576.
7. L. O. Purdon, "The Pardoner's Old Man," 334-49.
8. Takami Matsuda, "Death, Prudence, and Chaucer's *Pardoner's Tale*," 315.
9. Robert Miller, "Chaucer's Pardoner," 188 and 197.
10. Robert Barakat, "Odin," 213-14.
11. Peter Beidler, "Noah and the Old Man," 253.
12. Nelson Sherwin Bushnell, "The Wandering Jew," 456.

13. Mary Flowers Braswell, "Chaucer's Palimpsest," 303-10.
14. Alfred Kellogg, "An Augustinian Interpretation," 474.
15. Alexandra Hennessey Olsen, "'They shul desiren to dye,'" 367-71.
16. Elizabeth Hatcher, "Life without Death," 248.
17. Alfred David, "Criticism and the Old Man," 44.
18. Gudrun Richardson, "The Old Man," 333.
19. John Steadman, "Old Age and *Contemptus Mundi*," 130.
20. Helen Cooper, *Oxford Guides to Chaucer*, 269.
21. Roy Pearcy, "Chaucer's Amphibologies," 4.
22. Lisa Lampert-Weissig, "Chaucer's Pardoner," 340.

Chapter 15

1. W. W. Skeat, *An Etymological Dictionary of the English Language*, 484-85.
2. Paull F. Baum, "Chaucer's Puns," 227.
3. Jonathan Culler, "The Call of the Phoneme," 4.
4. John Pollack, *The Pun Also Rises*, xxii.
5. This overview of Chaucerian puns and the critical tradition relies heavily on Larry Benson, "The 'Queynte' Punnings," 24-25.
6. Thomas Lounsbury, *Studies in Chaucer*, 3.319.
7. John S. P. Tatlock, "Puns in Chaucer," 230 and 229.
8. Helge Kökeritz, "Rhetorical Word-Play," 940-41.
9. Paull F. Baum, "Chaucer's Puns: A Supplementary List," 167-70. See also Norman D. Hinton, "More Puns in Chaucer," 115-16.
10. Larry Benson, "The 'Queynte' Punnings," 47.
11. Archibald Hill, "Chaucer and the Pun-Hunters," 66.
12. Joseph Dane, "'Queynte,'" 498.
13. Ruth Fisher, "Cosyn and Cosynage," 168.
14. *MED*, s.v. "cosin" 1 (a).
15. Ruth Fisher, "Cosyn and Cosynage," 170.
16. David Abraham, "*Cosyn* and *Cosyngage*," 320.
17. *OED*, s.v. "trim" 7.
18. William Shakespeare, *Titus Andronicus*, 5.1.95-96.
19. G. Wapull, *The Tide Tarrieth No Man*, line 809.
20. T. Lupton, *All for Money*, line 1301.
21. Gerhard Joseph, "Chaucer's Coinage," 352.
22. Claude Jones, "Chaucer's *Taillynge Ynough*," 570.
23. Robert Caldwell, "Chaucer's *Taillynge Ynough, Canterbury Tales*, B 1624," 262-65. Some readers may be able to pinpoint the exact distinction between "a subtleness of innuendo" and a pun, yet it seems probable that in this discussion Caldwell is overarchingly concerned with diminishing Chaucer's reputation as a punster.
24. Marsha L. Dutton, "Chaucer's *Cunning*," 57.

Chapter 16

1. Heather Blurton and Hannah Johnson, *The Critics and the Prioress*, 5.
2. This brief history of Jewish life in and exile from medieval England is

adapted from Miriamne Ara Krummel and Tison Pugh, *Jews in Medieval England*, 1-2.

3. William of Norwich allegedly died in 1144, but Thomas of Monmouth began his narrative tracing Jewish conspiracies around the boy's death in 1150. On this issue, see Thomas of Monmouth, *The Life and Passion of William of Norwich*, x.

4. Jeffrey Jerome Cohen, *Stone*, 149.

5. This date of "readmission," 1659, generates some controversy; see David Katz, *Philo-Semitism*, 190-244.

6. Marion Turner, *Chaucer*, 113.

7. Nancy Bradley Warren, "Sacraments, Gender, and Authority," 394-95.

8. Merrall Llewelyn Price, "Sadism and Sentimentality," 201.

9. The identity of this grain has generated scholarly debate, but Kathleen Oliver convincingly identifies it as "a particle of the consecrated Host" in "Singing Bread."

10. Sylvia Tomasch, "Postcolonial Chaucer," 73.

11. Kathy Lavezzo, "The Minister and the Privy," 365.

12. Geraldine Heng, "England's Dead Boys," S67.

13. Florence Ridley, *The Prioress and the Critics*, 12.

14. *MED*, s.v. "sobre," 1 (a), 4, and 5 (a and b).

15. Lawrence Besserman, "Ideology, Antisemitism," 57.

16. Louise Fradenburg, "Criticism, Anti-Semitism," 84.

17. E. T. Donaldson, *Chaucer's Poetry*, 934.

18. Sherman Hawkins, "Chaucer's Prioress," 606.

19. Hardy Long Frank, "Chaucer's Prioress," 358.

20. John Archer, "The Structure of Anti-Semitism," 46.

21. Lee Patterson, "'The Living Witnesses,'" 542.

22. Michael Calabrese, "Performing the Prioress," 72.

23. Stephen Spector, "Empathy and Enmity," 218.

24. Albert Friedman, "The *Prioress's Tale*," 119.

Chapter 17

1. While the critical consensus agrees that the *Tale of Sir Thopas* is a parody, for an opposing view see Kenneth Eckert, "Harry Bailly and Chaucer-Pilgrim's 'Quiting.'"

2. Derek Pearsall, *The Canterbury Tales*, 161-62.

3. J. A. Cuddon, *The Penguin Dictionary of Literary Terms*, 682.

4. Dwight McDonald, *Parodies*, xiii-xiv.

5. Jessica Brantley, "Reading the Forms," 417.

6. J. A. Burrow, "*Sir Thopas*," 58.

7. Seth Lerer, "'Now holde youre mouth,'" 183.

8. *OED*, s.v. "doggerel."

9. Judith Tschann, "The Layout of *Sir Thopas*," 7.

10. Marianne Børch, "Writing Remembering Orality," 134.

11. Martin Stevens, "The Royal Stanza," 67.

12. Alan Gaylord, "Chaucer's Dainty 'Dogerel,'" 275.

13. Alan Gaylord, "Chaucer's Dainty 'Dogerel,'" 280.

14. John Matthews Manly, "The Stanza-Forms of *Sir Thopas*," 144.

15. Marie Boroff, *Traditions and Renewals*, 87-88.

16. Richard Hurd, *Letters on Chivalry and Romance*, 172.
17. C. David Benson, *Chaucer's Drama of Style*, 31.
18. Lindsey Jones, "Chaucer's Anxiety of Poetic Craft," 303.

Chapter 18

1. C. David Benson, "Their Telling Difference," 70.
2. Edward Foster, "Has Anyone Here Read Melibee?," 398.
3. Jeremy Tambling, *Allegory*, 17.
4. Richard Firth Green, *Poets and Princepleasers*, 143.
5. Lynn Staley, *Languages of Power*, 332–33.
6. Carolyn Collette, "Heeding the Counsel," 419.
7. C. David Benson, "Their Telling Difference," 71.
8. Paul Strohm, "The Allegory of the *Tale of Melibee*," 34.
9. *MED*, s.v. "contrarie" 1 and 2(a).
10. Stephen Yeager, "Chaucer's Prudent Poetics," 309–10.
11. Jamie Taylor, "Chaucer's *Tale of Melibee*," 96.
12. Ruth Waterhouse and Gwen Griffiths, "'Swete words,'" 346.
13. David Aers, "Chaucer's *Tale of Melibee*," 81.
14. Chad Crosson, "Chaucer's Corrective Form," 259.
15. William Witherle Lawrence, "The Tale of Melibeus," 100 and 110.
16. Diane Bornstein, "Chaucer's *Tale of Melibee*," 241.
17. Edward Foster, "Has Anyone Here Read Melibee?," 398–99 and 401.
18. John Gardner, *The Life and Times of Chaucer*, 291.

Chapter 19

1. M. C. Seymour, "Chaucer's Early Poem," 165.
2. On Seneca's influence on the Monk's conception of tragedy, see Renate Haas, "Chaucer's *Monk's Tale*."
3. Henry Ansgar Kelly, "The Evolution," 410.
4. Jonathan Hsy, "Diverging Forms," 86.
5. Eleanor Johnson, "Tragic Nihilism," 13.
6. Kemp Malone, *Chapters on Chaucer*, 172.
7. Robert Boenig, "Is the *Monk's Tale* a Fragment?," 264.
8. R. E. Kaske, "The Knight's Interruption," 253.
9. Shawn Normandin, "Reading Chaucer's *Monk's Tale*," 191.

Chapter 20

1. Peter Travis, *Disseminal Chaucer*, 1.
2. Morton Bloomfield, "The Wisdom," 70.
3. Sigmund Freud, *Wit*, 114.
4. Piero Boitani, "'My tale is of a cock,'" 33.
5. John Finlayson, "Reading Chaucer's *Nun's Priest's Tale*," 494.
6. For example, see Craik, *The Comic Tales*, 81n, and Paul Thomas, "'Have ye no mannes herte?'" 188.

7. Dolores Warwick Frese, "The *Nun's Priest's Tale*," 336 and 338-39.

Chapter 21

1. Karen Arthur, "Equivocal Subjectivity," 219.
2. Carolyn Collette, "Critical Approaches to the *Prioress's Tale*," 100 and 95.
3. This reading of the *Second Nun's Tale* is adapted from my *Chaucer's (Anti-) Eroticisms*, 192-203.
4. Margery Kempe, *The Book of Margery Kempe*, 25; archaic letters modernized.
5. Dyan Elliott, *Spiritual Marriage*, 65.
6. Mary Beth Long, "'O sweete and wel biloved spouse deere,'" 166.
7. Elizabeth Robertson, "Apprehending the Divine," 118.
8. Lynn Staley Johnson, "Chaucer's Tale of the Second Nun," 326.
9. Lucia Impelluso, *Nature*, 334.
10. Roger Ellis, *Patterns of Religious Narrative*, 89-90.
11. V. A. Kolve, "Chaucer's *Second Nun's Tale*," 141, 143.
12. Paul Strohm, *Theory and the Premodern Text*, 202.

Chapter 22

1. *MED*, s.v. "leued" 1 (a); and John S. P. Tatlock and Arthur Kennedy, *A Concordance*, 522.
2. Paul Clogan, "Literary Genres," 201.
3. Cato, *The Distichs*, 1.17, at pp. 18-19.
4. *Rhetorica ad Herennium*, 1661.
5. *MED*, s.v. "descensorie" 1; s.v. "sublymatorie" 1; and s.v. "cucurbite" 1 (a).
6. Edgar Duncan, "The Literature of Alchemy," 638.
7. Robert Cook, "The Canon's Yeoman," 29-30.
8. Jackson Campbell, "The Canon's Yeoman," 176.
9. Helen Cooper, *Oxford Guides to Chaucer*, 379.
10. Egbert of Liège, *The Well-Laden Ship*, 5.
11. Joseph Grennen, "Chaucer's Characterization," 281.
12. Joseph Grennen, "Chaucer's Characterization," 283.
13. John Reidy, "Explanatory Notes of the *Canon's Yeoman's Prologue*," *Riverside Chaucer*, 946-51, for line 1117.
14. George Keiser, "The Conclusion of the *Canon's Yeoman's Tale*," 1.
15. Geberus, *Summa perfectionis magisterii*, qtd. in Edgar Duncan, "The Literature of Alchemy," 642.
16. Ann Astell, *Chaucer and the Universe of Learning*, 136.
17. Theophilus, *On Divers Arts*, 13.

Chapter 23

1. Brian Striar, "The *Manciple's Tale*," 176.
2. Britton Harwood, "Language and the Real," 271.
3. Michaela Paasche Grudin, "Chaucer's *Manciple's Tale*," 332.
4. David Raybin, "The Death of a Silent Woman," 31.

5. Ann Astell, "Nietzsche, Chaucer," 331–32.
6. Michael Kensak, "Apollo *exterminans*," 149.
7. Helen Phillips, "Why Does Chaucer's Manciple Tell a Tale about a Crow?," 118.
8. Celeste Patton, "False 'Rekenynges,'" 413.

Chapter 24

1. Anne Hudson, *Selections from English Wycliffite Writings*, 24–29.
2. Frances McCormack, "Chaucer and Lollardy," 36.
3. Jill Mann, *Chaucer and Medieval Estates Satire*, 56.
4. R. S. Loomis, "Was Chaucer a Laodicean?," 303.
5. Katherine Little, "Chaucer's Parson," 226.
6. Andrew Cole, *Literature and Heresy*, 78.
7. Richard Newhauser, "The *Parson's Tale*," 46.
8. Karen Winstead, "Chaucer's *Parson's Tale*," 243.
9. Frances McCormack, *Chaucer and the Culture of Dissent*, 62.
10. Anne Hudson, *Selections from English Wycliffite Writings*, 88.
11. Charlotte Gross, "'The Goode Wey,'" 181.

Conclusion

1. Tristanne Connolly, "Falling in Love with Bad Poetry," 9.

Works Cited

Abraham, David. "*Cosyn* and *Cosyngage*: Pun and Structure in the *Shipman's Tale*." *Chaucer Review* 11.4 (1977): 319-27.

Addison, Joseph. *The Poetical Works of Joseph Addison; Gay's "Fables", and Somerville's "Chase"*. Ed. George Gilfillan. James Nichol, 1859.

Aers, David. "Chaucer's Tale of Melibee: Whose Virtues?" *Medieval Literature and Historical Inquiry: Essays in Honor of Derek Pearsall*. Ed. David Aers. D. S. Brewer, 2000. 69-81.

Alderson, William L., and Arnold C. Henderson. *Chaucer and Augustan Scholarship*. University of California Press, 1970.

Algander, Per. "Bad Art and Good Taste." *Journal of Value Inquiry* 53 (2019): 145-54.

Allen, Judson Boyce, and Theresa Anne Moritz. *A Distinction of Stories: The Medieval Unity of Chaucer's Fair Chain of Narratives for Canterbury*. Ohio State University Press, 1981.

Archer, John. "The Structure of Anti-Semitism in the *Prioress's Tale*." *Chaucer Review* 19.1 (1984): 46-54.

Arnold, Matthew. *The English Poets: Selections with Critical Introductions*. Vol. 1, *Chaucer to Donne*. Ed. Thomas Humphry Ward. Macmillan, 1903.

Arthur, Karen. "Equivocal Subjectivity in Chaucer's *Second Nun's Prologue* and *Tale*." *Chaucer Review* 32.3 (1998): 217-31.

Astell, Ann. *Chaucer and the Universe of Learning*. Cornell University Press, 1996.

Astell, Ann. "Nietzsche, Chaucer, and the Sacrifice of Art." *Chaucer Review* 39.3 (2005): 323-40.

Baechle, Sarah, and Carissa M. Harris. "The Ethical Challenges of Chaucerian Scholarship in the Twenty-First Century." *Chaucer Review* 56.4 (2021): 311-21.

Bakhtin, Mikhail. *Rabelais and His World*. Trans. Hélène Iswolsky. Indiana University Press, 1984.

Barakat, Robert. "Odin: Old Man of the *Pardoner's Tale*." *Southern Folklore Quarterly* 28 (1964): 210-15.

Barnett, Pamela. "'And shortly for to seyn they were aton': Chaucer's Deflection of Rape in the *Reeve's* and *Franklin's Tales*." *Women's Studies* 22 (1993): 145-62.

Baugh, Albert. "The Original Teller of the *Merchant's Tale*." *Modern Philology* 35.1 (1937): 15-26.

Baum, Paull F. "Chaucer's Puns." *PMLA* 71.1 (1956): 225-46.

Baum, Paull F. "Chaucer's Puns: A Supplementary List." *PMLA* 73.1 (1958): 167-70.

Bayless, Martha. *Sin and Filth in Medieval Culture: The Devil in the Latrine*. Routledge, 2012.

Beidler, Peter, ed. *Masculinities in Chaucer: Approaches to Maleness in the "Canterbury Tales" and "Troilus and Criseyde."* D. S. Brewer, 1998.

Beidler, Peter. "Noah and the Old Man in the *Pardoner's Tale." Chaucer Review* 15.3 (1981): 250-54.

Bell, Quentin. *Bad Art.* University of Chicago Press, 1989.

Bennett, Alastair. "'The emprentyng of hire consolacioun': Engraving, Erosion, and Persistent Speech in the *Franklin's Tale." Studies in the Age of Chaucer* 41 (2019): 141-72.

Benson, C. David. *Chaucer's Drama of Style: Poetic Variety and Contrast in the "Canterbury Tales."* University of North Carolina Press, 1986.

Benson, C. David. "Their Telling Difference: Chaucer the Pilgrim and His Two Contrasting Tales." *Chaucer Review* 18.1 (1983): 61-76.

Benson, Donald. "The Marriage 'Encomium' in the *Merchant's Tale*: A Chaucerian Crux." *Chaucer Review* 14.1 (1979): 48-60.

Benson, Larry. "The 'Queynte' Punnings of Chaucer's Critics." *Studies in the Age of Chaucer, Proceedings* 1 (1984): 23-47.

Besserman, Lawrence. "Ideology, Antisemitism, and Chaucer's *Prioress's Tale." Chaucer Review* 36.1 (2001): 48-72.

Bestul, Thomas. "Chaucer's *Parson's Tale* and the Late-Medieval Tradition of Religious Meditation." *Speculum* 64.3 (1989): 600-619.

Biggs, Frederick. "The *Miller's Tale* and *Heile van Beersele." Review of English Studies* 56.226 (2005): 497-523.

Bird, Stephanie. "Death, Being, and the Place of Comedy in Representations of Death." *Women and Death 3: Women's Representations of Death in German Culture since 1500.* Ed. Claire Bielby and Anna Richards. Camden House, 2010. 134-51.

Bloch, R. Howard. "Chaucer's Maiden's Head: The *Physician's Tale* and the Poetics of Virginity." *Chaucer: Contemporary Critical Essays.* Ed. Valerie Allen and Ares Axiotis. St. Martin's, 1996. 145-56.

Bloomfield, Morton. "The Miller—An UnBoethian Interpretation." *Medieval Literature and Folklore Studies: Essays in Honor of Francis Lee Utley.* Ed. Jerome Mandel and Bruce Rosenberg. Rutgers University Press, 1971. 205-11.

Bloomfield, Morton. "The Wisdom of the *Nun's Priest's Tale." Chaucerian Problems and Perspectives: Essays Presented to Paul E. Beichner.* Ed. Edward Vasta and Zacharis Thundy. University of Notre Dame Press, 1979.

Blurton, Heather, and Hannah Johnson. *The Critics and the Prioress: Antisemitism, Criticism, and Chaucer's "Prioress's Tale."* University of Michigan Press, 2017.

Boccaccio, Giovanni. *The Decameron.* Trans. G. H. McWilliam. Penguin, 1972.

Boenig, Robert. "Is the *Monk's Tale* a Fragment?" *Notes and Queries* 43.3 (1996): 261-64.

Boitani, Piero. "'My tale is of a cock,' or, The Problems of Literal Interpretation." *Literature and Religion in the Later Middle Ages.* Ed. Richard Newhauser and John Alford. Cornell University Press, 1995. 25-42.

Børch, Marianne. "Writing Remembering Orality: Geoffrey Chaucer's *Sir Thopas." European Journal of English Studies* 10.2 (2006): 131-48.

Bornstein, Diane. "Chaucer's *Tale of Melibee* as an Example of the Style Clergial." *Chaucer Review* 12.4 (1978): 236-54.

Boroff, Marie. *Traditions and Renewals: Chaucer, the Gawain Poet, and Beyond.* Yale University Press, 2003.

Bourdieu, Pierre. *Distinction: A Social Critique of the Judgment of Taste.* Trans. Richard Nice. Harvard University Press, 1984.

Bowers, John, ed. *The "Canterbury Tales": Fifteenth-Century Continuations and Additions.* Medieval Institute Publications, 1992.

Bowler, Kate. *Blessed: A History of the American Prosperity Gospel.* Oxford University Press, 2013.

Bowman, Mary. "'Half as she were mad': Dorigen in the Male World of the *Franklin's Tale.*" *Chaucer Review* 27.3 (1993): 239-51.

Boyd, David Lorenzo. "Social Texts, Bodley 686, and the Politics of the *Cook's Tale.*" *Reading from the Margins: Textual Studies, Chaucer, and Medieval Literature.* Ed. Seth Lerer. Huntington Library, 1996. 81-97.

Brandeis, Arthur, ed. *Jacob's Well: An English Treatise on the Cleansing of Man's Conscience.* EETS o.s. 115. Kegan Paul, 1900.

Brantley, Jessica. "Reading the Forms of *Sir Thopas.*" *Chaucer Review* 47.4 (2013): 416-38.

Braswell, Mary Flowers. "Chaucer's Palimpsest: Judas Iscariot and the *Pardoner's Tale.*" *Chaucer Review* 29.3 (1995): 303-10.

Brewer, Derek, ed. *Chaucer: The Critical Heritage.* Vol. 1, *1385-1837,* and vol. 2, *1837-1933.* Routledge, 1978.

Brewer, Derek. "The Fabliaux." *Companion to Chaucer Studies.* Ed. Beryl Rowland. Rev. ed. Oxford University Press, 1979. 296-325.

Brown, Emerson. "Chaucer, the Merchant, and Their Tale: Getting beyond Old Controversies." *Chaucer Review* 13.2 (1978): 141-56.

Bryan, Jennifer. "'A berd! A berd!': Chaucer's Miller and the Poetics of the Pun." *Studies in the Age of Chaucer* 38 (2016): 1-37.

Bryant, Brantley. "'By extorcions I lyve': Chaucer's *Friar's Tale* and Corrupt Officials." *Chaucer Review* 42.2 (2007): 180-95.

Burger, Glenn. "Doing What Comes Naturally: The *Physician's Tale* and the Pardoner." *Masculinities in Chaucer: Approaches to Maleness in the "Canterbury Tales" and "Troilus and Criseyde."* Ed. Peter Beidler. D. S. Brewer, 1998. 117-30.

Burns, E. Jane. "Courtly Love: Who Needs It? Recent Feminist Work in the Medieval French Tradition." *Signs* 27.1 (2001): 23-57.

Burrow, Colin. *Epic Romance: Homer to Milton.* Clarendon, 1993.

Burrow, J. A. "Irony in the *Merchant's Tale.*" *Anglia* 75 (1957): 199-208.

Burrow, J. A. "*Sir Thopas:* An Agony in Three Fits." *Review of English Studies* 22.85 (1971): 54-58.

Bushnell, Nelson Sherwin. "The Wandering Jew and the *Pardoner's Tale.*" *Studies in Philology* 28.3 (1931): 450-60.

Cady, Diane. "Damaged Goods: Merchandise, Stories, and Gender in Chaucer's *Man of Law's Tale.*" *New Medieval Literatures* 17 (2017): 115-49.

Calabrese, Michael. "Performing the Prioress: 'Conscience' and Responsibility in Studies of Chaucer's *Prioress's Tale.*" *Texas Studies in Literature and Language* 44.1 (2002): 66-91.

Caldwell, Robert. "Chaucer's 'Taillynge Ynough,' *Canterbury Tales,* B 1624." *Modern Language Notes* 55.4 (2940): 262-65.

Campbell, Jackson. "The Canon's Yeoman as Imperfect Paradigm." *Chaucer Review* 17.2 (1982): 171-81.

Cannon, Christopher. "Chaucer and Rape: Uncertainty's Certainties." *Studies in the Age of Chaucer* 22 (2000): 67-92.

Cannon, Christopher. "Raptus in the Chaumpaigne Release and a Newly Discovered Document Concerning the Life of Geoffrey Chaucer." *Speculum* 68.1 (1993): 74–94.

Carlton, Eric. *Dancing in the Dark: Reflections on the Problem of Theodicy.* Fairleigh Dickinson University Press, 2005.

Carruthers, Mary. "The Wife of Bath and the Painting of Lions." *PMLA* 94.2 (1979): 209–22.

Casey, Jim. "Unfinished Business: The Termination of Chaucer's *Cook's Tale*." *Chaucer Review* 41.2 (2006): 185–96.

Cato. *The Distichs of Cato: A Famous Medieval Textbook.* Ed. Wayland Johnson Chase. University of Wisconsin, 1922.

Cels, Marc. "'An irous man': Anger and Authority in the *Summoner's Tale*." *Chaucer Review* 53.3 (2018): 308–35.

Chaucer, Geoffrey. *The Canterbury Tales: A Facsimile and Transcription of the Hengwrt Manuscript, with Variants from the Ellesmere Manuscript.* Ed. Paul G. Ruggiers. University of Oklahoma Press, 1979.

Chaucer, Geoffrey. *The Riverside Chaucer.* Ed. Larry D. Benson. 3rd ed. Houghton Mifflin, 1987.

Cicero. *Cicero on Oratory and Orators.* Trans. J. S. Watson. Southern Illinois University Press, 1970.

Cicero. *De inventione, De optimo genere oratorum, Topica.* Trans. H. M. Hubbell. Harvard University Press, 1949.

Clogan, Paul. "Literary Genres in a Medieval Textbook." *Medievalia et Humanistica* 11 (1982): 199–209.

Coghill, Nevill. *The Poet Chaucer.* 2nd ed. Oxford University Press, 1967.

Cohen, Jeffrey Jerome. *Stone: An Ecology of the Human.* University of Minnesota Press, 2015.

Cole, Andrew. *Literature and Heresy in the Age of Chaucer.* Cambridge University Press, 2008.

Collette, Carolyn. "Critical Approaches to the *Prioress's Tale* and the *Second Nun's Tale*." *Chaucer's Religious Tales.* Ed. C. David Benson and Elizabeth Robertson. D. S. Brewer, 1990. 95–107.

Collette, Carolyn. "Heeding the Counsel of Prudence: A Context for the *Melibee*." *Chaucer Review* 29.4 (1995): 416–33.

Connolly, Tristanne. "Falling in Love with Bad Poetry." *New Quarterly*, Winter 2014, 6–9.

Cook, Alexandra. "'O swete harm so queynte': Loving Pagan Antiquity in *Troilus and Criseyde* and the *Knight's Tale*." *English Studies* 91.1 (2010): 26–41.

Cook, Robert. "The Canon's Yeoman and His Tale." *Chaucer Review* 22.1 (1987): 28–40.

Cooney, Helen. "The *Parlement of Foules*: A Theodicy of Love." *Chaucer Review* 32.4 (1998): 339–76.

Cooper, Helen. *Oxford Guides to Chaucer: The "Canterbury Tales."* Oxford University Press, 1989.

Correale, Robert M., and Mary Hamel, eds. *Sources and Analogues of the "Canterbury Tales."* 2 vols. D. S. Brewer, 2005.

Craik, T. W. *The Comic Tales of Chaucer.* Barnes & Noble, 1964.

Crane, Susan. "Cat, Capon, and Pig in the *Summoner's Tale*." *Studies in the Age of Chaucer* 34 (2012): 319–24.

Crane, Susan. *Gender and Romance in Chaucer's "Canterbury Tales."* Princeton University Press, 1994.

Critchley, Simon. *Very Little . . . Almost Nothing: Death, Philosophy, Literature.* Routledge, 1997.

Crocker, Holly. "Affective Politics in Chaucer's *Reeve's Tale*: 'Cherl' Masculinity after 1381." *Studies in the Age of Chaucer* 29 (2007): 225-58.

Crocker, Holly. "Performative Passivity and Fantasies of Masculinity in the *Merchant's Tale*." *Chaucer Review* 38.2 (2003): 178-98.

Crosson, Chad. "Chaucer's Corrective Form: The *Tale of Melibee* and the Poetics of Emendation." *Studies in Philology* 115.2 (2018): 242-66.

Cuddon, J. A. *The Penguin Dictionary of Literary Terms and Literary Theory.* 3rd ed. Penguin, 1991.

Culler, Jonathan. "The Call of the Phoneme: Introduction." *On Puns: The Foundation of Letters.* Ed. Jonathan Culler. Blackwell, 1988. 1-16.

Dane, Joseph. "'Queynte': Some Rime and Some Reason on a Chaucer(ian) Pun." *Journal of English and Germanic Philology* 94.5 (1996): 497-514.

David, Alfred. "Criticism and the Old Man in Chaucer's *Pardoner's Tale*." *College English* 27.1 (1965): 39-44.

Desmond, Marilynn. *Ovid's Art and the Wife of Bath.* Cornell University Press, 2006.

Donaldson, E. T., ed. *Chaucer's Poetry: An Anthology for the Modern Reader.* Ronald Press, 1958.

Dubin, Nathaniel, trans. *The Fabliaux: A New Verse Translation.* Liveright, 2013.

Duncan, Edgar. "The Literature of Alchemy and Chaucer's *Canon's Yeoman's Tale*: Framework, Theme, and Characters." *Speculum* 43.4 (1968): 633-56.

Duplessis, Rachel Blau. "Endings and Contradictions." *Narrative Dynamics: Essays on Time, Plot, Closure, and Frames.* Ed. Brian Richardson. Ohio State University Press, 2002. 282-99.

Dutton, Marsha L. "Chaucer's *Cunning*: An Incarnational Pun and an Omission in the *Middle English Dictionary*." *Chaucer Review* 53.1 (2018): 36-59.

Dyck, John, and Matt Johnson. "Appreciating Bad Art." *Journal of Value Inquiry* 51 (2017): 279-92.

Dyer, Christopher. *Standards of Living in the Later Middle Ages: Social Change in England, c.1200-1520.* Cambridge University Press, 1989.

Eckert, Kenneth. "Harry Bailly and Chaucer-Pilgrim's 'Quiting' in the *Tale of Sir Thopas*." *Review of English Studies* 68.285 (2016): 471-87.

Edwards, A. S. G. "Gladly wolde he lerne? Why Chaucer Is Disappearing from the University Curriculum." *Times Literary Supplement*, 2 July 2021, 7-8.

Egbert of Liège. *The Well-Laden Ship.* Trans. Robert Gary Babcock. Harvard University Press, 2013.

Elliott, Dyan. *Spiritual Marriage: Sexual Abstinence in Medieval Wedlock.* Princeton University Press, 1993.

Ellis, Roger. *Patterns of Religious Narrative in the "Canterbury Tales."* Croom Helm, 1986.

Finlayson, John. "The *Knight's Tale*: The Dialogue of Romance, Epic, and Philosophy." *Chaucer Review* 27.2 (1992): 126-49.

Finlayson, John. "The *Merchant's Tale*: Literary Contexts, the Play of Genres, and Institutionalized Sexual Relations." *Anglia* 121.4 (2004): 557-80.

Finlayson, John. "Reading Chaucer's *Nun's Priest's Tale*: Mixed Genres and Multilayered Worlds of Illusion." *English Studies* 86.6 (2005): 493-510.

Fisher, Ruth. "Cosyn and Cosynage: Complicated Punning in Chaucer's *Shipman's Tale*." *Notes and Queries* 210 (1965): 168-70.

Foster, Edward. "Has Anyone Here Read Melibee?" *Chaucer Review* 34.4 (2000): 398-409.

Fradenburg, Louise. "Criticism, Anti-Semitism, and the *Prioress's Tale*." *Exemplaria* 1.1 (1989): 69-115.

Frank, Hardy Long. "Chaucer's Prioress and the Blessed Virgin." *Chaucer Review* 13.4 (1979): 346-62.

Frese, Dolores Warwick. "The *Nun's Priest's Tale*: Chaucer's Identified Masterpiece?" *Chaucer Review* 16.4 (1982): 330-43.

Freud, Sigmund. *Wit and Its Relation to the Unconscious.* Trans. A. A. Brill. 1922. Routledge, 1999.

Friedman, Albert. "The *Prioress's Tale* and Chaucer's Anti-Semitism." *Chaucer Review* 9.2 (1974): 118-29.

Frost, William. "A Chaucerian Crux." *Yale Review* 66 (1977): 551-61.

Frye, Northrop. *Anatomy of Criticism: Four Essays.* Princeton University Press, 1957.

Garbáty, Thomas Jay. "The Monk and the *Merchant's Tale*: An Aspect of Chaucer's Building Process in the *Canterbury Tales*." *Modern Philology* 67.1 (1969): 18-24.

Gardner, John. *The Life and Times of Chaucer.* Knopf, 1977.

Gaylord, Alan. "Chaucer's Dainty 'Dogerel': The 'Elvyssh' Prosody of *Sir Thopas*." *Chaucer's Humor: Critical Essays.* Ed. Jean Jost. Garland, 1994. 271-94.

Ginsberg, Warren. "Aesthetics *sine Nomine*." *Chaucer Review* 39.3 (2005): 234-40.

Grass, Günter. *The Tin Drum.* Trans. Ralph Manheim. 1959. Pantheon, 1961.

Graves, Robert. "What Is Bad Poetry?" *North American Review*, September 1923, 353-68.

Green, Richard Firth. *Poets and Princepleasers: Literature and the English Court in the Late Middle Ages.* University of Toronto Press, 1979.

Gregg, Joan Young. *Devils, Women, and Jews: Reflections of the Other in Medieval Sermon Stories.* State University of New York Press, 1997.

Grennen, Joseph. "Chaucer's Characterization of the Canon and His Yeoman." *Journal of the History of Ideas* 25.2 (1964): 279-84.

Gross, Charlotte. "'The Goode Wey': Ending and Not-Ending in the *Parson's Tale*." *Closure in the "Canterbury Tales": The Role of the "Parson's Tale."* Ed. David Raybin and Linda Tarte Holley. Medieval Institute Publications, 2000. 177-97.

Grudin, Michaela Paasche. "Chaucer's *Manciple's Tale* and the Poetics of Guile." *Chaucer Review* 25.4 (1991): 329-42.

Haas, Renate. "Chaucer's *Monk's Tale*: An Ingenious Criticism of Early Humanist Conceptions of Tragedy." *Humanistica Lovaniensia* 36 (1987): 44-70.

Haller, Robert. "*The Knight's Tale* and the Epic Tradition." *Chaucer Review* 1.2 (1966): 67-84.

Hamilton, Marie Padgett. "Death and Old Age in the *Pardoner's Tale*." *Studies in Philology* 36.4 (1939): 571-76.

Hanson, Thomas. "Chaucer's Physician as Storyteller and Moralizer." *Chaucer Review* 7.2 (1972): 132-39.

Harris, Carissa M. *Obscene Pedagogies: Transgressive Talk and Sexual Education in Late Medieval Britain.* Cornell University Press, 2018.

Harwood Britton. "Language and the Real: Chaucer's Manciple." *Chaucer Review* 6.4 (1972): 268-79.

Hatcher, Elizabeth. "Life without Death: The Old Man in Chaucer's *Pardoner's Tale*." *Chaucer Review* 9.3 (1975): 246-52.

Hawkins, Sherman. "Chaucer's Prioress and the Sacrifice of Praise." *Journal of English and Germanic Philology* 63.4 (1964): 599-624.

Heines, Sister Virginia, S.C.N., trans. *Libellus de alchimia: Ascribed to Albertus Magnus.* University of California Press, 1958.

Heller, Agnes. *Immortal Comedy: The Comic Phenomenon in Art, Literature, and Life.* Lexington, 2005.

Hendrix, Laurel. "'Pennance profytable': The Currency of Custance in Chaucer's *Man of Law's Tale.*" *Exemplaria* 6.1 (1994): 141-66.

Heng, Geraldine. "England's Dead Boys: Telling Tales of Christian-Jewish Relations before and after the First European Expulsion of the Jews." *MLN* 127.5 (2012): S54-S85.

Hill, Archibald. "Chaucer and the Pun-Hunters: Some Points of Caution." *On Language: Rhetorica, Phonologica, Syntactica.* Ed. Caroline Duncan-Rose and Theo Vennemann. Routledge, 1988. 66-78.

Hill, John M. "The Countervailing Aesthetic of Joy in *Troilus and Criseyde.*" *Chaucer Review* 39.3 (2005): 280-97.

Hinton, Norman D. "More Puns in Chaucer." *American Notes and Queries* 2 (1964): 115-16.

Hodges, Laura. *Chaucer and Costume: The Secular Pilgrims in the "General Prologue."* D. S. Brewer, 2000.

Hoffman, Richard. "Jephthah's Daughter and Chaucer's Virginia." *Chaucer Review* 2.1 (1967): 20-31.

Homar, Katie. "Chaucer's Novelized, Carnivalized Exemplum: A Bakhtinian Reading of the *Friar's Tale.*" *Chaucer Review* 45.1 (2010): 85-105.

Horowitz, Deborah. "An Aesthetic of Permeability: Three Transcapes of the *Book of the Duchess.*" *Chaucer Review* 39.3 (2005): 259-79.

Houlik-Ritchey, Emily. "Dwelling with Humans and Nonhumans: Neighboring Ethics in the *Franklin's Tale.*" *Studies in the Age of Chaucer* 41 (2019): 107-39.

Howard, Donald. *Chaucer: His Life, His Works, His World.* Dutton, 1987.

Howard, Donald. *The Idea of the "Canterbury Tales."* University of California Press, 1976.

Hsy, Jonathan. "Diverging Forms: Disability and the Monk's Tales." *Chaucer and the Subversion of Form.* Ed. Thomas Prendergast and Jessica Rosenfeld. Cambridge University Press, 2018. 85-98.

Hudson, Anne, ed. *Selections from English Wycliffite Writings.* University of Toronto Press, 1997. 24-29.

Hurd, Richard. *Letters on Chivalry and Romance, with the Third Elizabethan Dialogue.* Ed. Edith Morley. Henry Frowde, 1911.

Huxley, Aldous. *Point Counter Point.* 1928. Dalkey Archive, 1996.

Impelluso, Lucia. *Nature and Its Symbols.* Trans. Stephen Sartarelli. Getty Museum, 2003.

Ingham, Patricia Clare. "Little Nothings: The *Squire's Tale* and the Ambition of Gadgets." *Studies in the Age of Chaucer* 31 (2009): 53-80.

Innocent III. *De miseria condicionis humane.* Ed. Robert E. Lewis. University of Georgia Press, 1978.

Jobes, Gertrude. *Dictionary of Mythology, Folklore, and Symbols.* 2 vols. Scarecrow, 1962.

Johnson, Eleanor. "Tragic Nihilism in the *Canterbury Tales*: The Monk as Literary Theorist." *Journal of Medieval and Early Modern Studies* 49.1 (2019): 7-31.

Johnson, Lynn Staley. "Chaucer's Tale of the Second Nun and the Strategies of Dissent." *Studies in Philology* 89 (1992): 314-33.

Johnson, Samuel. *A Dictionary of the English Language.* 2 vols. Thomas Tegg, 1832.

Jones, Claude. "Chaucer's 'Taillynge Ynough.'" *Modern Language Notes* 52.8 (1937): 570.

Jones, Lindsey. "Chaucer's Anxiety of Poetic Craft: The *Squire's Tale.*" *Style* 41.3 (2007): 300-318.

Jones, Terry. *Chaucer's Knight: Portrait of a Medieval Mercenary.* Louisiana State University Press, 1980.

Jordan, Robert. "The Non-dramatic Disunity of the *Merchant's Tale.*" *PMLA* 78.4 (1963): 293-99.

Joseph, Gerhard. "Chaucer's Coinage: Foreign Exchange and the Puns of the *Shipman's Tale.*" *Chaucer Review* 17.4 (1983): 341-57.

Julian of Norwich. *Showings.* Trans. Edmund Colledge, O.S.A., and James Walsh, S.J. Paulist Press, 1978.

Kao, Wan-Chuan. "Conduct Shameful and Unshameful in the *Franklin's Tale.*" *Studies in the Age of Chaucer* 34 (2012): 99-139.

Kao, Wan-Chuan. "In the Lap of Whiteness." *New Literary History* 52.3-4 (2021): 535-61.

Karnes, Michelle. "Wonders, Marvels, and Metaphor in the *Squire's Tale.*" *ELH* 82.2 (2015): 461-90.

Kaske, R. E. "An Aube in the *Reeve's Tale.*" *ELH* 26.3 (1959): 295-310.

Kaske, R. E. "The Knight's Interruption of the *Monk's Tale.*" *ELH* 24.4 (1957): 249-68.

Katz, David. *Philo-Semitism and the Readmission of the Jews to England, 1603-1655.* Clarendon Press, 1982.

Keiser, George. "The Conclusion of the *Canon's Yeoman's Tale*: Readings and (Mis) Readings." *Chaucer Review* 35.1 (2000): 1-21.

Kellogg, Alfred. "An Augustinian Interpretation of Chaucer's Pardoner." *Speculum* 26.3 (1951): 465-81.

Kelly, Henry Ansgar. "The Evolution of the *Monk's Tale*: Tragical to Farcical." *Studies in the Age of Chaucer* 22 (2000): 407-14.

Kempe, Margery. *The Book of Margery Kempe.* Ed. Sanford Brown Meech. EETS. Oxford University Press, 1997.

Ker, W. P. *Epic and Romance: Essays on Medieval Literature.* Macmillan, 1922.

Kittredge, George Lyman. *Chaucer and His Poetry.* 1915. Harvard University Press, 1970.

Kline, Daniel. "Jephthah's Daughter and Chaucer's Virginia: The Critique of Sacrifice in the *Physician's Tale.*" *Journal of English and Germanic Philology* 107.1 (2008): 77-103.

Knapp, Peggy A. "Aesthetic Attention and the Chaucerian Text." *Chaucer Review* 39.3 (2005): 241-58.

Knapp, Peggy A. *Chaucerian Aesthetics.* Palgrave Macmillan, 2008.

Kohanski, Tamarah. "In Search of Malyne." *Chaucer Review* 27.3 (1993): 228-38.

Kökeritz, Helge. "Rhetorical Word-Play in Chaucer." *PMLA* 69.4 (1954): 937-52.

Kolve, V. A. *Chaucer and the Imagery of Narrative: The First Five Canterbury Tales.* Stanford University Press, 1984.

Kolve, V. A. "Chaucer's *Second Nun's Tale* and the Iconography of Saint Cecilia." *New Perspectives in Chaucer Criticism.* Ed. Donald Rose. Pilgrim, 1981. 137-74.

Kruger, Steven F. "Claiming the Pardoner: Toward a Gay Reading of Chaucer's *Pardoner's Tale*." *Exemplaria* 6.1 (1994): 115-39.

Krummel, Miriamne Ara, and Tison Pugh, eds. *Jews in Medieval England: Teaching Representations of the Other*. Palgrave Macmillan, 2017.

Lacan, Jacques. *The Seminar of Jacques Lacan*: Book VII, *The Ethics of Psychoanalysis, 1959-1960*. Ed. Jacques-Alain Miller. Trans. Dennis Porter. Norton, 1986.

Ladd, Roger. "The Mercantile (Mis)Reader in the *Canterbury Tales*." *Studies in Philology* 99.1 (2002): 17-32.

Lambdin, Laura C., and Robert T. Lambdin, eds. *Chaucer's Pilgrims: An Historical Guide to the Pilgrims in the "Canterbury Tales."* Greenwood, 1996.

Lampert-Weissig, Lisa. "Chaucer's Pardoner and the Jews." *Exemplaria* 28.4 (2016): 337-60.

Laskaya, Anne. *Chaucer's Approach to Gender in the "Canterbury Tales."* D. S. Brewer, 1995.

Lavezzo, Kathy. "The Minister and the Privy: Rereading the *Prioress's Tale*." *PMLA* 126.2 (2011): 363-82.

Lawrence, William Witherle. "The Tale of Melibeus." *Essays and Studies in Honor of Carleton Brown*. New York University Press, 1940. 100-110.

Leicester, H. Marshall, Jr. *The Disenchanted Self: Representing the Subject in the "Canterbury Tales."* University of California Press, 1990.

Lenaghan, R. T. "The Irony of the *Friar's Tale*." *Chaucer Review* 7.4 (1973): 281-94.

Lerer, Seth. "'Now holde youre mouth': The Romance of Orality in the *Thopas-Melibee* Section of the *Canterbury Tales*." *Oral Poetics in Middle English Poetry*. Ed. Mark Amodio. Routledge, 1994. 181-205.

Levitan, Alan. "The Parody of Pentecost in Chaucer's *Summoner's Tale*." *University of Toronto Quarterly* 40.3 (1971): 236-46.

Lindley, Arthur. "'Vanysshed was this daunce, he nyste where': Alisoun's Absence in the *Wife of Bath's Prologue* and *Tale*." *ELH* 59.1 (1992): 1-21.

Little, Katherine. "Chaucer's Parson and the Specter of Wycliffism." *Studies in the Age of Chaucer* 23 (2001): 225-53.

Lomperis, Linda. "Unruly Bodies and Ruling Practices: Chaucer's *Physician's Tale* as Socially Symbolic Act." *Feminist Approaches to the Body in Medieval Literature*. Ed. Linda Lomperis and Sarah Stanbury. University of Pennsylvania Press, 1993. 21-37.

Long, Mary Beth. "'O sweete and wel biloved spouse deere': A Pastoral Reading of Cecilia's Post-nuptial Persuasion in the *Second Nun's Tale*." *Studies in the Age of Chaucer* 39 (2017): 159-90.

Loomis, R. S. "Was Chaucer a Laodicean?" *Chaucer Criticism: The "Canterbury Tales."* Ed. Richard Schoeck and Jerome Taylor. Notre Dame University Press, 1960. 291-310.

Lounsbury, Thomas. *Studies in Chaucer: His Life and Writings*. 3 vols. Harper, 1892.

Luecke, Janemarie. "Dorigen: Marriage Model or Male Fantasy." *Journal of Women's Studies in Literature* 1 (1979): 107-21.

Lupton, T. *All for Money: English Morality Plays and Moral Interludes*. Ed. Edgar Schell and J. D. Shuchter. Holt, Rinehart, 1969. 419-73.

Malone, Kemp. *Chapters on Chaucer*. Johns Hopkins University Press, 1951.

Manly, John Matthews. *Some New Light on Chaucer: Lectures Delivered at the Lowell Institute*. Henry Holt, 1926.

Manly, John Matthews. "The Stanza-Forms of *Sir Thopas*." *Modern Philology* 8.1 (1910): 141-44.

Manly, John Matthews, and Edith Rickert, eds. *The Text of the "Canterbury Tales": Studies on the Basis of All Known Manuscripts.* 8 vols. University of Chicago Press, 1940.

Mann, Jill. *Chaucer and Medieval Estates Satire: The Literature of Social Classes and the "General Prologue" to the "Canterbury Tales."* Cambridge University Press, 1973.

Manne, Kate. *Down Girl: The Logic of Misogyny.* Oxford University Press, 2017.

Martin, Jennifer. "The 'Crossing' of the Wife of Bath." *The "Canterbury Tales" Revisited: 21st Century Interpretations.* Ed. Kathleen Bishop. Cambridge Scholars, 2008. 60-74.

Matsuda, Takami. "Death, Prudence, and Chaucer's *Pardoner's Tale.*" *Journal of English and Germanic Philology* 91.3 (1992): 313-24.

McCall, John P. "The Squire in Wonderland." *Chaucer Review* 1 (1966): 103-9.

McCallum, J. Ramsay. *Abelard's Christian Theology.* Richwood, 1976.

McCormack, Frances. "Chaucer and Lollardy." *Chaucer and Religion.* Ed. Helen Phillips. D. S. Brewer, 2010. 35-40.

McCormack, Frances. *Chaucer and the Culture of Dissent: The Lollard Context and Subtext of the "Parson's Tale."* Four Courts, 2007.

McDonald, Dwight, ed. *Parodies: An Anthology from Chaucer to Beerbohm—and After.* Random House, 1960.

McDonie, Jacob. "'Ye gete namoore of me': Narrative, Textual, and Linguistic Desires in Chaucer's *Merchant's Tale.*" *Exemplaria* 24.4 (2012): 313-41.

McFarland, Ian. "Prosperity Gospel." *The Cambridge Dictionary of Christian Theology.* Ed. Ian McFarland, David Fergusson, Karen Kilby, and Iain Torrance. Cambridge University Press, 2011. 414-15.

Merrix, Robert. "Sermon Structure in the *Pardoner's Tale.*" *Chaucer Review* 17.3 (1983): 235-49.

Middleton, Anne. "The *Physician's Tale* and Love's Martyrs: 'Ensamples mo than ten' as a Method in the *Canterbury Tales.*" *Chaucer Review* 8.1 (2973): 9-32.

Miller, Robert. "Chaucer's Pardoner, the Scriptural Eunuch, and the *Pardoner's Tale.*" *Speculum* 30.2 (1955): 180-99.

Miller, Robert. "Chaucer's Rhetorical Rendition of Mind: The *Squire's Tale.*" *Chaucer and the Craft of Fiction.* Ed. Leigh Arrathoon. Solaris, 1986. 219-40.

Minnis, A. J., and A. B. Scott, eds. *Medieval Literary Theory and Criticism, c. 1100—c. 1375: The Commentary Tradition.* Rev. ed. Clarendon, 1991.

Mitchell, J. Allan. *Ethics and Exemplary Narrative in Chaucer and Gower.* D. S. Brewer, 2004.

Morse, Charlotte. "The Exemplary Griselda." *Studies in the Age of Chaucer* 7 (1985): 51-86.

Moss, Rachel E. "Chaucer's Funny Rape: Addressing a Taboo in Medieval Studies." Rachelemoss.com, 11 September 2014.

Mroczkowski, Przemyslaw. "The *Friar's Tale* and Its Pulpit Background." *English Studies Today.* Ed. G. A. Bonnard. 2nd series. Francke Verlag, 1961. 107-20.

Nakley, Susan. "'Rowned she a pistel': National Institutions and Identities according to Chaucer's Wife of Bath." *Journal of English and Germanic Philology* 114.1 (2015): 61-87.

Newhauser, Richard. "The *Parson's Tale* and Its Generic Affiliations." *Closure in the "Canterbury Tales": The Role of the Parson's Tale.* Ed. David Raybin and Linda Tarte Holley. Medieval Institute Publications, 2000. 45-76.

Normandin, Shawn. "'Non intellegant': The Enigmas of the *Clerk's Tale*." *Texas Studies in Literature and Language* 58.2 (2016): 189-223.

Normandin, Shawn. "Reading Chaucer's *Monk's Tale*." *Viator* 47.2 (2016): 183-204.

Olderr, Steven. *Symbolism: A Comprehensive Dictionary.* McFarland, 1986.

Oliver, Kathleen. "Singing Bread, Manna, and the Clergeon's 'Greyn.'" *Chaucer Review* 31.4 (1997): 357-64.

Olsen, Alexandra Hennessey. "'They shul desiren to dye, and deeth shal flee fro hem': A Reconsideration of the Pardoner's Old Man." *Neuphilologische Mitteilungen* 84.3 (1983): 367-71.

Olson, Glending. "Measuring the Immeasurable: Farting, Geometry, and Theology in the *Summoner's Tale*." *Chaucer Review* 43.4 (2009): 414-27.

O'Neill, Patrick. "The Comedy of Entropy: The Contexts of Black Humour." *Dark Humor.* Ed. Harold Bloom and Blake Hobby. Chelsea House, 2010. 79-103.

Otaño Gracia, Nahir I. "Borders and the Global North Atlantic: Chaucer, Pilgrimage, and Crusade." *English Language Notes* 58.2 (2020): 35-49.

Otis-Cour, Leah. "True Lover / False Lover, *franquise / dete*: Dichotomies in the *Franklin's Tale* and Their Analogues in Richard de Fournival's *Consaud d'amours*." *Chaucer Review* 47.2 (2012): 161-86.

Ovid. *Heroides and Amores.* Trans. Grant Showerman. 2nd ed. Harvard University Press, 1986.

Patterson, Lee. "'The Living Witnesses of Our Redemption': Martyrdom and Imitation in Chaucer's *Prioress's Tale*." *Journal of Medieval and Early Modern Studies* 31.3 (2001): 507-60.

Patterson, Lee. *Temporal Circumstances: Form and History in the "Canterbury Tales."* Palgrave Macmillan, 2006.

Patton, Celeste. "False 'Rekenynges': Sharp Practice and the Politics of Language in Chaucer's *Manciple's Tale*." *Philological Quarterly* 71.4 (1992): 399-417.

Pearcy, Roy. "Chaucer's Amphibologies and 'the Old Man' in the *Pardoner's Tale*." *English Language Notes* 41.4 (2004): 1-10.

Pearsall, Derek. *Arthurian Romance: A Short Introduction.* Blackwell, 2003.

Pearsall, Derek. *The Canterbury Tales.* Allen & Unwin, 1985.

Pearsall, Derek. "The *Canterbury Tales* II: Comedy." *Chaucer's Humor: Critical Essays.* Ed. Jean Jost. Garland, 1994. 101-23.

Phillips, Helen. "Why Does Chaucer's Manciple Tell a Tale about a Crow?" *Nottingham Medieval Studies* 54 (2010): 113-19.

Pinti, Daniel. "Governing the *Cook's Tale* in Bodley 686." *Chaucer Review* 30.4 (1996): 379-88.

Pitcher, John. "Chaucer's Wolf: Exemplary Violence in the *Physician's Tale*." *Genre* 36 (2003): 1-28.

Plummer, John. "Hooly Chirches Blood: Simony and Patrimony in Chaucer's *Reeve's Tale*." *Chaucer Review* 18 (1983): 49-60.

Pollack, John. *The Pun Also Rises: How the Humble Pun Revolutionized Language, Changed History, and Made Wordplay More Than Some Antics.* Gotham, 2011.

Price, Merrall Llewelyn. "Sadism and Sentimentality: Absorbing Antisemitism in Chaucer's Prioress." *Chaucer Review* 43.2 (2008): 197-214.

Prior, Sandra Pierson. "Virginity and Sacrifice in Chaucer's *Physician's Tale*." *Constructions of Widowhood and Virginity in the Middle Ages.* Ed. Angela Jane Weisl and Cindy Carlson. St. Martin's Press, 1999. 165-80.

Pugh, Tison. *Chaucer's (Anti-) Eroticisms and the Queer Middle Ages.* Ohio State University Press, 2014.

Purdon, L. O. "The Pardoner's Old Man and the Second Death." *Studies in Philology* 89.3 (1992): 334-49.

Quinn, William. "String Theory and the *Man of Law's Tale*: Where Is Constancy?" *Critical Survey* 29.3 (2017): 48-64.

Raybin, David. "The Death of a Silent Woman: Voice and Power in Chaucer's *Manciple's Tale*." *Journal of English and Germanic Philology* 95.1 (1996): 19-37.

Raybin, David. "'Goddes instrumentz': Devils and Free Will in the *Friar's* and *Summoner's Tales*." *Chaucer Review* 46.1 (2011): 93-100.

Raybin, David, and Susanna Fein. "Chaucer and Aesthetics." *Chaucer Review* 39.3 (2005): 225-33.

Raybin, David, and Linda Tarte Holley, eds. *Closure in the "Canterbury Tales": The Role of the "Parson's Tale."* Medieval Institute Publications, 2000.

Revard, Carter. "Four Fabliaux from London, British Library MS Harley 2253, Translated into English Verse." *Chaucer Review* 40.2 (2005): 111-40.

Rhetorica ad Herennium. Trans. Harry Caplan. Harvard University Press, 1954.

Richardson, Gudrun. "The Old Man in Chaucer's *Pardoner's Tale*: An Interpretive Study of His Identity and Meaning." *Neophilologus* 87 (2003): 323-37.

Rickert, Edith. "Chaucer's 'Hodge of Ware.'" *Times Literary Supplement*, 20 October 1932, 761.

Ridley, Florence. *The Prioress and the Critics.* University of California Press, 1965.

Rigby, Stephen H., ed. *Historians on Chaucer: The "General Prologue" to the "Canterbury Tales."* Oxford University Press, 2014.

Robertson, Elizabeth. "Apprehending the Divine and Choosing to Believe: Voluntarist Free Will in Chaucer's *Second Nun's Tale*." *Chaucer Review* 46.1-2 (2011): 111-30.

Robinson, F. N. *The Works of Geoffrey Chaucer.* 2 vols. 2nd ed. Houghton Mifflin, 1957.

Roger, Euan, and Sebastian Sobecki. "Geoffrey Chaucer, Cecily Chaumpaigne, and the Statute of the Laborers: New Records and Old Evidence Reconsidered." *Chaucer Review* 57.4 (2022): 407-37.

Rose, Christine. "Women's 'Pryvete,' May, and the Privy: Fissures in the Narrative Voice in the *Merchant's Tale*, 1944-86." *Chaucer Yearbook* 4 (1997): 61-77.

Rossi-Reder, Andrea. "Male Movement and Female Fixity in the *Franklin's Tale* and *Il Filocolo*." *Masculinities in Chaucer: Approaches to Maleness in the "Canterbury Tales" and "Troilus and Criseyde."* Ed. Peter Beidler. D. S. Brewer, 1998. 105-16.

Ruskin, John. *The Stones of Venice.* 3 vols. 1851-53. Dana Estes, 1913.

Scala, Elizabeth. "Canacee and the Chaucer Canon: Incest and Other Unnarratables." *Chaucer Review* 30.1 (1995): 15-39.

Scattergood, V. J. "*Goodfellas*, Sir John Clanvowe, and Chaucer's *Friar's Tale*: 'Occasions of Sin.'" *Chaucer's Poetry: Words, Authority, and Ethics.* Ed. Clíodhna Carney and Frances McCormack. Four Courts, 2013. 15-36.

Scattergood, V. J. "Perkyn Revelour and the *Cook's Tale*." *Chaucer Review* 19.1 (1984): 14-23.

Schell, Edgar, and J. D. Shuchter, eds. *English Morality Plays and Moral Interludes.* Holt, Rinehart, 1969.

Schrock, Chad. "Neoplatonic Theodicy in Chaucer's *Legend of Philomela*." *Studies in Philology* 108.1 (2011): 27-43.

Schwebel, Leah. "Redressing Griselda: Restoration through Translation in the *Clerk's Tale*." *Chaucer Review* 47.3 (2013): 274-99.

Schweizer, Bernard, ed. *Approaches to the Anglo and American Female Epic, 1621–1982.* Ashgate, 2006.

Seal, Samantha Katz. "Reading Like a Jew: Chaucer's *Physician's Tale* and the Letter of the Law." *Chaucer Review* 52.3 (2017): 298-317.

Seal, Samantha Katz. "Whose Chaucer? On Cecily Chaumpaigne, Cancellation, and the English Literary Canon." *Chaucer Review* 57.4 (2022): 484-97.

Seymour, M. C. "Chaucer's Early Poem *De casibus virorum illustrium.*" *Chaucer Review* 24.2 (1989): 163-65.

Seymour, M. C. "Of This Cokes Tale." *Chaucer Review* 24.3 (1990): 259-62.

Shakespeare, William. *Titus Andronicus. The Riverside Shakespeare.* Ed. G. Blakemore Evans. Houghton Mifflin, 1997. 1065-100.

Sharon-Zisser, Shirley. "The *Squire's Tale* and the Limits of Non-mimetic Function." *Chaucer Review* 26.4 (1992): 377-94.

Sidhu, Nicole Nolan. "'To late for to crie': Female Desire, Fabliau Politics, and Classical Legend in Chaucer's *Reeve's Tale.*" *Exemplaria* 21.1 (2009): 3-23.

Sidney, Sir Philip. *The Prose Works of Sir Philip Sidney.* Ed. Albert Feuillerat. 4 vols. Cambridge University Press, 1968.

Sigal, Gale. *Erotic Dawn-Songs of the Middle Ages: Voicing the Lyric Lady.* University of Florida Press, 1996.

Skalak, Chelsea. "The Unwilling Wife: Marital Rape in the *Canterbury Tales.*" *Chaucer Review* 55.2 (2020): 119-46.

Skeat, W. W. *An Etymological Dictionary of the English Language.* Rev. ed. 1882. Clarendon, 1963.

Smith, Barbara Herrnstein. *Poetic Closure: A Study of How Poems End.* University of Chicago Press, 1968.

Sontag, Susan. "Notes on 'Camp.'" *Against Interpretation and Other Essays.* Delta, 1966. 275-92.

Spearing, A. C. *Medieval to Renaissance in English Poetry.* Cambridge University Press, 1985.

Spector, Stephen. "Empathy and Enmity in the *Prioress's Tale.*" *The Olde Daunce: Love, Friendship, Sex, and Marriage in the Medieval World.* Ed. Robert Edwards and Stephen Spector. State University of New York Press, 1991. 211-28.

Spenser, Edmund. *The Faerie Queene.* Ed. A. C. Hamilton. Longman, 1977.

Staley, Lynn. *Languages of Power in the Age of Richard II.* Pennsylvania State University Press, 2005.

Stanley, E. G. "Of This Cokes Tale Maked Chaucer Na Moore." *Poetica* 5 (1976): 36-59.

Steadman, John. "Old Age and *Contemptus Mundi* in the *Pardoner's Tale.*" *Medium Ævum* 33.2 (1964): 121-30.

Stein, Gertrude. *Everybody's Autobiography.* Random House, 1937.

Stevens, Martin. "The Royal Stanza in Early English Literature." *PMLA* 94.1 (1979): 62-76.

Striar, Brian. "The *Manciple's Tale* and Chaucer's Apolline Poetics." *Criticism* 33.2 (1991): 173-204.

Strohm, Paul. "The Allegory of the *Tale of Melibee.*" *Chaucer Review* 2.1 (1967): 32-42.

Strohm, Paul. "Jean of Angoulême: A Fifteenth-Century Reader of Chaucer." *Neuphilologische Mitteilungen* 72.1 (1971): 69-76.

Strohm, Paul. *Theory and the Premodern Text.* University of Minnesota Press, 2000.

Stroud, T. A. "Chaucer's Friar as Narrator." *Chaucer Review* 8.1 (1973): 65-69.

Sturges, Robert. *Chaucer's Pardoner and Gender Theory: Bodies of Discourse.* St. Martin's, 2000.

Tambling, Jeremy. *Allegory.* Routledge, 2010.

Tatlock, John S. P. "Puns in Chaucer." *Flügel Memorial Volume.* Stanford University Press, 1916. 228-32.

Tatlock, John S. P., and Arthur Kennedy. *A Concordance to the Complete Works of Geoffrey Chaucer and to the "Romaunt of the Rose."* Peter Smith, 1963.

Taylor, Jamie. "Chaucer's *Tale of Melibee* and the Failure of Allegory." *Exemplaria* 21.1 (2009): 83-101.

Taylor, Karla. "Chaucer's Reticent Merchant." *The Idea of Medieval Literature: New Essays on Chaucer and Medieval Culture in Honor of Donald R. Howard.* Ed. James M. Dean and Christian Zacher. University of Delaware Press, 1992. 189-205.

Taylor, Karla. "Social Aesthetics and the Emergence of Civic Discourse from the *Shipman's Tale* to *Melibee.*" *Chaucer Review* 39.3 (2005): 298-322.

Taylor, Mark. "Sergeant and Lord / Lady and Wife: "The *Franklin's Tale* and Traditions of Courtly and Conjugal Love." *Chaucer Review* 32.1 (1997): 64-81.

Theophilus. *On Divers Arts.* Trans. John Hawthorne and Cyril Stanley Smith. Dover, 1979.

Thomas, A. H., ed. *Calendar of Plea and Memoranda Rolls, 1364-1381.* Cambridge, 1929.

Thomas, Paul R. "'Have ye no mannes herte?': Chauntecleer as Cock-Man in the *Nun's Priest's Tale.*" *Masculinities in Chaucer: Approaches to Maleness in the "Canterbury Tales" and "Troilus and Criseyde."* Ed. Peter Beidler. D. S. Brewer, 1998. 187-202.

Thomas of Monmouth. *The Life and Passion of William of Norwich.* Ed. and trans. Miri Rubin. Penguin, 2014.

Tomasch, Sylvia. "Postcolonial Chaucer and the Virtual Jew." *Chaucer and the Jews: Sources, Contexts, Meaning.* Ed. Sheila Delany. Routledge, 2002. 69-85.

Travis, Peter. *Disseminal Chaucer: Rereading the "Nun's Priest's Tale."* Notre Dame University Press, 2010.

Tschann, Judith. "The Layout of *Sir Thopas* in the Ellesmere, Hengwrt, Cambridge Dd.4.24, and Cambridge Gg.4.27 Manuscripts." *Chaucer Review* 20.1 (1985): 1-13.

Turner, Marion. *Chaucer: A European Life.* Princeton University Press, 2019.

Walts, Dawn Simmons. "Tricks of Time in the *Miller's Tale.*" *Chaucer Review* 43.4 (2009): 400-413.

Wapull, G. "The Tide Tarrieth No Man." *English Morality Plays and Moral Interludes.* Ed. Edgar Schell and J. D. Shuchter. Holt, Rinehart, 1969. 309-66.

Warren, Nancy Bradley. "Sacraments, Gender, and Authority in the Prioress's *Prologue* and *Tale* and *Pearl.*" *Christianity and Literature* 66.3 (2017): 385-403.

Waterhouse, Ruth, and Gwen Griffiths. "'Swete wordes' of Non-sense: The Deconstruction of the Moral *Melibee*: Part I." *Chaucer Review* 23.4 (1989): 338-61.

Weisl, Angela Jane. *Conquering the Reign of Femeny: Gender and Genre in Chaucer's Romance.* D. S. Brewer, 1995.

West, Lindy. *Shrill: Notes from a Loud Woman.* Hachette, 2016.

Wetherbee, Winthrop. "Romance and Epic in Chaucer's *Knight's Tale.*" *Exemplaria* 2.1 (1990): 303-28.

Wheeler, Bonnie. "Trouthe without Consequences: Rhetoric and Gender in Chaucer's *Franklin's Tale.*" *Feminea Medievalia I: Representations of the Feminine in the Middle Ages.* Ed. Bonnie Wheeler. Academia Press, 1993. 91-116.

Whitaker, Cord J. *Black Metaphors: How Modern Racism Emerged from Medieval Race-Thinking.* University of Pennsylvania Press, 2019.

Winstead, Karen. "Chaucer's *Parson's Tale* and the Contours of Orthodoxy." *Chaucer Review* 43.3 (2009): 239-59.

Wood, Chauncey. "Chaucer's Man of Law as Interpreter." *Traditio* 23 (1967): 149-90.

Yeager, Stephen. "Chaucer's Prudent Poetics: Allegory, the *Tale of Melibee,* and the Frame Narrative to the *Canterbury Tales.*" *Chaucer Review* 48.3 (2014): 307-21.

Žižek, Slavoj. *The Metastases of Enjoyment: Six Essays on Women and Causality.* 1994. Verso, 2005.

Index